Data on the Web

FROM RELATIONS
TO SEMISTRUCTURED DATA AND XML

Data on the Web

From Relations
to Semistructured Data and XML

Serge Abiteboul
Peter Buneman
Dan Suciu

Morgan Kaufmann Publishers
San Francisco, California

Sponsoring Editor	Diane Cerra
Director of Production and Manufacturing	Yonie Overton
Production Editor	Heather Collins
Editorial Coordinator	Belinda Breyer
Cover Design	Martin Heirakuji
Text Design	Mark Ong
Composition and Illustration	Windfall Software, using ZzTEX
Copyeditor	Ken Della Penta
Proofreader	Carol Leyba
Indexer	Steve Rath
Printer	Courier Corporation

Cover credits: Vasily Kandinsky, *Composition VIII*, July 1923 Photograph by David Heald © The Solomon R. Guggenheim Foundation, New York. © 2000 Artist Rights Society (ARS), New York/ADAGP, Paris.

Morgan Kaufmann Publishers
Editorial and Sales Office
340 Pine Street, Sixth Floor
San Francisco, CA 94104-3205
USA
Telephone 415 / 392-2665
Facsimile 415 / 982-2665
Email *mkp@mkp.com*
WWW *http://www.mkp.com*

04 03 02 01 00 5 4 3 2 1

Library of Congress Cataloging-in-Publication Data

Abiteboul, S. (Serge)
   Data on the web : from relations to semistructured data and XML / Serge Abiteboul, Peter Buneman, Dan Suciu.
      p. cm.
   Includes bibliographical references.
   ISBN 1-55860-622-X
    1. Database management.   2. XML (Document markup language).   3. Word Wide Web (Information retrieval system).   I. Buneman, Peter, 1943– II. Suciu, Dan.   III. Title.
QA76.9.D3 A258   2000
005.7′2—dc21
                                              99-046708
                                                CIP

Foreword

All information is moving online. Today, much of it is unstructured text data. As the size and complexity of Web sites grow, designers are recasting the data as semistructured XML files, as object-oriented network databases, and as classical record-oriented databases.

This is an area and era of great intellectual ferment. It is the collision between three cultures: the everything-is-a-document culture, the everything-is-an-object culture, and the everything-is-a-relation culture. Each group sees different aspects of the elephant.

This book bridges the gaps among those three cultures. XML is the one thing all three groups agree on (minus a few details). It, or one of its children, will become the intergalactic dataspeak: the standard way to interchange semistructured and structured data among computer systems. So, first the book views XML from the three cultural perspectives.

The book then explores the issues of how one accesses XML-like data. How do schemas and subschemas work? What kind of query language is needed? How should the query engine work? How can updates be managed? How can data interchange work? Semistructured data raises new issues in each of these areas.

The book is an excellent combination of the underlying theory and the state of the art. Serge Abiteboul, Peter Buneman, and Dan Suciu are leaders in this emerging field. Their book is founded on their research and on their participation in the development of some leading semistructured database systems: Lore, UnQL, Strudel, and XML-QL. It is an excellent introduction to this exciting new approach to data management, data fusion, and data interchange.

Jim Gray

Contents

Acknowledgments

This book is an account of recent research and development in the database and web communities. Our first debt of gratitude is to our colleagues in those communities. More specifically we would like to thank our colleagues at our home institutions: The Verso Project at Inria, the Database Group at the University of Pennsylvania, AT&T Laboratories, and the Database Group at Stanford. Many individuals have helped us by commenting on parts of the book or by enlightening us on various topics. They include François Bancilhon, Sophie Cluet, Susan Davidson, Alin Deutsch, Wenfei Fan, Mary Fernandez, Daniela Florescu, Sophie Gammerman, Alon Levy, Hartmut Liefke, Arnaud Sahuguet, Jerôme Siméon, WangChiew Tan, Frank Tompa, Anne-Marie Vercoustre and Jennifer Widom. This list is, of course, partial. We apologize to the people we have omitted to acknowledge, and also—in the likely event that we have misrepresented their ideas—to those whom we have acknowledged.

Diane Cerra of Morgan Kaufmann guided us through the materialization and publication of this book. We thank her and Jim Gray for their enthusiasm for the project. The hard work of the reviewers also helped us greatly. Finally, we would like to thank the Bioinformatics Center at Penn for providing a stable CVS repository.

1

Introduction

Until a few years ago the publication of electronic data was limited to a few scientific and technical areas. It is now becoming universal. Most people see such data as Web documents, but these documents, rather than being manually composed, are increasingly generated automatically from databases. The documents therefore have some regularity or some underlying structure that may or may not be understood by the user. It is possible to publish enormous volumes of data in this way, and we are now starting to see the development of software that extracts structured data from Web pages that were generated to be readable by humans. From a document perspective, issues such as efficient retrieval, version control, change management, and sophisticated methods of querying documents, which were formerly the province of database technology, are now important. From a database perspective, the Web has generated an enormous demand for recently developed database architectures such as data warehouses and mediation systems for database integration, and it has led to the development of *semistructured* data models with languages adapted to this model.

The emergence of XML as a standard for data representation on the Web is expected greatly to facilitate the publication of electronic data by providing a simple syntax for data that is both human- and machine-readable. While XML is itself relatively simple, it is surrounded by a confusing number of XML-enabled systems by various software vendors and an alphabet soup of proposals (RDF, XML-Data, XML-Schema, SOX, etc.) for XML-related standards.

Although the document and database viewpoints were, until quite recently, irreconcilable, there is now a convergence in technologies brought about by the development of XML for data on the Web and the closely related development of semistructured data in the database community. *This book is primarily about this convergence.* Its main goal is to present foundations for the management of data found on the Web. New shifts of paradigms are needed from an architecture and a data model viewpoint. These form the core of the book. A constant theme is bridging the gap between logical representation of data and data modeling on the one hand and syntax and functionalities of document systems on the other. We hope this book will help clarify these concepts and make it easier to understand the variety of powerful tools that are being developed for Web data.

1.1   AUDIENCE

The book aims at laying the foundations for future Web-based data-intensive applications. As such it has several potential audiences.

The primary audience consists of people developing tools or doing research related to the management of data on the Web. Most of the topics presented in the book are today the focus of active research. The book can serve as an entry point to this rapidly evolving domain. For readers with a data management background, it will serve as an introduction to Web data and notably to XML. For people coming from Web publishing, this book aims to explain why modern database technology is needed for the integrated storage and retrieval of Web data. It will present a perhaps unexpected view of the future use of XML as a *data exchange format*, as opposed to a standardized document markup language.

A second audience consists of students and teachers interested in semistructured data and in the management of data on the Web. The book contains an extensive survey of the literature and can thus serve as a basis for an advanced seminar.

A third audience consists of information systems managers in charge of publishing data on Web sites. This book is intended to take them away from their day-to-day struggle with new tools and changes of standards. It is hoped that it may help them understand the main technical solutions as well as bottlenecks and give them a feeling of longer-term goals in the representation of data. This book may help them achieve a better vision of the new breed of information systems that will soon pervade the Web.

1.2   WEB DATA AND THE TWO CULTURES

Today's Web The Web provides a simple and universal standard for the exchange of information. The central principle is to decompose information into units that can be named and transmitted. Today, the unit of information is typically a file that is created by one Web user and shared with others by making available its name in the form of a URL (Uniform Resource Locator). Other users and systems keep the URL in order to retrieve the file when required. Information, however, has structure. The success of the Web is derived from the development of HTML (Hypertext Markup Language), a means of structuring text for visual presentation. HTML describes both an intradocument structure (the layout and format of the text), and an interdocument structure (references to other documents through hyperlinks). The introduction of HTTP as a standard and the use of HTML for composing documents are at the root of the universal acceptance of the Web as the medium of information exchange.

The Database Culture There is another long-standing view of the structure of information that is almost orthogonal to that of textual structure—the view developed for data management systems. People working in this field use the vocabulary of relational database schemas and entity relationship diagrams to describe structure. Moreover, their view of the mechanisms for sharing information is very different. They are concerned with query languages to access information and with mechanisms for concurrency control and for recovery in order to preserve the integrity of the structure of their data. They also want to separate a "logical" or "abstract" view of a database from its physical implementation. The former is needed in order to understand and to query the data; the latter is of paramount importance for efficiency. Providing efficient implementations of databases and query languages is a central issue in databases.

The Need for a Bridge That we need convergence between these two approaches to information exchange is obvious, and it is part of the motivation for writing this book. Consider the following example of a common situation in data exchange on the Web. An organization publishes financial data. The source for this data is a relational database, and Web pages are generated on demand by invoking an SQL query and formatting its output into HTML. A second organization wants to obtain some financial analyses of this data but only has access to the HTML page(s). Here, the only solution is to write software to parse the HTML and convert it into a structure suitable for the analysis software. This solution has two serious defects: First, it is brittle, since a minor formatting change in the source could break the parsing program. Second, and more serious, is that the software may have to download an entire underlying database through repeated requests for HTML pages, even though the analysis software only requires something such as an average value of a single column of a table that could easily have been computed by the inaccessible underlying SQL server.

XML is a first step toward the convergence of these two views on information structure. Since XML is syntactically related to HTML (it is a fragment of SGML), tools have been developed to convert XML to HTML. However, its primary purpose is not to describe textual formats but to transmit structured data. In that sense it is related to, and may supplant, other data formats that have been developed for this purpose. So, in our scenario of data exchange through Web pages, while XML will solve the first problem of providing a robust interface with stable parsing tools that are independent of any display format, it will not per se solve the second problem of efficiently extracting the required portion of the underlying data. The solution to that, we believe, will come from the parallel database developments in semistructured data. This allows us to bring the efficient storage and extraction technology developed for highly structured database systems to bear upon the relatively loosely structured format specified by XML.

To summarize, let us list the technologies that the two cultures bring to the table. The Web has provided us with

- a global infrastructure and set of standards to support document exchange
- a presentation format for hypertext (HTML)
- well-engineered user interfaces for document retrieval (information retrieval techniques)
- a new format, XML, for the exchange of data with structure

Of course, we must not forget the most important fact that the Web is—by orders of magnitude—the largest database ever created.

In contrast, database technology has given us

- storage techniques and query languages that provide efficient access to large bodies of highly structured data
- data models and methods for structuring data
- mechanisms for maintaining the integrity and consistency of data
- a new model, that of semistructured data, which relaxes the strictures of highly structured database systems

It is through the convergence of the last points, XML and semistructured data, that we believe a combining technology for Web data will emerge.

A Shift in Paradigm In contrast to conventional database management systems, communication with data on the Web presents an essential shift of paradigm. The standard database approach is based on a client/server architecture (see Figure 1.1). The client (a person or a program) issues a query that is processed, compiled into an optimized code, and executed. Answer data is returned by the server. By contrast, data processing in a Web context is based on a "multitier"

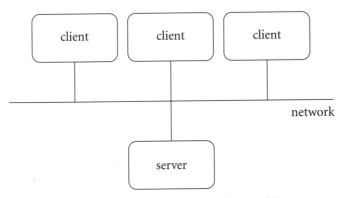

Figure 1.1 Traditional client/server database architecture.

approach (see Figure 1.2). The lowest tier consists of *data sources*, also called *servers*. These may be conventional database servers; they may also be legacy systems, file servers, or any application that produces data. No matter what data a source stores, it translates it into a common logical data model and a common format (most likely XML). The highest tier, the *client* tier, consists of user interfaces or applications such as analysis packages that consume data. In between there can be a whole collection of intermediate tiers, often called *middleware*—the software that transforms, integrates, or otherwise adds value to the data.

In the simplest scenario, there is no middle layer and the interaction is directly between clients and servers. Data flows from servers to clients, while queries are shipped in the opposite direction. The query processing at the server side now consists in *translating* the query into the server's own data model, processing it using the underlying query engine, then translating the result back into the common logical data model.

Database researchers interested in data integration have worked extensively on the issue of middleware. One approach is *data warehousing*. The middleware imports data from the sources and stores it in a specially constructed intermediate database (the warehouse), which is queried by the client. The main difficulty with this approach is keeping the database current when the sources are updated. A second approach is a *mediator system*, in which queries from the client are transformed and decomposed directly into queries against the source data. Partial results from several sources are integrated by the mediator on the fly; this solves the update problem, but shifts the burden on communication and query transformation. We should remark that while updates for data warehouses have been extensively studied, data warehousing technology has yet to prove itself for transaction-intensive applications.

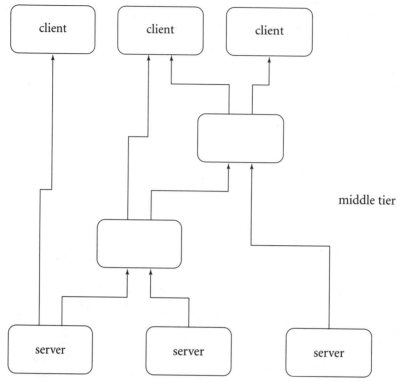

Figure 1.2 Web-based application architecture.

The Three Levels of Data Abstraction Over a 30-year period, the database community has found it useful to adopt a model of three levels of abstraction for representing the implementation and functionality of a database system. First there is the physical data level describing *how* the data is stored; this level is concerned with physical storage and what indexes are available. Above this is the logical level which, for example, dictates what queries are valid. The distinction between the logical and physical layers is perhaps the most important general idea in databases, and it is essentially the same as the notion of abstraction in programming languages. It enables us to modify the representation—perhaps to make it more efficient—without destroying the correctness of our existing interfaces to the data. Finally, the third is the external level; it provides a number of views—interfaces that individual users have to the data.

At present this distinction between the logical and physical layers has not been recognized for Web data, and there is no reason why it should when the main function of the Web is to deliver short pieces of hypertext. That will change. Take, for example, the case of a scientific database consisting of a few million entries each of several kilobytes. Such databases exist and are held in some data format. We could consider this a single 100-gigabyte XML file, but the actual physical representation may be a compressed version of the file, or a relational database, or a large collection of files stored in a deep Unix directory hierarchy, or the data may not be stored at all, but requests for data entries may be redirected to the appropriate servers.

To summarize, we can think of XML as a physical representation—a data format—or as a logical representation. In this book we will promote the second view, for the logical representation is that of semistructured data. Indeed, much of this book will be concerned with the development of query languages for this representation, just as relational query languages have been developed for another highly successful logical representation, relational databases.

Data Diversity Another issue that we will discuss extensively in this book is data diversity—the heterogeneous structure of data sources. Again, reconciling heterogeneous data has been a major focus of database research for some time. Heterogeneity occurs at all levels. Typically, the hard or insoluble problems occur at the *conceptual level*. People simply disagree on how data should be represented even when they are using the same data model. However, if agreement is reached, reconciliation at the *logical level* is possible, though far from straightforward. In fact only relatively recently have tools been developed for integrating the variety of logical representations of data that exist in standard (relational, object-oriented) database systems by providing a uniform query interface to those systems.

XML and query languages for XML emerge strongly as a solution to the logical diversity problem. However, XML is not the only solution ever considered. Almost every area has developed one or more data formats for serializing structured data into a byte stream suitable for storage and transmission. Most of these formats are domain specific; for example, we could probably not use a format developed for satellite imagery to serialize genetic data. However, some of these formats are, like XML, general-purpose, and a comparison with XML is informative. NetCDF, for example, is a format that is primarily designed for multidimensional array data, but can also be used to express relational data. ASN.1 was developed as a format for data transport between two layers of a network operating system, but is now widely used for storing and communicating bibliographic and genetic data. ACeDB (a database developed for the genetics of a small worm—we can hardly get more domain specific) has a model and format with remarkable affinities to the model we shall develop for semistructured data. Finally, we should not forget that most database management systems have a "dump" text format, which could be used, with varying degrees of generality, as data exchange formats.

If we are right in assuming that XML and semistructured data will emerge as a solution to the logical diversity problem, then the study of languages for that model and of type systems that relate to that model is of paramount importance, and that is what this book is about.

What This Book Is Not About There are important facets of Web data management that we do not address in this book. Perhaps the most important one is change control, since Web data is often replicated under various formats. We also ignore here transaction management, concurrency control, recovery, versions, and so on, which, while equally important for Web data management, deserve in our opinion separate treatment. Finally, we do not address here document retrieval, including information retrieval techniques and search engines, which have received the most attention in connection with the Web.

1.3 ORGANIZATION

This book contains four parts. The first part, "Data Model," describes the novel semistructured data model. Chapter 2 relates it to traditional relational and other data models. Chapter 3 introduces XML, shows its remarkably close connection with semistructured data, and discusses some of the related data modeling issues.

The second part, "Queries," presents the query component of the model. There have been several query languages proposed for semistructured data. The features common to all these proposals are introduced in Chapter 4, mostly based on the syntax found in the Lorel and UnQL query languages. These concepts are illustrated for XML in Chapter 5, which presents the language XML-QL and compares it with XSL. Following this, Chapter 6 describes the relationship between semistructured query languages and other query formalisms. It deals with the construction of new objects, structural recursion, cyclic data, and some features of other query languages.

The third part, "Types," is the newest and most dynamic research topic presented in the book, and is by necessity incomplete. Chapter 7 presents some foundations for types in semistructured data: a logic-based approach, and an approach based on simulation and bisimulation.

The fourth part, "Systems," discusses a few implementation issues and presents two systems: Lore, a general-purpose semistructured data management system, and Strudel, a Web site management system.

I

Data Model

2

A Syntax for Data

SEMISTRUCTURED DATA is often explained as "schemaless" or "self-describing," terms that indicate that there is no separate description of the type or structure of data. Typically, when we store or program with a piece of data, we first describe the structure (type, schema) of that data and then create instances of that type (or populate) the schema. In semistructured data we directly describe the data using a simple syntax. We start with an idea familiar to Lisp programmers, association lists, which are nothing more than label-value pairs and are used to represent recordlike or tuplelike structures:

```
{name: "Alan", tel: 2157786,  email: "agb@abc.com"}
```

This is simply a set of pairs such as name: "Alan" consisting of a label and a value. The values may themselves be other structures as in

```
{name: {first: "Alan",  last: "Black"},
 tel: 2157786,
 email: "agb@abc.com"
}
```

We may represent this data graphically as a node that represents the object, connected by edges to values (see Figure 2.1).

However, we depart from the usual assumption made about tuples or association lists that the labels are unique, and we will allow duplicate labels as in

```
{name: "Alan, tel:  2157786, tel: 2498762 }
```

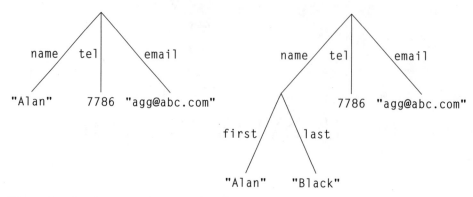

Figure 2.1 Graph representations of simple structures.

The syntax makes it easy to describe sets of tuples as in

```
{ person:
    {name: "Alan", phone: 3127786, email: "agg@abc.com"},
  person:
    {name: "Sara", phone: 2136877, email: "sara@math.xyz.edu"},
  person:
    {name: "Fred", phone: 7786312, email: "fds@acme.co.uk"}
}
```

We are not constrained to make all the person tuples the same type. One of the main strengths of semistructured data is its ability to accommodate variations in structure. While there is nothing to prevent us from building and querying completely random graphs, we usually deal with structures that are "close" to some type. The variations typically consist of missing data, duplicated fields, or minor changes in representation, as in

```
{person:
    {name: "Alan", phone: 3127786, email: "agg@abc.com"},
  person:
    {name: {first: "Sara", last: "Green"},
     phone: 2136877,
     email: "sara@math.xyz.edu"
    },
```

```
person:
    {name: "Fred", Phone: 7786312  Height: 183}
}
```

In a programming language such as C++, it may be possible, by a judicious combination of tuple types, union types, and some collection type such as a list, to give a type to each of the examples above. However, such a type is unlikely to be stable. A small change in the data will require a revision of the type. In semistructured data, we make the conscious choice of forgetting any type the data might have had, and we serialize it by annotating each data item explicitly with its description (such as name, phone, etc.). Such data is called *self-describing*. The term *serialization* means converting the data into a byte stream that can be easily transmitted and reconstructed at the receiver. Of course self-describing data wastes space (if naively stored), since we need to repeat these descriptions with each data item, but we gain interoperability, which is crucial in the Web context. On the other hand, no information is lost by dropping the type, and we show next how easily familiar forms of data can be represented by this syntax.

2.1 BASE TYPES

The starting point for our syntactic representation of data is a description of the *base types*. In our examples these consist of numbers (135, 2.7, etc.), strings ("Alan", "sara@rome.edu", etc.), and labels (name, height, etc.). These can be distinguished by their syntax: numbers start with a digit, strings with a quotation mark, and so on. However, we would not want to limit ourselves to these types alone. There are many other types, with defined textual encodings, such as date, time, gif, wav, and so on, that we would like to include. For such types we need to develop a notation such as (date, "1 May 1997"), (gif ": M1TE&.#=A=P!E'/<','.h ...")—the syntax is purely fictional—in which each value has a tag that indicates its type and an encoding. Such encodings have been developed for a number of data formats, and there is no need to reinvent them here. For simplicity we shall take labels, strings, and numbers as our examples, and we shall not use any explicit tagging of base types in our model. However, when we come to query languages we shall want basic operations that allow us to ask about the types of the values stored in semistructured data.

2.2   REPRESENTING RELATIONAL DATABASES

A relational database is normally described by a schema such as r1(a,b,c) r2(c,d). In these expressions, r1 and r2 are the names of the relations, and a,b,c and c,d are the column names of the two relations. In practice we also have to specify the types of those columns. An instance of such a schema is some data that conforms to this specification, and while there is no agreed syntax for describing relational instances, we typically depict them as rows in tables (see Figure 2.2).

We can think of the whole database instance as a tuple consisting of two components, the r1 and r2 relations. Using our notation, we describe this as {r1: i_1, r2: i_2}, where i_1 and i_2 are representations of the data in the two relations, each of which can be described as a set of rows:

```
{r1: {row: {a: a1, b: b1,  c: c1},
      row: {a: a2, b: b2,  c: c2}
      },
 r2: {row: { c: c2,  d: d2},
      row: { c: c3,  d: d3},
      row: { c: c4,  d: d4}
      }
}
```

It is worth remarking here that this is not the only possible representation of a relational database. Figure 2.3 shows tree diagrams for the syntax we have just given and for two other representations of the same relational database.

r1:	a	b	c		r2:	c	d
	a1	b1	c1			c2	d2
	a2	b2	c2			c3	d3
						c4	d4

Figure 2.2 Examples of relations.

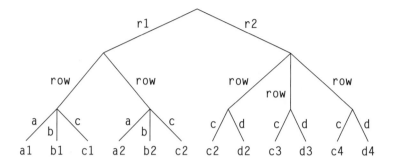

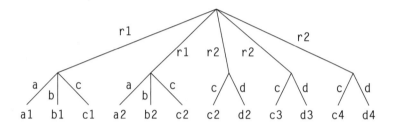

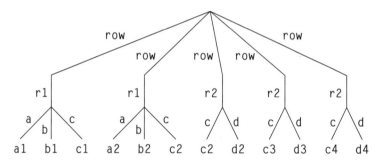

Figure 2.3 Three representations of a relational database.

2.3 REPRESENTING OBJECT DATABASES

Modern database applications handle objects, either through an object-relational or an object database. Such data can be represented as semistructured data too. Consider for example the following collection of three persons, in which `Mary` has two children, `John` and `Jane`. Object identities may be used when we want to construct structures with references to other objects:

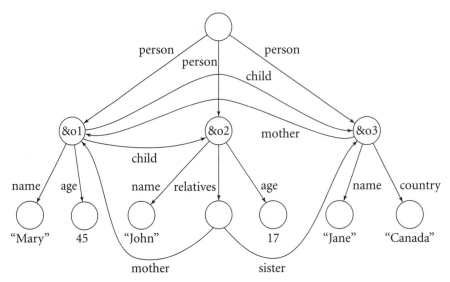

Figure 2.4 A cyclic structure.

```
{person: &o1{name:    "Mary",
             age:      45,
             child:   &o2,
             child:   &o3
            },
 person: &o2{name:    "John",
             age:     17,
             relatives: {mother: &o1,
                         sister: &o3}
            },
 person: &o3{name:   "Jane",
             country: "Canada",
             mother: &o1
            }
}
```

The presence of a node label such as &o1 before a structure binds &o1 to the identity of that structure. We are then able to use that label—as a value—to refer to that structure. In our graph representation we allow ourselves to build graphs with shared substructures and cycles, as shown in Figure 2.4. The names &o1,

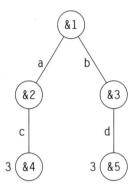

Figure 2.5 A structure
with object identities.

&o2, &o3 are called *object identities,* or oids. In this figure, we have placed arrows
on the edges to indicate the direction, which is no longer implicitly given by the
treelike structure.

At this point the data is no longer a tree but a graph, in which each node has a
unique oid. We shall freely refer to nodes as *objects* throughout this book. Note
that even the terminal nodes have identities. In Figure 2.5, we have drawn circles
around the object identities to differentiate the values stored at terminal nodes
from the object identities for those nodes. This suggests that we could also place
data (i.e., atomic values) at internal nodes in a structure. We shall not do this in
our initial formalism for semistructured data; atomic values will be allowed only
on leaves, since this simple formalism suffices to represent any data of practical
interest.

Since oids are just strings or integers, their meaning is restricted to a certain
domain. Although oids have a logical meaning, it is important to understand
what they denote physically. For data loaded in memory, an oid can be a seen
as a pointer to the memory location corresponding to a node and is only valid
for the current application. For data stored on disk, an oid may be an address on
the disk for the node, or an entry in a translation table that provides the address.
In this case, the same oid is valid across several applications, on all machines on
the local network sharing that disk. In the context of data exchange on the Web,
however, an object identifier becomes part of a global namespace. We may use, for
instance, a URL followed by a query that, at that URL, would extract the object.
Indeed, we need this or another means of *locating* an object. In the same data
instance, oids from different domains may coexist and may be translated during

data exchange. For example, the oid of an object on the Web may be translated into a disk-local oid when that object is fetched on the local disk, then translated into a pointer when it is loaded in memory.

In our simple syntax for semistructured data, we allow both nodes with explicit oids and nodes without oids: the system will explicitly assign a unique oid automatically, when the data is parsed. Thus {a:&o1{b:&o2 5}} and {a:{b:5}} denote isomorphic graphs, as does {a:&o1{b:5}}.

This convention requires us to take some care about what is denoted by this syntax. Consider the simple structure

```
{a: {b: 3}, a: {b: 3}}
```

Since a separate object identifier is assigned to each component, each of the repeated {b: 3} components will have a different identifier. Thus this represents a set with *two* elements (there are two edges from the root in the graph representation). If this were a representation of a relation, we might treat this as a structure with *one* tuple, equivalent to {a: {b: 3}}. To start with, we shall assume that each node in the graph is given a unique oid when loaded by the system, so that this is a set of two objects. Later, in Chapter 6, we shall examine an alternative semantics in which object identities are not added.

2.4　SPECIFICATION OF SYNTAX

At this point it is worth summarizing the syntax we have developed so far. We shall call our semistructured data expressions *ssd-expressions;* the evocation of Lisp's s-expressions is deliberate.

We assume some standard syntax for labels and for atomic values (numbers, strings, etc.). We shall normally write object identifiers with an initial ampersand, for example, &123.

$$\langle ssd{-}expr \rangle ::= \langle value \rangle \mid \texttt{oid} \langle value \rangle \mid \texttt{oid}$$

$$\langle value \rangle ::= \texttt{atomicvalue} \mid \langle complexvalue \rangle$$

$$\langle complexvalue \rangle ::= \{ \texttt{label} : \langle ssd{-}expr \rangle, \dots, \texttt{label} : \langle ssd{-}expr \rangle \}$$

We say that an object identifier o is *defined* in an ssd-expression s if either s is of the form $o\, v$ for some value v or s is of the form $\{l_1 : e_1, \dots, l_n : e_n\}$ and o is defined in one of the $e_1 \dots e_n$. If it occurs in any other way in s, we say it is *used* in s. For an ssd-expression s to be consistent it must satisfy the following properties:

- Any object identifier is defined at most once in *s*.
- If an object identifier *o* is used in *s*, it must be defined in *s*.

The previous definition has to be extended if we want to consider *external* resources and external oids.

2.5 THE OBJECT EXCHANGE MODEL (OEM)

Self-describing data formats have been used for a long time for exchanging data between applications. Their use for exchange between heterogeneous systems is more recent. The Object Exchange Model (OEM) was explicitly defined for that purpose in the context of Tsimmis, a system for integrating heterogeneous data sources. Since then variants of OEM have been used in several projects, making it the de facto semistructured data model. We describe here briefly its original presentation. An OEM object is a quadruple (`label`, `oid`, `type`, `value`), where `label` is a character string, `oid` is the object's identifier, and `type` is either `complex` or some identifier denoting an atomic type (like `integer`, `string`, `gif-image`, etc.). When `type` is `complex`, then the object is called a *complex object*, and `value` is a set (or list) of oids. Otherwise the object is an *atomic object,* and `value` is an atomic value of that type. Thus OEM data is essentially a graph, like the semistructured data described in this section, but in which labels are attached to nodes rather than edges.

Since its introduction, many systems have used a variant of OEM in which labels are attached to edges, rather than nodes. We follow this variant throughout the book. Thus we shall take our data as an edge-labeled graph. This is a model that is prevalent in work on semistructured data, but it is not the only possibility: we could consider node-labeled graphs or graphs in which both nodes and edges are labeled.

2.6 OBJECT DATABASES

Modern applications use some form of object-oriented model for their data. Following our description of relational databases, we shall consider a basic object-oriented data model following the ODMG [Cat94] specifications. This forms the standard of object databases, also sometimes called object-oriented databases. We shall briefly describe how to express ODMG data in the syntax of semistructured data. For now we shall ignore the representation of methods.

```
class State
    (extent states)
{       attribute string scode;
        attribute string sname;
        attribute City capital;
        relationship set<City> cities-in
            inverse City::state-of;
}
class City
    (extent cities)
{       attribute string ccode;
        attribute string cname;
        relationship State state-of
            inverse State::cities-in;
}
```
Figure 2.6 An ODMG schema.

Figure 2.6 shows a simple schema expressed in ODL, the Object Definition Language of ODMG. It illustrates important constructs that are common to all object database management systems. First, ODMG includes some built-in tuple and collection types. For collections, ODMG provides set, list, multiset, and array types. Second, ODMG provides some persistent roots or *handles* to the objects in the database. In this case, states and cities consist of collections of objects. Indeed, they form the *extents* of two classes, State and City, respectively. The sets states and cities are both global names. The type of elements in cities is set<City>. Since it happens to be the extent of City, this set contains all objects created by the constructor of City and not removed. In ODMG, the constructors are defined in the database/language bindings (e.g., ODMG/C++ or ODMG/Java) rather than in the ODL syntax. Similarly, the language bindings decide the style of destruction of objects, that is, by explicit destruction or by unreachability and garbage collection.

Objects of type City have a precise structure that specifies their attributes, ccode, cname, state-of. This last attribute is interesting because it illustrates a last feature we will mention, namely, *relationship*. Relationships are like attributes as far as a query language is concerned. However, they allow the expression of inverse constraints. The fact that state-of in City and cities-in in State are inverse of each other indicates in particular that for each State object s, and each City object c in s.cities-in, c.state-of is s.

```
{states: {state: &s1{scode:       "ID",
                      sname:       "Idaho",
                      capital:     &c1,
                      cities-in:  {City: &c1, City: &c3, ...}
                     },
          state: &s2{scode:       "NE",
                      sname:       "Nevada",
                      capital:     &c2
                      cities-in:  {City: &c2, ...}
                     },
                 .
                 .
                 .
         },
 cities: {city: &c1{ccode: "BOI", cname: "Boise",       state-of: &s1},
          city: &c2{ccode: "CCN", cname: "Carson City", state-of: &s2},
          city: &c3{ccode: "MOC", cname: "Moscow",      state-of: &s1},
            .
            .
            .
         }
}
```

Figure 2.7 Representation of ODMG data.

The process of describing ODMG data as semistructured data is straightforward. Figure 2.7 is an example. It follows the same technique used to describe relational databases, but we now have to make use of names for object identities in order to describe attribute values that are objects. We have used, arbitrarily, lowercase type names (such as city) on edges that denote set membership rather than the neutral row that we used for relations. There is no assertion about types in the semistructured representation nor is there any assertion that the data should satisfy an inverse relationship. From the point of view of semistructured data, both types and inverse relationships are special forms of constraints. We shall discuss such constraints later in this book.

The ODMG standards also include an informal specification for an Object Interchange Format (OIF) that is intended for specifying a textual dump and load format for an object database. There is a straightforward translation from OIF into our format. The only detail to be taken care of is the translation of arrays, which can be handled in a variety of ways.

2.7   OTHER REPRESENTATIONS

So far we have dealt with how to represent data that conforms to standard data models in our syntax. However, there are already numerous syntactic forms for describing data. There are, for example, formats that have been designed for the exchange and archiving of scientific data. These have been designed to be both machine- and human-readable, but they are mostly specific to some domain. For example, it is unlikely that a data format designed for a specific geographical information system will be usable as a biological database.

There are some data formats that are generic, even though they are mostly "structured" in the sense that a type or schema is needed to interpret the data. Two of them, however, ACeDB and XML, have very close affinities with the model we develop here. We shall briefly mention ACeDB here. XML will be the topic of the next chapter.

2.7.1 ACeDB

ACeDB (A *C. elegans* Database) is not well-known as a general database management system [TMD92]. It was, as its name indicates, originally developed as a database for genetic data of a specific organism. However, the data model is quite general. It is popular with biologists for several reasons: the ability to deal with missing data, some extremely good user interfaces (some general and some specific to genetic sequence data), and some good browsing tools.

Some of these qualities derive from a simple and elegant data model that underlies ACeDB. An ACeDB schema is given in Figure 2.8 together with a matching data value. Both schema and data can be seen as edge-labeled trees. In the example, ?Book is a class name, and to its right are various attributes (a tuple specification). In turn, some of those attributes may be tuples. When we encounter a type name such as Int, we should think of that as a node followed by an infinite set of edges, each labeled with a distinct integer. Similarly for Text. Thus the schema can be thought of as an infinitely branching tree and the data instance as a finite subtree of this. The keyword UNIQUE specifies that any data instance may choose at most one label. In the case of UNIQUE followed by english, french, other, we are allowed to select at most one branch, so this is effectively an enumerated type.

```
?Book title UNIQUE Text
      authors Text
      chapters int UNIQUE Text
      language UNIQUE english
                      french
                      other
      date UNIQUE month Int
                   year Int


&hock2 title     "Computer Simulation Using Particles"
      authors    "Hockney"
                 "Eastwood"
      chapters 1 "Computer Experiments"
               2 "A One-Dimensional Model"
               .
               .
               .
      language english
```
Figure 2.8 An ACeDB schema and data.

As an example of the expressive power of this model,

```
array Int UNIQUE Int
```

specifies a (sparse) array. The schema is a node with an infinite number of integer out-edges, each leading to node with an infinite number of integer out-edges. An instance is specified by a finite number of top-level integer edges (the array indices), each followed by at most one integer edge (the associated value).

The edges may be labeled with any base type including labels. From a given vertex in the data tree, there can be many outgoing edges unless UNIQUE is specified in the corresponding position in the schema tree. Thus after a title edge there can be at most one string (text), but there can be several string edges after an author edge. Note the use of integer-labeled edges to create arrays and UNIQUE to specify a form of union or variant type.

ACeDB allows any label other than the top-level object identifier (e.g., Hock2) to be missing. Also, the object identifiers are provided by the user; they are not provided by the system.

While ACeDB requires a schema, the fact that data may be missing and the fact that label data is treated uniformly with that of other base types make it a close relative of the semistructured data model. An ACeDB representation of the cities/states example is given in Figure 2.9. Note that ACeDB has provisions for

```
?State    scode UNIQUE Text              &id scode "ID",
          sname UNIQUE Text                  sname "Idaho"
          capital UNIQUE ?City              capital &boi
          cities-in ?City XREF state-of    cities-in &boi
                                                      &moc
?City     ccode UNIQUE Text                        ...
          cname UNIQUE Text              &ne scode "NE",
          state-of  ?State XREF cities-in    sname "Nevada"
                                             capital &ccn
                                             cities-in: &ccn

                                                      ...

                                         ...
                                         &boi ccode "BOI"
                                              cname "Boise"
                                              state-of &id
                                         &ccn ccode "CCN"
                                              cname "Carson City"
                                              state-of &ne
                                         &moc ccode "MOC"
                                              cname  "Moscow"
                                              state-of &id
                                         ...
```

Figure 2.9 ACeDB schema and data showing cross-references.

ensuring "relationship" constraints. It will be apparent that the syntax for ACeDB data is only superficially different from that of ssd-expressions.

2.8 TERMINOLOGY

The terminology used to describe semistructured data is that of basic graph theory and can be found in any book on that topic or in any good introduction to computer science. However, the terminology varies slightly, and a brief summary of terminology used in this book may be appropriate for readers in need of a brief review.

A *graph* (N, E) consists of a set N of *nodes* and a set E of *edges*. Associated with each edge $e \in E$ there is an (ordered) pair of nodes, the source node $s(e)$ and the target node $t(e)$. A *path* is a sequence $e_1, e_2, \ldots, e_k$ of edges such that $t(e_i) = s(e_{i+1})$, $1 \leq i \leq k - 1$. Such a path is called a path from the source $s(e_1)$ of e_1 to the target $t(e_k)$ of e_k. The number of edges in this path, k, is its *length*. A node r is a *root* for a graph (N, E) if there is a path from r to n for every $n \in N$, $n \neq r$. A *cycle* in a graph is a path between a node and itself. A graph with no

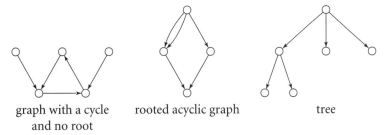

graph with a cycle   rooted acyclic graph   tree
    and no root

Figure 2.10 Terminology for unlabeled graphs.

cycles is called *acyclic*. A rooted graph is a *tree* if there is a unique path from r to n for every $n \in N$, $n \neq r$. Note that a tree is necessarily acyclic and cannot have more than one root. A node is *terminal node* or a *leaf* if it is not the source of any edge in E.

Figure 2.10 illustrates some of these terms. In this figure, nodes are drawn as small circles and edges as arrows with the target node being at the head of the arrow and the source node at its back.

Variations in terminology include *vertex* or *point* for node and *line* for *edge*. The only graphs we consider are directed, and they are usually rooted. It is common to call a directed acyclic graph a DAG. Our definition of a graph allows for more than one edge between two nodes. Also, according to our definition, if there is a path between a node and itself, it has length of at least one. However, we shall often assume that there is a "trivial" path, of length 0, from any node to itself.

As we have already stated, our model of semistructured data is that of an *edge-labeled graph*. That is, we have a labeling function $F_E : E \to \mathcal{L}_E$, where $\mathcal{L}_E$ is the domain of edge labels. The model usually also includes node labels, though the labels on nodes are typically confined to terminal nodes. This is the case in OEM (Section 2.5). However, in some models, for example, UnQL (Section 4.4) and ACeDB (Section 2.7.1), node labels are absent and the data is carried entirely on the edge labels. We should mention that in most computer implementations of graphs the nodes are implemented through the use of references or indexes. These act as internal names for the nodes and are often called, in database jargon, *object identifiers,* or *oids* for short. Edge identifiers, even if they are present in the implementation, are less important. We shall discuss later the issue of whether there is an order on the edges leading from a vertex.

To complete this section on basic terminology, we have used the term *ssd-expression* to describe a syntax for constructing semistructured data. We shall use the term *data graph* to describe the graphical representation of the data.

2.9 BIBLIOGRAPHIC REMARKS

The current development of interest in semistructured data starts with the OEM model developed first for the Tsimmis project at Stanford around 1995 [H+95, CGMH+94, PGMW95]. At about the same time, a related project at Stanford, Lore [AQM+97, MAG+97] introduced the edge-labeled variant of OEM, which we follow in this book. An alternative data model, based on bisimulation, was proposed in UnQL [BDS95, BDHS96]. The syntax used in this chapter and throughout the book is based on that used in Lore and UnQL. Tutorials and overviews on semistructured data can be found in [Abi97, Bun97, Suc98].

There is a huge literature on data formats. Most data formats have been developed for specific domains, so that a biological data format EMBL [RTSCF96] would be of little use in a situation in which multidimensional array data [NCS99] is needed. However, some data formats such as netCDF [RD90], even though they are biased toward array data, are reasonably generic, and some [NOA73] already allow semistructured features such as the addition of new fields.

The need to exchange data in a platform/language-independent way has a history that predates the Web by decades. For this purpose various serialization techniques for general data types have been proposed. Notable among these is ASN.1 [ISO87], which is widely used not only for data exchange but also for the implementation of databases. ASN.1 data requires a schema, and even the format for data alone has several built-in types. In addition, object database systems [Cat94] and data exchange systems [OMG92] come equipped with a definition of how to serialize data.

The idea that data may be profitably modeled as an edge-labeled graph appears in Graphlog [CM90b] and in ACeDB [TMD92]; the latter, as we have noted, has a particularly interesting data model in that edge labels carry most of the data.

3

XML

XML IS A NEW STANDARD adopted by the World Wide Web Consortium (W3C) to complement HTML for data exchange on the Web. In this chapter, we describe XML by relating it to the semistructured data model that was previously discussed. The chapter is not intended to contain a full description of XML; see the "Bibliographic Remarks" section (Section 3.7) for references to comprehensive XML. Rather, it presents XML from a database perspective.

Most readers will have seen HTML, the language for describing Web pages. HTML consists of text interspersed with tag fields such as <i> . . . </i> to describe the layout of the page, hyperlinks, the inclusion of pictures, forms and so on. As we noted in the introduction, much data on the Web is now published in HTML pages. For example, it is common to find a database relation displayed as an HTML table or an HTML list. Figure 3.1 illustrates a simple way to display a small table with three persons in HTML and its rendering with the Netscape browser. The HTML tags used here are <h1> for header (the text will be printed with a larger font), <p> for paragraph (start a new line), <b> for boldface, and <i> for italic. While the rendering is human-readable, there is nothing in the HTML text to make it easy for other programs to understand the structure and content of such data. Applications that need to read Web data must contain a "screen scraping" software component dedicated to extracting structured data from the Web. Such software, called a *wrapper*, is brittle because it can break as a result of minor changes in the format and has to be hand-tuned for each data extraction task. For example, a wrapper for the data in Figure 3.1 may break when the email address is changed from italic <i> to teletype <t>. The problem is that HTML was designed specifically to describe the presentation, not the content.

27

```
<h1>People on the fourth floor </h1>
<p> <b>Alan</b>, 42 years, <i>agb@abc.com</i> </p>
<p> <b>Patsy</b>, 36 years, <i>ptn@abc.com</i> </p>
<p> <b>Ryan</b>, 58 years, <i>rgz@abc.com</i> </p>
```

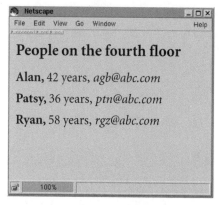

Figure 3.1 An example of an HTML file
and its presentation with Netscape.

XML (Extensible Markup Language) was designed specifically to describe content, rather than presentation. It differs from HTML in three major respects:

1. New tags may be defined at will.
2. Structures can be nested to arbitrary depth.
3. An XML document can contain an optional description of its grammar.

XML allows users to define new tags to indicate structure. For example, the textual structure enclosed by <person> . . . </person> would be used to describe a person tuple. Unlike HTML, an XML document does not provide any instructions on how it is to be displayed. Such information may be included separately in a *stylesheet*. Stylesheets in a specification language called XSL (XML Stylesheet Language) are used to translate XML data to HTML. The resulting HTML pages can then be displayed by standard browsers. XSL will be described in Chapter 5.

In its basic form, XML is simply a syntax for transmitting data, much in the spirit of the syntax described in Chapter 2. As such, it is very likely to become a major standard for data exchange on the Web. For an organization or a group of users, XML allows a specification that facilitates data exchange and reuse by multiple applications. On the assumption that XML will become a universal data exchange format, many software vendors are building tools for importing and exporting XML data. The presentation of XML in this chapter emphasizes its role as a data exchange format, and not that of a document markup language. However, it is important to keep in mind XML's roots as a document markup language, which pose certain problems when used in the context of data exchange.

The use of XML also brings as a bonus tools such as parsers or syntax-driven editors as well as APIs like SAX and DOM. However XML's "type definition" (the DTD) in some ways falls short of what we might call a database schema language. For example, there is only one base type (text), and references to other parts of a document cannot be typed. This has led to a host of extensions to XML that provide some sort of added type system such as DCD, XML-Data, RDF, which we shall briefly discuss.

3.1 BASIC SYNTAX

3.1.1 XML Elements

XML is a textual representation of data. The basic component in XML is the *element*, that is, a piece of text bounded by matching tags such as `<person>` and `</person>`. Inside an element we may have "raw" text, other elements, or a mixture of the two. Consider the following XML example:

```
<person>
    <name> Alan </name>
    <age> 42 </age>
    <email> agb@abc.com </email>
</person>
```

An expression such as `<person>` is called a start-tag and `</person>` an end-tag. Start- and end-tags are also called markups. Such tags must be balanced; that is, they should be closed in inverse order to that in which they are opened, like parentheses. Tags in XML are defined by users; there are no predefined tags, as in HTML. The text between a start-tag and the corresponding end-tag, including the embedded tags, is called an *element*, and the structures between the tags are referred to as the *content*. The term *subelement* is also used to describe the relation between an element and its component elements. Thus `<email>` . . . `</email>` is a subelement of `<person>` . . . `</person>` in the example above.

As with semistructured data, we may use repeated elements with the same tag to represent collections. Figure 3.2 contains an example in which several `<person>` tags occur next to each other.

```
<table>
    <description> People on the fourth floor </description>
    <people>
        <person>
            <name> Alan </name>
            <age> 42 </age>
            <email> agb@abc.com </email>
        </person>
        <person>
            <name> Patsy </name>
            <age> 36 </age>
            <email> ptn@abc.com </email>
        </person>
        <person>
            <name> Ryan </name>
            <age> 58 </age>
            <email> rgz@abc.com </email>
        </person>
    </people>
</table>
```
Figure 3.2 XML data.

It is interesting to compare XML to HTML. The information in the HTML document in Figure 3.1 is essentially the same as that in the XML document in Figure 3.2: both describe three persons, living on the fourth floor. But while HTML describes the presentation, XML describes the content. An application can easily understand the XML data (e.g., separate names from ages from emails); on the other hand, there is no indication in XML on how the data should be displayed.

Observe that the quotation marks around the character strings have disappeared; all data is treated as text. This is because XML evolved as a language for document markup, and the data—that part of the syntax not enclosed within angle brackets ⟨. . .⟩—is taken to be the text of the document. This data is often referred to as PCDATA (Parsed Character Data). The details of PCDATA have been carefully developed to allow the exchange of data in many languages. XML uses characters in Unicode (e.g., "&#x0152" for the letter *mem* in Hebrew).

Finally, XML has a useful abbreviation for empty elements. The following:

```
<married> </married>
```

can be abbreviated to

```
<married/>
```

3.1.2 XML Attributes

XML allows us to associate *attributes* with elements. Here we have to be a little careful with terminology. Attributes in the relational sense of the term have so far been expressed in XML by tags. XML uses the term "attribute" for what is sometimes called a "property" in data models. In XML, attributes are defined as (name,value) pairs. In the example below, attributes are used to specify the language or the currency:

```
<product>
    <name language="French">trompette six trous</name>
    <price currency="Euro"> 420.12 </price>
    <address format="XLB56" language="French">
        <street>31 rue Croix-Bosset</street>
        <zip>92310</zip> <city>Sevres</city>
        <country>France</country>
    </address>
</product>
```

As with tags, users may define arbitrary attributes, like language, currency, and format above. The value of an attribute is always a string and must be enclosed in quotation marks.

There are differences between attributes and tags. A given attribute may only occur once within a tag, while subelements with the same tag may be repeated. Also the value associated with an attribute is a string, while the structure enclosed between a start- and end-tag may contain subelements.

Attributes reveal XML's origin as a document markup language. In data exchange they introduce ambiguity as to whether to represent information as attributes or elements. For example, we could represent the information about Alan as

```
<person> <name> Alan </name>
  <age> 24 </age>
  <email> agb@abc.com </email>
</person>
```

or as

```
<person name="Alan" age="42" email="agb@abc.com"/>
```

or as

```
<person age="42">
```

```
   <name> Alan </name>
   <email> agb@abc.com </email>
</person>
```

3.1.3 Well-Formed XML Documents

So far we have presented the basic XML syntax. There are very few constraints
that have to be matched: tags have to nest properly, and attributes have to be
unique. In XML parlance we say that a document is *well-formed* if it satisfies
these two constraints. Being well-formed is a very weak constraint; it does little
more than ensure that XML data will parse into a labeled tree.

   We now have a (rough) general picture of XML. An element may contain other
elements and data. Inside an element, the ordering of subelements and pieces of
data is relevant.

3.2   XML AND SEMISTRUCTURED DATA

The basic XML syntax is perfectly suited for describing semistructured data.
Recall the syntax for ssd-expressions in Chapter 2. The simple XML document

```
<person>
   <name> Alan </name>
   <age> 42 </age>
   <email> agb@abc.com </email>
</person>
```

has the following representation as an ssd-expression:

```
{person :  {name: "Alan", age: 42,  email: "agb@abc.com"}}
```

   For trees the translation from ssd-expressions to XML can be easily automated.
Let us call T the translation function. Referring to the grammar in Section 2.4,
the translation is

$$T(\mathtt{atomicvalue}) = \mathtt{atomicvalue}$$

$$T(\{l_1 : v_1, \ldots, l_n : v_n\}) = < l_1 > T[v_1] < /l_1 > \ldots < l_n > T[v_n] < /l_n >$$

   Beyond this simple analogy, however, XML and semistructured data are not
always easy to reconcile. In addition to the ambiguity introduced by attributes,
there are some other differences that we discuss here.

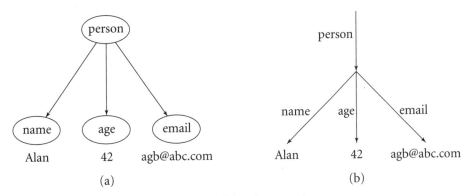

Figure 3.3 Trees for (a) XML data and (b) ssd-expression.

3.2.1 **XML Graph Model**

There is a subtle distinction between an XML element and an ssd-expression. An ssd-expression is a set of label/subtree pairs, while an element has just one top-level label. The distinction, while minor, is nevertheless important and worthwhile understanding. Ssd-expressions denote graphs with labels on edges, while XML denotes graphs with labels on nodes. Figure 3.3 illustrates the graph for the XML data above, and the graph for the corresponding ssd-expression. In the case of tree data, it is easy to convert back and forth between the two. Starting from the XML tree, we simply "lift" each label from the node to the edge entering that node. To do the same for the root, we add a new incoming edge. This transforms the left tree into the right tree in Figure 3.3. When the data is a graph, however, the distinction between the two models may become important. We describe how XML represents graphs next.

3.2.2 **XML References**

So far all our XML examples described trees. We show here XML's mechanism for defining and using references and, hence, for describing graphs rather than trees.

XML allows us to associate unique identifiers to elements, as the value of a certain attribute. For the moment, we will assume that the particular attribute is called id; we discuss later (Section 3.3) how to choose a different attribute for that purpose. In the example below, we associate the identifier s2 with a <state> element:

```
<state id="s2">
   <scode> NE </scode>
   <sname> Nevada </sname>
</state>
```

We can refer to that element by using the attribute idref attribute. (Again, we will show later how we can control which attribute serves that purpose.) For example:

```
<city id="c2">
   <ccode> CCN </ccode>
   <cname> Carson City </cname>
   <state-of idref="s2"/>
</city>
```

Note that <state-of> is an empty element; its only purpose is to reference, via an attribute value, another element. This technique allows us to build representations of cyclic/recursive data structures that commonly occur in object databases. Figure 3.4 illustrates such an example.

With references, the analogy between XML and semistructured data is less clean. For example consider the semistructured data instance in Figure 3.5. We could encode this in XML either as

```
<a> <b id="&o123"> some string </b> </a>
<a c="&o123"/>
```

and assume that the attribute c is a reference attribute, or as

```
<a b="&o123"/>
<a> <c id="&o123"> some string </b> </a>
```

assuming that b is now a reference attribute.

3.2.3 Order

The semistructured data model we described earlier is based on unordered collections, while XML is ordered. For example the following two pieces of semistructured data are equivalent:

```
person:{firstname:"John", lastname:"Smith"}
person:{lastname:"Smith",firstname:"John"}
```

while the following two XML documents are not equivalent:

```
<geography>
    <states>
        <state id = "s1">
            <scode> ID </scode>
            <sname> Idaho </sname>
            <capital idref="c1"/>
            <cities-in idref="c1"/> <cities-in idref="c3"/> . . .
        </state>
        <state id="s2">
            <scode> NE </scode>
            <sname> Nevada </sname>
            <capital idref="c2"/>
            <cities-in idref="c2"/> . . .
        </state>
        . . .
    </states>
    <cities>
        <city id="c1">
            <ccode> BOI </ccode>
            <cname> Boise </cname>
            <state-of idref="s1"/>
        </city>
        <city id="c2">
            <ccode> CCN </ccode>
            <cname> Carson City </cname>
            <state-of idref="s2"/>
        </city>
        <city id="c3">
            <ccode> MOC </ccode>
            <cname> Moscow </cname>
            <state-of idref="s1"/>
        </city>
        . . .
    </cities>
</geography>
```

Figure 3.4 XML representation of cross-references.

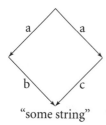

"some string"

Figure 3.5 Simple semi-structured data instance.

```
<person><firstname>John</firstname>
        <lastname>Smith</lastname> </person>
<person><lastname>Smith</lastname>
        <firstname>John</firstname></person>
```

To make matters worse, attributes are *not* ordered in XML; hence, the following two XML documents are equivalent:

```
<person firstname="John" lastname="Smith"/>
<person lastname="Smith" firstname="John"/>
```

The emphasis on order in XML also stems from its origin as a document markup language. In documents, order is critical; while in data applications, unordered data is prevalent. Unordered data can be processed more efficiently than ordered data, and all commercial database systems exploit this fact in their implementations. For example, consider a request for all persons in a database whose age is between 30 and 32. A database optimizer may use an index to retrieve efficiently all answers. The use of the index, however, may report the results in a different order than stored on disc. If that order were important, additional bookkeeping and processing are necessary to recover it. In the cases when order is important, databases deal with it separately, for example, with ordered collections (lists, arrays) and through the orderedby clause in SQL.

Applications that use XML for data exchange are likely to ignore order.

3.2.4 Mixing Elements and Text

XML allows us to mix PCDATA and subelements within an element:

```
<Person>
    This is my best friend
    <Name> Alan </Name>
    <Age> 42 </Age>
```

```
I am not too sure of the following email
  <Email> agb@abc.com </Email>
</Person>
```

From a database perspective this seems a little unnatural, but from a document perspective it is reasonable: we want to embed text in structured data and vice versa. Note that in order to translate XML back into the syntax of ssd-expressions, we would have to add some surrounding standard tag for the PCDATA.

3.2.5 Other XML Constructs

XML has additional constructs required in document applications that have little or no use for data exchange. We mention them here only briefly.

Comments in XML are written as

```
<!-- this is a comment -->
```

Comments are allowed anywhere except inside markups. Somewhat surprisingly, they are part of the XML document (although not part of the *character data*) and can be passed to the application.

Another construct is the processing instruction (PI), which allows documents to contain instructions for applications. A PI has a target (the name of the application) and an optional free text. In the example below, xml-stylesheet is the target, and all the rest is free text:

```
<?xml-stylesheet href="book.css" type="text/css"?>
```

There is no semantics associated to PIs except that they have to be passed to the applications. An XML document starts with an optional construct that looks like a PI but is not considered to be a PI by the XML standard. The construct is

```
<?xml version="1.0"?>
```

Currently XML's version is 1.0, but, of course, this will change in the future. Some additional information describing the character encoding of the document may follow the version number.

A third construct is CDATA (character data), used to write escape blocks containing characters that would be otherwise recognized as markup. CDATA sections start with <![CDATA[and end with]]>, as in the following example:

```
<![CDATA[<start>this is an incorrect element</end>]]>
```

A fourth construct is entities, which are a form of macros. One kind of entity starts with &, is followed by a name, and ends with ;. For example < is an entity reference for the character <. Another kind starts with %. Users can define new entities in XML. Entities are quite elaborate in XML, and a good portion of the language definition deals with them. However, they are of little use in data applications, so we mention them only briefly.

Finally, an XML document may have an optional *document type definition* (DTD), which defines the document's grammar. This has the form

```
<!DOCTYPE name [markupdeclarations]>
```

Thus, the document type definition consists of the name of the root document tag, optionally followed by several markup declarations that declare the tags permitted in the document and their associated structure.

Summarizing, a complete XML document has the following form, in which the first two lines are optional:

```
<?xml . . .?>
<!DOCTYPE name [markupdeclarations]>
<name> . . . </name>
```

where name is some element tag.

3.3   DOCUMENT TYPE DEFINITIONS

A document type definition (DTD) serves as grammar for the underlying XML document, and it is part of the XML language. To some extent a DTD can also serve as schema for the data represented by the XML document; hence our interest here. As schema formalisms, DTDs are somewhat unsatisfactory, and several proposals have been made after the adoption of the XML standard for better schema formalisms. However, no consensus exists so far beyond the basic DTDs.

3.3.1   A Simple DTD

Consider an XML document consisting of an arbitrary number of person elements like

```
<db><person> <name> Alan </name>
             <age> 42 </age>
             <email> agb@abc.com </email>
    </person>
    <person> . . . </person>
    . . .
</db>
```

A DTD for it might be

```
<!DOCTYPE db [
    <!ELEMENT db (person*)>
    <!ELEMENT person (name,age,email)>
    <!ELEMENT name (#PCDATA)>
    <!ELEMENT age (#PCDATA)>
    <!ELEMENT email (#PCDATA)>
]>
```

The first line says that the root element is <db>. The next five lines are markup declarations stating that <db> may contain an arbitrary number of <person> elements, each containing <name>, <age>, and <email> elements. The latter contain only character data (no elements). Here person* is a regular expression, meaning any number of person elements. Other regular expressions are e+ (one or more occurrences), e? (zero or one), e | e' (alternation), and e,e' (concatenation).

3.3.2 DTDs as Grammars

A DTD is precisely a context-free grammar for the document. In particular, the example above imposes that <name>, <age>, and <email> appear *in that order* in a <person> element. Grammars can be recursive, as in the following DTD describing binary trees:

```
<!ELEMENT node (leaf | (node,node))>
<!ELEMENT leaf (#PCDATA)>
```

An example of such an XML document is

```
<node>
    <node>
        <node> <leaf> 1 </leaf> </node>
        <node> <leaf> 2 </leaf> </node>
    </node>
    <node>
        <leaf> 3 </leaf>
    </node>
</node>
```

3.3.3 DTDs as Schemas

DTDs can be used to a certain extent as schemas. The db DTD requires that person elements have a name field. In this sense they resemble types, though the types that can be expressed using DTDs are not as extensive as someone coming from the world of structured databases might wish. As an example, consider the relational schema r1(a,b,c), r2(c,d), and the following representation in XML (see also Figure 2.3):

```
<db><r1><a> a1 </a> <b> b1 </b> <c> c1 </c> </r1>
    <r1><a> a2 </a> <b> b2 </b> <c> c2 </c> </r1>
    <r2><c> c2 </c> <d> d2 </d> </r2>
    <r2><c> c3 </c> <d> d3 </d> </r2>
    <r2><c> c4 </c> <d> d4 </d> </r2>
</db>
```

In this representation we have taken the names of the relations r1, r2 as tags for the tuples in the relation. A DTD for such data is

```
<!DOCTYPE db [
  <!ELEMENT db (r1*, r2*)>
  <!ELEMENT r1 (a,b,c)>
  <!ELEMENT r2 (c,d)>
  <!ELEMENT a (#PCDATA)>
  <!ELEMENT b (#PCDATA)>
  <!ELEMENT c (#PCDATA)>
  <!ELEMENT d (#PCDATA)>
]>
```

The DTD correctly constrains r1 elements to contain three components a, b, c and r2 elements to contain the components c, d. But it also forces c, d to occur in that order. Obviously, the order d, c is equally acceptable for relational data, so we may modify the DTD to

```
<!ELEMENT r2 ((c,d)|(d,c))>
```

This becomes more verbose for r1, where we have to list six orders. Another problem is that r1 elements are constrained to appear before r2 elements. The following change allows them to be interspersed:

```
<!ELEMENT db ((r1|r2)*)>
```

On the bright side, DTDs make it easy for us to describe optional or repeated components. For example, we could modify r1 to

```
<!ELEMENT r1 (a,b?,c+)>
```

stating that exactly one a is required, that b is optional, and that c is required, but may have several occurrences.

So far we have included all the schema inside the XML document, as in

```
<!DOCTYPE db [<!ELEMENT . . .> . . .]>
```

We can alternatively store the schema in a separate file, say, schema.dtd, and refer to it as

```
<!DOCTYPE db SYSTEM "schema.dtd">
```

The schema can reside at a different URL, and then we refer to it as

```
<!DOCTYPE db SYSTEM "http://www.schemaauthority.com/schema.dtd">
```

This allows many sites on the Web to share a common schema, thus facilitating exchange.

3.3.4 Declaring Attributes in DTDs

DTDs also allow us to assert the type of attributes. Consider an XML document containing products like

```
<product>
   <name language="French" department="music">
                   trompette six trous </name>
   <price currency="Euro"> 420.12      </price>
</product>
```

In addition to the element declarations for product, name, price we have

```
<!ATTLIS name language   CDATA #REQUIRED
             department CDATA #IMPLIED>
<!ATTLIS price currency  CDATA #IMPLIED>
```

The declaration says that <name> has two attributes, language and department; the first is required, while the second one is optional. Similarly, <price> has the attribute currency, which is optional. All attributes are of "type" CDATA, which means strings in XML slang.

   Of particular importance are declarations of types ID, IDREF, and IDREFS. The type ID declares that the particular attribute defines the entity's unique identifier; we have used id for attributes of that type in Section 3.2, but of course any name can be used. Similarly, the type IDREF means that the attribute's value is some other element's identifier; IDREFS means that its value is a list of identifiers, separated by spaces.

As a simple example of the use of references, here is a family tree specification:

```
<!DOCTYPE family [
  <!ELEMENT family (person)*>
  <!ELEMENT person (name)>
  <!ELEMENT name (#PCDATA)>
  <!ATTLIST person id       ID    #REQUIRED
                   mother   IDREF #IMPLIED
                   father   IDREF #IMPLIED
                   children IDREFS #IMPLIED>
]>
```

A very simple XML element that conforms to this DTD is

```
<family>
  <person  id="jane"  mother="mary" father="john">
    <name> Jane Doe </name>
  </person>
  <person id="john" children="jane jack">
    <name> John Doe </name>
  </person>
  <person id="mary" children="jane jack">
    <name> Mary Smith </name>
  </person>
  <person  id="jack"  mother="smith"  father="john">
    <name> Jack Smith </name>
  </person>
</family>
```

As a richer example of a DTD involving references, here is a DTD for the example in Figure 3.4.

```
<!DOCTYPE geography [
  <!ELEMENT geography (state|city)*>
  <!ELEMENT state (scode,sname,capital,cities-in*)>
    <!ATTLIST state  id ID #REQUIRED>
  <!ELEMENT scode (#PCDATA)>
  <!ELEMENT sname (#PCDATA)>
  <!ELEMENT capital EMPTY>
    <!ATTLIST capital idref IDREF #REQUIRED>
  <!ELEMENT cities-in EMPTY>
    <!ATTLIST cities-in idref IDREF #REQUIRED>
```

```
<!ELEMENT city (ccode,cname,state-of)>
  <!ATTLIST city id ID>
<!ELEMENT ccode (#PCDATA)>
<!ELEMENT cname (#PCDATA)>
<!ELEMENT state-of EMPTY>
  <!ATTLIST state-of idref IDREF #REQUIRED>
]>
```

EMPTY in the place of an element content means that the element is empty. For example, capital can only occur as

```
<capital idref=". . ."/>
```

The attribute type IDREFS allows an attribute to refer to multiple entities. For example, we could change the DTD above as follows:

```
<!DOCTYPE geography [
  . . .
  <!ELEMENT state (scode,sname,capital,cities-in)>
  . . .
  <!ELEMENT cities-in EMPTY>
    <!ATTLIST cities-in idrefs IDREFS #REQUIRED>
  . . .
]>
```

The cities-in elements could then be written as <cities-in idref="c1 c2"/>. There are other ways of representing this data even more compactly. For example, we could make both capital and cities-in attributes of State, as in

```
<!ATTLIST State id ID #REQUIRED
                capital IDREF  #REQUIRED
                cities-in IDREFS  #REQUIRED>
```

Finally, we conclude our discussion of DTDs with an example illustrating entities to refer to external data using a URL. Such external references may be useful in data exchange. We give an example in Figure 3.6 of an XML document that uses external documents. Consider the abstract defined in the prologue. We define abstract as an "entity" consisting of some external XML file. The use of %abstract; in the report results in inserting the entire abstract document at that position. Thus, the document includes explicitly only the elements meta (some meta information about the report), and title; the abstract and content are fetched from other documents.

```
<?xml version "1.0"?>
<!DOCTYPE report [
<!ENTITY %abstract SYSTEM "/u/abitebou/LEBOOK/abstract">
<!ENTITY %content SYSTEM "/u/suciu/LEBOOK/lebook">
]>
<report>
   <meta keywords="xml,www,web,semistructured"
         author="Abiteboul,Buneman,Suciu"
         date="25.12.98"/>
   <title>Data on the Web</title>
   %abstract;
   %content;
</report>
```
Figure 3.6 Using external resources.

3.3.5   Valid XML Documents

Recall that a well-formed XML document is one that, essentially, has matching
markups. A *valid* XML document is one that, in addition, has a DTD, and that
conforms to that DTD. That is, elements may be nested only in the way described
by the DTD and may have only the attributes allowed by the DTD. For identifiers
and references the requirements are very weak: the values of all attributes of type
ID must be distinct, and all references of type IDREF or IDREFS must be to existing
identifiers. The DTD does not impose any constraint on the type of the referenced
element.

3.3.6   Limitations of DTDs as Schemas

We have seen that one limitation is the fact that DTDs impose order. Another
is that there is no notion of atomic types. We would like to say, for instance,
that the content of an age element has to be an integer; instead the only atomic
type is #PCDATA, which means strings. In addition to that we would need range
specifications, for example, the ability to constrain the age between 0 and
140.

   A subtle limitation is that the type associated with an element, more correctly
with the tag, is global. For example, in an object database, a name field might
have one structure in a person class and another in a course class. XML does
not allow that. In translating to XML, one would have to use two distinct tag
names, for example, personname and coursename. XML offers a partial solution
in the form of *namespaces*. We would define two namespaces called person and

course, then rename the tags to `person:name` and `course:name`. Associated to each namespace is a DTD defining the element `name`.

Finally, a serious limitation is that DTDs do not constrain the type of `IDREF`s. One would like to say, for example, that the `idref` attribute in `state-of` must be an identifier of a `state` element, while that of `cities-in` must be of "type" `city`.

In conclusion, from a database perspective the typing offered by DTDs may be regarded as inadequate. There are, in fact, many extensions to XML that deal with these and other issues. We give a brief review here.

3.4 DOCUMENT NAVIGATION

XML Links (XLink) and XML Pointers (XPointer) allow us to navigate the entire Web by pointing to arbitrary positions in documents. For that, we can use an ID of the document or a relative position (e.g., the chapter just after that with the string "Query" in the title). Links are elements that own a particular attribute *xml:link* and other attributes determining the nature of the linking. In the simpler cases, we find simple links as in HTML:

```
<A xml:link="simple" HREF="http:www-rocq.inria.fr/verso">
                          Verso Group</A>
<A HREF="mailto:Serge.Abiteboul@inria.fr">Serge</A>
```

An example of relative addressing is given by

```
<node xml:link="simple" HREF=
     "report.xml#root().child(2,section).child(3,subsection)">
```

The following is a more complex example from [Mic98] with "behavioral" semantics attached to links:

```
<payment-choice xml:link="extended"
   inline="true"
   role="form"
   title="choose form of payment" >
 <target xml:link="locator"
    href="http://foo.bar.fr/visa-form.xml"
    role="form"
    title="visa"
    show="embed"
    actuate="user"
    behavior="type;field=1;no-scroll" />
```

```
<target xml:link="locator"
   href="http://foo.bar.fr/klee-form.xml"
   role="form"
   title="kleebox"
   show="embed"
   actuate="user"
   behavior="type;field=1;no-scroll" />
</payment-choice>
```

This may be presented to the user with a title *choose form of payment*. If the user clicks on this anchor, a pop-up menu appears with an alternative between *visa* and *kleebox*, the two accepted forms of payment. The choice of one triggers the inclusion of the appropriate form.

The linking process is quite rich. Indeed, a link between an element in a document d_1 and a document d_2 may be defined *externally* to both d_1 and d_2. Thus, we may link a document to others without actually modifying it. XLink also allows us to create links that have several targets.

XLink and Xpointer are not yet fully standardized. We will not discuss them in more detail. To conclude this section, observe in Figure 3.6 the specification in the prologue of metadata that are used, for instance, for indexing by search engines.

3.5   DCD

DCD (Document Content Description) [DCD99] is used to define the typing of some XML data more precisely than just with a DTD. We will discuss more generally the notion of typing semistructured data in Chapter 7. This area is not as well established as XML. DCD is just a proposal in the spirit of previous proposals such as XML-Data and XML-Schema. We briefly consider some aspects of DCD here to express some issues that typing for XML data should address.

First, DCDs are used to "type" terminal elements (PCDATA). We illustrate this aspect with a simple example taken from [DCD99]. Recall that <ElementDef/> is just a shorthand for <ElementDef> </ElementDef>.

```
<DCD>
<ElementDef Type="Booking" Model="Elements" Content="Closed">
 <Description>Describes an airline reservation</Description>
  <Group RDF:Order="Seq">
   <Element>LastName</Element> <Element>FirstInitial</Element>
   <Element>SeatRow</Element> <Element>SeatLetter</Element>
```

```
    <Element>Departure</Element> <Element>Class</Element>
  </Group>
</ElementDef>

<!-- example omits boring field declarations -->
<ElementDef Type="SeatRow" Model="Data" Datatype="i1"
                          Min="1" Max="72" />

<ElementDef Type="SeatLetter" Model="Data" Datatype="char"
                          Min="A" Max="K"/>
<ElementDef Type="Class" Model="Data" Datatype="char"
                          Default="1"/>

</DCD>
```

This specification imposes some constraints for documents in an airline reservation service. Observe the specification of types such as "i1" or "char", range constraints such as between 1 and 72, and the specification of default values such as "1".

Also, recall that a DTD applies to a particular document, that is, a single resource. DCDs also allow you to relate a number of resources. For instance, an encyclopedia may be defined by one or several DTDs that specify the structure of the elementary documents, the articles. A DCD may be used to impose a conceptual structure to the set of articles. In particular, it may specify relationships such as *subcategory* or *is-an-instance-of*.

It should be observed that our presentation covers very little of the rich typing world of DCD. It must also be said that none of this is yet a standard.

3.6 PARAPHERNALIA

XML is only a piece (although an important one) of a much larger picture. In this section, we briefly mention three essential components of this larger picture.

3.6.1 RDF

The Resource Description Framework (RDF) is a proposal for representing metadata in XML. Its intended applications include

- providing better search engine capabilities in resource discovery
- cataloging for describing the content and content relationships available at a particular Web site
- allowing intelligent software agents to share and exchange knowledge

RDF consists of a data model and a syntax; a separate proposal is RDF-Schema. We briefly mention here the data model and syntax only.

In its simplest form, the RDF data model is that of an edge-labeled graph, exactly like OEM. Nodes are called *resources*, and edge labels are called *properties*. RDF's syntax is a convention for representing this model in XML. For example, Figure 3.3(b) would be represented in RDF as follows:

```
<rdf:description ID="&o1">
    <person> <rdf:description ID="&o2">
                <name> Alan </name>
                <age>  42   </age>
                <email> agb@abc.com </email>
            </rdf.description>
    </person>
</rdf:description>
```

The `<rdf:description>` element describes a resource. In this example we chose to create two new resources and give them unique ids (the `ID` attribute). The other choice is to talk about an existing resource and give its URL reference. The properties in this example are `person`, `name`, `age`, and `email`. An edge in RDF is called a *statement*. Thus, the above example makes four statements: resource `&o1` has property `person` whose value is resource `&o2`; resource `&o2` has property `name` with value `Alan`, and so on.

RDF's data model extends the basic graph model in several ways. First, it has containers: a container can be a bag, a sequence, or an alternative. The first two roughly correspond to the bag type and list type in ODMG. Second, it extends the model with higher-order statements. That is, RDF provides syntax for expressing something like `John` *says that the email of resource* `&o2` *is* `agb@abc.com`. Here the resource is `John`, the property is `says`, and its value is another statement.

3.6.2 Stylesheets

We already mentioned that HTML dominates the Web. HTML combines data and presentation, and is the only language understood by browsers. Since XML contains only data, we need to convert it into HTML first, in order to display it with a browser. Stylesheets [Sty99] are special-purpose languages expressing this conversion. There are two, somewhat competing proposals for stylesheets. The first is lightweight: it is called Cascading Style Sheets (CSS), and we briefly illustrate it here. The other is a transformation language, called XSL, and is described in more detail in Chapter 5.

The main idea in CSS is to associate with each element type a presentation. For instance, we could use for *address* elements

```
<STYLE TAG="address">
  <FONT-SIZE V=10>
  <FONT-FAMILY V="Times New Roman">
</STYLE>
```

The stylesheet information may be included in the document or it may be found elsewhere. We can use a processing instruction to attach a stylesheet to the document. For instance,

```
<?STYLESPEC "company-desc" "style23.ssh" ?>
```

is an example of the use of a processing instruction to specify that the format "company-desc" found in file "style23.ssh" should be applied to the document. In general, processing instructions contain indications to be used by particular applications.

Observe that we can use different presentations of the same document, for example, customize the presentation to various uses or users.

3.6.3 SAX and DOM

These are two very different APIs for XML documents. SAX is more syntax driven, whereas DOM offers an array of the functionalities to develop applications with XML data.

SAX (Simple API for XML) is a standard for parsing XML data. A SAX parser reads the flow of some XML data, parses it, and detects *events* when interpreting the tags. These events are sent back to the application. This provides a simple API for handling XML.

An alternative is to compile the entire document directly and construct a tree representation for it. This is provided by an alternative API, namely, DOM (Document Object Model) [DOM99]. DOM is an API for XML documents. It offers an object-oriented view of the XML document, as opposed to an abstract data type view. That is, each document component defines an interface specifying its behavior; the data can be accessed only via this interface. DOM defines a Node interface, and subclasses Element, Attribute, and Character-Data interfaces inheriting from Node. The Node interface defines methods for accessing a node's components. For example, parentNode() returns the parent node; childNodes() returns the set of children. In addition there are methods for modifying the node and for creating new nodes. Thus, an application can completely restructure the document via this interface. In some sense, DOM is rather close to the *data* (vs. document) view of XML that is promoted in this book.

To conclude this section, we should mention some specific applications that are enriching the XML world, for example, MathML for mathematical data or SMIL for multimedia [W3C].

3.7   BIBLIOGRAPHIC REMARKS

There are numerous books on XML: more than 66 were available from ama-zon.com in 1999. We refer here to three: [McG98, GP98, Mic98]. An easy introduction to XML Internet applications can be found in [LLF98]. The author-itative source on XML is the language definition [XML98] from the World Wide Web Consortium (W3C) site [W3C]; although pretty terse for a first lecture, you should have no problems following it after reading this chapter. The W3C site provides information on, for instance, DCD [DCD99], DOM [DOM99], stylesheets [Sty99], XSL [XSL98], XLink [XLI98], XPointer [XPO98], and RDF [RDF99].

An excellent paper spelling out crisply the rationale behind XML is Jon Bosak's [Bos97].

HTML is based on SGML, while XML is a fragment of SGML. SGML is described in [ISO86]. XSL is described in [XSL98].

There is a huge literature on tools for extracting data from HTML pages (such programs are sometimes called wrappers). Some entry points are [KM98, Ade98, HGMC⁺97, SA98].

II

Queries

4

Query Languages

In Chapter 1, we described a fundamental difference between the document and database views of how data is accessed. In the document world, we provide a URL and retrieve a whole HTML page; in the database world, we construct a query, the query is shipped to a server, and an answer is returned. The difference is in part illusory because HTML pages are frequently constructed on the fly in response to a query that is generated at the user interface. Thus, some form of query is already being generated at the user interface. Still, there is a major difference in granularity: HTML documents offer a fixed level of granularity, while queries can group or divide data to arbitrary level of granularity.

A query language is essential for Web data. We have already discussed how we would represent databases as XML documents, but the size of the resulting document may prohibit its transmission as a single page. Moreover, a large XML document would most likely be a view of a large database, and a user will typically want only a fragment of that data. How we select and transform information from large sources is the topic of query languages. One very simple and widely used form of query is provided by an indexed file. Much scientific data is held in documents that consist of a large number of complex records, each with a similar structure. The purpose of the index is to retrieve one/some of these records when a record entry (e.g., a key) is provided as input. This in itself is a query language. Indexing systems such as SRS for biological data are probably the most widely used form of query for documents structured in this way. However, we would like to do better. We would like our query language, in the spirit of database query languages, to be able to use complex predicates on the data. It should be able to do joins (e.g., combine data from different sources) and perform some form of data restructuring.

David Maier has recently laid out a number of desiderata for an XML query language. Several of them are completely independent of the specific format (XML) and would apply to any query language for semistructured data. The following list does not correspond directly to Maier's list, but many of the points are inspired by it.

- *Expressive power.* We can write down an informal list of the kinds of operations that a query language should express. We can be somewhat more precise by saying that if we represent, say, relational data as semistructured data, then we would like our query language to be capable of expressing the operations corresponding to those in some standard relational language such as relational algebra or SQL. However, this is certainly not a complete requirement. An interesting issue is that of *restructuring* semistructured data. There are simple restructuring problems that defeat all of the query languages we shall describe. Moreover, there is no accepted notion of *completeness* for semistructured data restructuring. Therefore, it is yet unclear what expressive power should capture a query language for semistructured data.

- *Semantics.* Precise semantics are called for. Without this we cannot start to discuss query transformation or optimization. Here an interesting issue is what, if anything, the semantics adds to (or takes from) the syntax in which data is expressed. This is especially important for XML, whose specification is entirely syntactic.

- *Compositionality.* This requirement states that the output of a query can be used as the input of another query and is essential, among other things, for constructing views. The requirement has both semantic and syntactic consequences. Semantically it states that our queries must stay within the same data model. They cannot take data in one model and produce output in another. Syntactically it requires that our languages are referentially transparent. Wherever we use a name or variable that denotes semistructured data, we may replace that name with an expression denoting the same value without changing the meaning of a query.

- *Schema.* Although we have stated that semistructured data does not have a separate schema, later sections of this book, such as Chapter 7, will deal extensively with structure. Query languages for semistructured data should be "structure conscious." When structure is defined or inferred, a query language should be capable of exploiting the structure for type checking, optimization, and so on.

■ *Program manipulation.* It is important to remember that most SQL queries
are not written by programmers but are generated by other programs. The
same is true of query languages. For program generation, a simple though
verbose *core* language (such as the one we present below) may be more
appropriate than one user-friendly language with unclear semantics.

In this chapter, we shall introduce the syntax of a simple core language for
semistructured data and then describe two extensions that have resulted in working prototypes. The development of query languages for semistructured data,
and in particular for XML, is very much in its infancy, and it is anyone's guess
as to what will emerge as a standard. The two languages we shall describe here,
Lorel and UnQL, are very similar in expressive power. They are presented in this
fashion so that the reader should be able to appreciate that there is not a huge
difference between query languages based on a database standard query language
such as OQL and those, like XSL and XML-QL, that are based on pattern matching on the syntax of the underlying data format. Be aware that there are *semantic*
differences between these various languages that will be discussed in later chapters. However, these differences will not be important in the informal account of
query languages in this chapter.

4.1   PATH EXPRESSIONS

One of the main distinguishing features of semistructured query languages is
their ability to reach to arbitrary depths in the data graph. To do this they all
exploit, in some form, the notion of a *path expression.* Recall our model of data
as an edge-labeled directed graph. A sequence of edge labels $l_1.l_2.\ldots.l_n$ is called
a *path expression.* We view a path expression as a simple query whose result, for a
given data graph, is a set of nodes. For example, the result of the path expression
"biblio.book" in Figure 4.1(a) is the set of nodes {n1, n2}. The result of the
path expression "biblio.book.author" is the set of nodes with the associated
set of strings {"Combalusier", "Roux", "Smith"}.

In general, the result of the path expression $l_1.l_2.\ldots.l_n$ on a data graph is the
set of nodes v_n such that there exist edges $(r, l_1, v_1), (v_1, l_2, v_2), \ldots, (v_{n-1}, l_n, v_n)$
in the data graph, where r is the root. Thus, path expressions result in sets of
nodes. They do not (yet) result in pieces of semistructured data.

Rather than specify a path completely, we may want to specify it by some
property. This property may be a property of the path (e.g., the path must traverse
a paper edge) or it may be a property on an individual edge label (e.g., the edge
label contains the substring "bib".) We shall use *regular expressions*, at two levels,

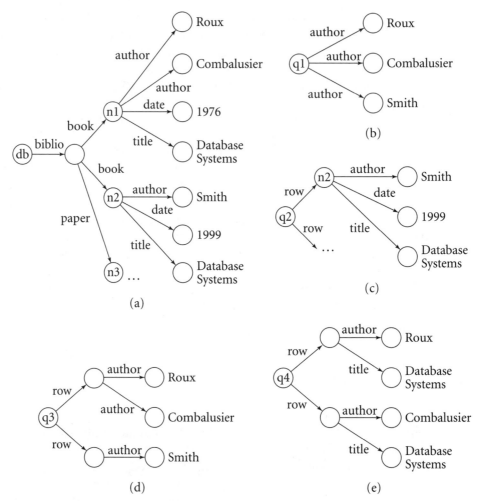

Figure 4.1 Database and answers.

both on the alphabet of edge labels and on the alphabet of (ASCII) characters that comprise labels, to describe such path properties. Starting with the alphabet of edge labels, a regular expression such as book|paper matches either a book edge or a paper edge. In the database of Figure 4.1, it could be used in the query
biblio.(book|paper).author

Another useful pattern is a "wild card," which matches any edge label. We shall use the symbol _. Thus biblio._.author matches any path consisting of a biblio edge followed by any edge followed by a author edge. We can also consider a Kleene closure operation, denoted $*$, which specifies arbitrary repeats of a regular expression. For instance, `biblio._*.author` specifies nodes at the end of a path that starts with a `biblio` label, ends with an `author` label, and has an arbitrary sequence of edges between.

The general syntax of regular expressions on paths is

$$e ::= l \mid \epsilon \mid \_ \mid e'.'e \mid '('e')' \mid e'—'e \mid e'*' \mid e'+' \mid e'?'$$

where l ranges over labels, e over expressions, and ϵ is the empty expression. The expression $e*$ stands for 0 or more repeats of e, that is, for

$$\epsilon \mid e \mid e.e \mid e.e.e \mid e.e.e.e \mid \ldots$$

Also, $e+$ stands for one or more repeats, and e? for zero or one occurrence of e.

So far, we can either specify completely a label or use the $\_$ wild card. To specify more complex label patterns, we shall use the established syntax of grep. For example, the pattern

```
((s|S)ection|paragraph)(s)?
```

matches any six labels: `section`, `Section`, `sections`, `Sections`, `paragraph`, and `paragraphs`. To avoid ambiguities between the regular expressions for labels and those for path expressions we enclose the former in quotation marks. (Note that the period is used as a character wild card in grep, but it is used as the concatenation operator for path expressions.) As an example of a generalized path expression that contains both forms of matching, the pattern

```
biblio ._*.section.("[tT]itle" | paragraph.".*heading.*")
```

matches any path that starts with a `biblio` label and ends with a `section` label followed by either a (possibly capitalized) `title` or a `paragraph` edge followed by an edge that contains the string `heading`.

In some models of semistructured data, the edge labels are not limited to being strings. They may be integers or some other category of strings. A query language that makes use of path expressions may coerce all these types to an underlying string representation and match a regular expression to this representation.

When the data graph has cycles, it is possible to specify paths of arbitrary length. Referring to Figure 2.7, the path expressions

```
cities.state-of
cities.state-of.capital
cities.state-of.capital.state-of
cities.state-of.capital.state-of.capital
```

all match the data graph. Moreover the regular expression _* matches an infinite number of paths whenever there is a cycle. The set of nodes specified by this path expression is still finite, being a subset of the nodes in the data graph, but we need to exercise more care when computing the result of a regular exprssion on a data graph with cycles.

In general, given a regular expression e and a data graph D, the result of e on D is computed as follows. First, construct some automaton A that is equivalent to the regular expression e; any nondeterministic automaton would do.[1] Let $\{x_1, x_2, \ldots\}$ be the set of nodes in D, with x_1 being the root, and let $\{s_1, s_2, \ldots\}$ be the set of states in A, with s_1 being the initial state. Compute a set *Closure* as follows. Initially *Closure* $= \{(x_1, s_1)\}$. Repeat the following, until *Closure* does not change any more. Choose some pair $(x, s) \in$ *Closure*, and consider some edge $x \xrightarrow{a} x'$ in the datagraph D, and some transition $s \xrightarrow{a} s'$ in A, labeled with the same label (denote here a); add the pair (x', s') to *Closure*. After *Closure* reaches a fixpoint, the result of e on D consists of the set of nodes x such that *Closure* contains some pair (x, s), with s a terminal state in A. Note that this procedure always terminates. In the worst case, it has to visit each node x in the data graph as many times as states in the automaton A. However, in practice, it will visit most nodes at most once and may not visit portions of the database at all.

4.2   A CORE LANGUAGE

Path expressions, although they are an essential feature of semistructured query languages, only get us some distance toward a query language. They can only return a subset of nodes in the database. They cannot construct new nodes, they cannot perform the equivalent of a relational database join, and they cannot test values stored in the database. Path expressions form the basic building block of the language. Standard query language features will do the rest.

The syntax of languages that have been developed so far is in a state of flux. We shall adopt a rather conservative approach and then deal with various extensions. We shall base our core syntax on Lorel and UnQL, which, to within very minor syntactic details, agree on this core.

---

1. This construction is described in detail in many textbooks, for example, [HU79].

4.2.1 The Basic Syntax

As in Lorel, our basic syntax is based on OQL and illustrated with the following query:

```
% Query q1
select author: X
from    biblio.book.author X
```

which computes the set of book authors. Informally, the semantics of the query is to bind the variable X to each node specified by the path expression. The effect of the query is to form one new node and connect it with edges labeled author to the nodes resulting from the evaluation of the path expression biblio.book.author. The result of the query is a new data graph shown in Figure 4.1(b) whose output corresponds to the ssd-expression

```
{author: "Roux", author: "Combalusier", author: "Smith"}
```

In our next example, we restrict the output by use of a condition in the where clause of the query:

```
% Query q2
select row: X
from    biblio._ X
where  "Smith" in X.author
```

whose output shown in Figure 4.1(c) corresponds to the ssd-expression

```
{row: {author: "Smith",
       date: 1999,
       title: "Database Systems"}, ...}
```

The notation X.author is also a path expression whose root is taken as the node denoted by X. In general, the result of this expression is a set, and the predicate "Smith" in X.author is a predicate that tests for set membership.

Assuming a predicate matches for matching strings to regular expressions, we can write the following:

```
select author:Y
from    biblio._ X,
        X.author Y,
        X.title Z
where  matches(".*(D|d)atabase.*", Z)
```

This collects all the authors of publications whose title contains the word "database". Note how each line of the from clause introduces a new variable.

In general, the semantics of a query `select E from B where C` is defined in three steps. The first deals with `from`, the second with `where`, and the last with `select`. Assume that B defines three variables, X, Y, Z. In the first step, we find the set of all bindings of these variables specified by B; each binding maps the variables to oids in the data graph. In the second step, we filter the bindings that satisfy C. Let this set be

$$\{(x_1, y_1, z_1), \ldots, (x_n, y_n, z_n)\}.$$

Here each value $x_1, \ldots, z_n$ is an oid from the input graph. In our illustration, this is a ternary relation, but in general it is a relation whose arity is the number of variables defined in B. In the last step, we construct the ssd-expression that forms the result

$$\{E(x_1, y_1, z_1), \ldots, E(x_n, y_n, z_n)\}.$$

Each $E(x_i, y_i, z_i)$ denotes E in which x_i, y_i, z_i are substituted for X, Y, Z. Finally, the result corresponds to an ssd-expression.

Illustrating the example above, in the first step we find the set of all values for X, Y, Z such that `biblio._ X, X.author Y, X.title Z`. In the second step, we keep only those such that `matches(".*(D_d)atabase.*",Z)`. Let

$$\{(x_1, y_1, z_1), \ldots, (x_n, y_n, z_n)\}$$

be this set. In the last step, we construct the result: {`author:`y_1, `author:`y_2, ..., `author:`y_n}. The query therefore creates just one new node in the data graph (the root).

Some queries create more than one new node. For instance, consider

```
select row: { title: Y, author: Z}
from   biblio.book X, X.title Y, X.author Z
```

Here the result will be constructed as

{`row:{title:`y_1, `author:`z_1}, ..., `row:{title:`y_n, `author:`z_n}}.

A new node is used for the entire result. Plus for each binding (x_i, y_i, z_i), a new node is constructed to represent the row {`title:`y_i, `author:`z_i}.

Another means of creating many new nodes is by nesting subqueries in the select clause since each instance of the nested subquery will potentially create new objects. This is illustrated in the following two queries:

```
% Query q3
select row:( select author: Y
             from   X.author Y)
from   biblio.book X
```

```
% Query q4
select row: ( select author: Y, title: T
              from    X.author Y,
                      X.title  T)
from  biblio.book X
where "Roux" in X.author
```

The output of q3 corresponds to the ssd-expression:

```
{ row: {author:  "Roux", author: "Combalusier"},
  row: {author: "Smith"} }
```

The data graph of the result is shown in Figure 4.1(d) and should be compared with the output from query q1.

The more complex query q4 implements a generalized form of projection and selection. The output is shown in Figure 4.1(e).

We can also express joins. Consider for instance a relational schema r1(a,b), r2(b,c), for which the following ssd-expression represents an instance:

```
{ r1: { row: {a: 1, b: 2},
        row: {a: 1, b: 3} },
  r2: { row: {b: 2, c: 4},
        row: {b: 2, c: 3} } }
```

Consider the query

```
% Query q-join
select a: A, c: C
from    r1.row X,
        r2.row Y,
        X.a A, X.b B, Y.b B', Y.c C
where   B = B'
```

where X and Y range, respectively, over the rows in r1 and r2. The query computes the join of the two relations on their B attributes, that is, their natural join, and projects on the A and C attributes.

Suppose that rows are allowed multiple B values. This query also computes the "join." But we have to be careful about what we mean by a join. Two rows match if they have some common B value. As another example of a join with a more sophisticated condition, the following query asks for authors that are referred to at least twice in some paper with "Database" in the title:

```
select row: W
from    biblio.paper X, X.refers-to Y, Y.author W,
        X.refers-to Z
```

```
where  NOT ( Y = Z )
  and  W in Z.author
  and  matches("*Database*", X.title)
```

4.3   MORE ON LOREL

The core language is, as we have noted, a fragment of Lorel, the query language in Lore (Lightweight Object REpository), a system for managing semistructured data. Lorel was essentially derived by adapting OQL to querying semistructured data. We now complete the description of Lorel, which provides for terser queries through the use of syntactic shortcuts and coercions that may make the language more attractive to, say, an SQL programmer.

The first of these concerns the omission of labels. Consider

```
select X
from   biblio.book.author X
```

Since we have not placed any label in the select clause, it is not a priori clear how this query is to produce semistructured data. Lorel adds a default label. To be consistent with other examples, we shall assume here that row is chosen as the default. (The default in Lorel would be answer). The result of the query is therefore

```
{row: "Roux", row: "Combalusier", row: "Smith"}.
```

Lorel also allows us to use path expressions in the select clause.

```
% Query q3'
select X.author
from   biblio.book X
```

Observe that for each X, X.author denotes a set of nodes. Indeed, we may understand X.author as the nested query

```
select author: Y
from   X.author Y
```

In general, an expression of the form X.p.1, where p is an arbitrarily complex path expression, is understood as the nested query

```
select 1: Y
from   X.p.1 Y
```

Now, in general, the semantics associated to path expressions in the `select` clause is understood by rewriting them into nested queries. In particular, query q3′ above corresponds to

```
select row: (select author: Y
             from   X.author Y)
from  biblio.book X
```

Thus, q3′ is the same query as q3.

A second use of overloading in Lorel occurs in the use of comparison predicates, especially equality. For instance, consider

```
select row: X
from biblio.paper X
where X.author = "Smith"
```

Note that `X.author` is strictly speaking a *set* of authors. Here we are using an equality predicate on disparate types. The intended meaning is `"Smith"` in `X.author`, that is,

```
select row: X
from biblio.paper X
where exists Y in X.author ( Y = "Smith" )
```

A similar rewriting is performed for other predicates as well. For instance, the selection condition in

```
select row: X
from biblio.paper X
where X.year > 1993
```

is understood as `exists Y in X.year ( Y > 1993 )`.

The previous syntactic extensions can be viewed as providing some form of coercion. The user compares an atomic value 1993 to a set `X.year` and the system introduces a membership test. In the same spirit, the user should not have to care about exact atomic types, for example, whether a date is stored as an integer, a string, or in a particular `date` sort known by the system. So, the semantics of the language is that the comparison of two atomic values succeeds if both values can be coerced to the same type and the comparison succeeds in this type. The comparison `X.date > 1995` thus succeeds for a date such as 1998—an integer—or for the string `"1998"`.

We should also mention at this point that Lorel allows both label and path variables. These are described later (Section 4.5).

4.3.1 Less Essential Syntactic Sugaring

It is a tradition in query languages to introduce syntactic sugaring to avoid using
variables as much as possible. This is the case in SQL, where relation names can be
used implicitly in place of tuple variables. This leads to nice and intuitive simple
queries but is also the cause of lots of complication and ambiguities when queries
get more complex. Similar ideas have penetrated the field of semistructured data.
One such idea is in the spirit of using relation names as variables.

```
% Query q5---authors of 1997 papers
select biblio.paper.author
from   biblio.paper
where  biblio.paper.year = 1997
```

In q5, we are using biblio.paper as a variable over the set of objects denoted by
that expression. So this query is a shorthand for the following query that explicitly
uses a variable:

```
select X.author
from   biblio.paper X
where  X.year = 1997
```

We could further sugar the syntax of query q5 in an SQL style by omitting X
in the select and where clauses:

```
select author
from   biblio.paper
where  year = 1997
```

The idea is that label author can only apply to an object denoted by biblio.
paper (or more precisely to an object denoted by the variable this expression
stands for).

4.4   UNQL

UnQL (Unstructured Query Language) is a language that is based upon a somewhat different data model and interpretation than that of Lorel. However, in its
basic form it is simply an extension of our core language that uses patterns, allowing the user to express concisely complex conditions on the structure. In contrast
to Lorel, UnQL does not make use of coercion, so a more precise knowledge of
the structure of data is needed to express queries. In this section, we shall de-

scribe only the `select` fragment of UnQL. There is a more general query form in UnQL that allows complex restructuring; this is described later in Section 6.4.

In UnQL a pattern is specified simply by augmenting our syntax for ssd-expressions (Chapter 2) with variables. To simplify this part of the exposition, variables are taken as uppercase and (constant) labels as lowercase names.[2] Examples of a pattern are

```
{biblio: X}
{biblio: {book: {author: Y, title: Z}}}
```

Patterns are used to bind variables to nodes. A pattern specifies a data graph that may be matched to some larger graph. For this, we use the syntax *p* in *e* to match a pattern *p* against a data graph specified by *e*. For example,

```
{biblio: {paper: X}} in db
```

will match the variable X to the `paper` node in Figure 4.1(a). That is, it will have the same effect as `biblio.paper X` in our previous examples. We now assume an explicit name, db for the root. The following example shows how patterns may be used in an UnQL query:

```
% Query q6:
select title: X
where   {biblio: {paper: {title: X, year:Y}}} in db,
        Y > 1989
```

The `from` clause, which was previously used to introduce variable bindings, is not needed since they can now be introduced by patterns. The `where` clause contains two kinds of syntactic structures: *generators* such as `{biblio: {paper: X}} in db`, which introduce variables and bind them, and *conditions* such as Y > 1989, which operate as before. Conditions and generators are separated by commas, which, when appearing between conditions, act as conjunctions.

We have thus extended the meaning of `in` to perform pattern matching; however, once again this is syntactic sugar. Query q6 may back into our core language by translating the patterns that occur in the `where` clause into variable bindings `from` clause. The example above can be rewritten as

---

2. This is done for readability. In XML-QL (Chapter 5) variables are marked with a $. In the original UnQL, the introduction of a variable in a pattern was marked by ?. This is necessary in order to use pattern matching in a query language that conforms to the normal scoping rules for programming languages.

```
select title: X
from   biblio.paper Z,
       Z.title X,
       Z.year Y
where  Y > 1989
```

A pattern such as {biblio: {paper: X}} that describes a tree consisting of a single path is said to be *linear*. We shall adopt the syntax $l_1.l_2. \ldots l_n.e$ for linear patterns $\{l_1 : \{l_2 : \ldots \{l_n : e\} \ldots\}\}$. This is a *path pattern*. Thus biblio.paper.X in db is equivalent to biblio.paper X. As an example, the following UnQL query produces the titles of papers written by "Smith":

```
select title: X
where biblio.paper.{author: "Smith", title: X} in db
```

Patterns are also useful for the multiple bindings that are needed to express joins:

```
select row: {a: X, c: Z}
where r1.row.{a: X, b: Y} in db,
      r2.row.{b: Y, C: Z} in db
```

This should be compared to query q-join.

4.5   LABEL AND PATH VARIABLES

The use of label variables allows some interesting queries that combine what would normally be regarded as schema and data information. Label variables are used in both Lorel and UnQL. In the following we shall continue our assumption that variables are capitalized (Lorel and UnQL use different conventions for flagging label variables). Consider the queries

```
select L: X
from   biblio._*.L X
where  matches(".*Shakespear.*", X)
```

```
select new-person: (select L: Y
                    from   X.L Y
                    where  not (L = salary))
from   db.person X
```

The first of these finds all the occurrences of a string in the database matching a regular expression. It returns a tuple showing the labels that lead to a string, for example,[3]

```
{author: "William Shakespear",
 title: "Shakespeare's Tragedies", ...}
```

The second of these "hides" the salary attribute of an employee. Unlike a conventional query language, we do not need to know the attributes that are to be preserved in order to formulate this query.

It is also convenient to turn labels into data and vice versa.

```
select publication: {type: L, title: T}
from   biblio.L X, X.title T
where  X.Year > 1989
```

This is a commonly required transformation. Rather than have the type of a publication node described by the label on the edge that leads to the node, we give a common label publication to all publications and describe the type of the publication by a subsidiary type edge. Typical output from this query would be

```
{ publication: {type: "book",
                title: "Database Systems"},
  publication: {type: "paper",
                title: "Semistructured data"},   ... }
```

which shows how a leaf node may carry label data rather than string data.

Another way to use labels as data is to effect a "group-by" operation. The following example groups papers under edges labeled by their year of publication.

```
select Y: (select X
           from   biblio.paper X
           where  X.year = Y)
from   biblio.paper.year Y
```

Note that some year Y may occur in the result several times, once for each paper published that year. All occurrences will be equal (each contains all papers published that year); hence, we need to perform duplicate elimination. We will discuss duplicate elimination in Section 6.4.3.

---

3. The misspelling is deliberate; Shakespeare himself sometimes used it.

4.5.1 Paths as Data

As a brief sequel to discussing labels as data, we mention the possibility of using paths as data. Suppose we wanted to know *where* the string "ubiquitin" occurs in the data reachable from a root, say, db1. We are presumably asking for a path to that string and would like to write something like

```
select @P
from   db1 @P.X
where  matches(".*(U|u)biquitin.*",X)
```

where we have arbitrarily chosen @P as a syntax for a path variable, one that is bound to a sequence of edges. Such power comes at a price, however. As observed in Section 4.1, there may be an infinite number of paths. Hence, while path expressions worked well on cyclic data, they don't work any more when we have path variables. There are various unsatisfactory solutions. One is to terminate arbitrarily any path when it crosses itself; another is to produce the smallest subgraph of the data graph that contains all the paths (this can be expressed in UnQL). The first may still be a very large set, and the second may give back most of the data graph. The problem appears to be endemic to our model of semistructured data, which does not provide any notion of a canonical path to a node.

4.6   MIXING WITH STRUCTURED DATA

Why can't we be fully satisfied with this model? Why reintroduce structure? To see that, we have to reconsider the notion of structure and analyze in some depth where it comes in as essential. This will be the topic of Chapter 7. But for now, we can briefly mention the following motivations for typing the data at least partially:

1. When we know about the type of some data elements (perhaps because we loaded this data from some structured sources), ignoring this type would be losing information.
2. The presence of regularities facilitates querying by graphical or form-based interfaces. Also, it simplifies explaining the content of (portions of) databases to users.
3. Although updates are not the topic here, the presence of regular typing allows better protection against (in)voluntary incorrect updates.

4. Even when the data is semistructured, we might want to define more regular (structured) views of it to simplify access and/or improve performance by materializing the view.

5. The presence of regular typing may allow more optimization. For example, the regular typing of some data will result in a much more regular physical data organization, allowing more efficient processing.

For these reasons, considering only a pure semistructured data model seems a bad idea. An orthogonal issue is whether a user has to know about such typing information. We can certainly imagine applications that handle both typed and semistructured data, but present only an untyped view of the data to naive users and use schema information to rewrite the user query into a more efficient typing-aware query. In such a context, typing is important even if not visible to naive users.

Because the language presented so far is in some sense an extension of OQL, it is relatively easy, taking advantage of the ODMG syntax, to consider querying databases containing both semistructured data and structured ODMG data.

Consider the ODMG model extended with a particular class OEM of semistructured data objects. For an OEM object *o* and a label *l*, an *l*-subobject of *o* may be either an OEM object or an ODMG object. Similarly, we allow the class OEM to occur in the type definition of an ODMG object. To illustrate, suppose the database is specified as follows:

```
class Project
  type tuple (name: String;
              manager: Person;
              description: OEM)
class Person
  type tuple (name: String;
              birth-year: integer)
  method age(): integer;
name mydb: OEM;
```

Suppose further that mydb has some project subobjects of type Project, and some project subobjects that are directly of type OEM.

Consider the following query that entirely ignores type information:

```
r1 = select X.description.member.picture
     from   mydb.project X, X.name Y
     where  Y = "Verso"
```

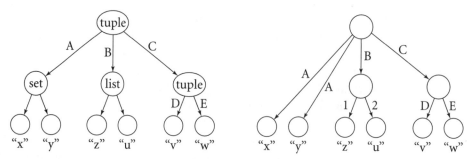

Figure 4.2 Conversion from ODMG to OEM.

This query navigates through structured ODMG and OEM data, ignoring the distinction between them. In particular, note that some of the Xs may be ODMG objects and others OEM. Similarly, some Ys may be ODMG strings and others OEM objects. All happens as if a semistructured data view of the data is provided by the system. This translation is straightforward: ODMG atomic values are transformed into OEM atomics, all kinds of ODMG collections are transformed into the unique form of OEM collections. For instance, a possible translation from ODMG to OEM is illustrated in Figure 4.2.

Note that we do not have to convert a priori ODMG data into OEM data. This conversion remains virtual and is performed only when we attempt to access some ODMG data as OEM data. The problem becomes even more interesting when methods are considered. For instance, the query

```
r2 = select  X.name
     from    mydb.project X
     where   X.manager.age < 32
```

returns the names of projects whose managers are less than 32 years old. Some managers may be stored as OEM objects, in which case the age is the value of an OEM atomic object. Others may be Person objects, in which case age is a method applied to the object.

Observe that, from a typing viewpoint, once we cross the frontier to OEM, we remain logically in the OEM world even if we pass by ODMG portions of the database. So, in particular, if we start from an OEM root of persistence, the result is forced to be of type OEM. We may want to use a feature of ODMG, namely, casting, to move logically back to the ODMG world, as in

```
select unique struct(name:Y.name,desc:Y.description)
from    mydb.project X, (Project X) = Y
```

This query returns a set of tuples with an ODMG value in one field and an OEM object in the second. The casting (Project X) succeeds when X is an object of the class project. It does not yield an error for project subobjects that are OEM since there is no runtime error in the OEM world. On the other hand, the query:

```
select Y.ceo
from   mydb.project X, (Project X) = Y
```

would yield a static type error since Y is of type Project and this class does not have an attribute ceo.

4.7 BIBLIOGRAPHIC REMARKS

David Maier's desiderata list for an XML query language is taken from [QL98].

The basic language we have described here draws on Lorel [AQM+97] and on UnQL [BDHS96]. As mentioned in the introduction to this chapter, the languages considered here primarily draw on the syntax of OQL, which was originally proposed in [BCD89] and adopted in modified form as part of the ODMG proposals [Cat94]. The core language makes substantial use of regular expressions. It may be best to consult [LP81] for the underlying theory or [FO97] for the syntax of grep and practical issues. The detailed syntax of UnQL (which we have not described) is based on comprehension syntax of functional programming languages [Tur85, FHPJW92]. Phil Wadler [Wad92] studied properties of the comprehension construct over arbitrary monads. Query languages based on the comprehension syntax were introduced in [BLS+94], and their associated optimization techniques were studied in [Won94].

There has been a very important body of literature on query languages from various perspectives, calculus, algebra, functional, and deductive (see [Ull88, Ull89, AHV94]), concerning structured data. Although developed with different motivations, languages to query documents satisfy some of the needs of querying semistructured data. For instance, query languages for SGML and structured documents such as POQL [CACS94] and integration with information retrieval tools [ACC+97, CM95] share many goals with the issues that we are considering. The work on query languages for hypertext structures (e.g., [MW95, BK90, CM90a, MW93]) is relevant. Query languages and interpreters related to OQL have also been developed for the complex types occuring in scientific data formats [BNTW95, DOTW97]. We should also remark that ACeDB [TMD92] has a limited query and update language that exploits a form of path expression, and that file indexing systems such as SRS [EA93] come equipped with a limited query language that, in some respects, uses a semistructured view of data.

With the popularity of the Web, query languages for the Web have attracted much recent attention, for example, W3QL [KS95] which focuses on extensibility; WebSQL [MMM96] which provides a formal semantics and introduces a notion of locality; or WebLog [LSS96] which is based on a Datalog-like syntax. A theory of queries of the Web is proposed in [AV97b] and in [MM97]. W3QL is typical of this line of work. It notably allows the use of Perl regular expressions and calls to Unix programs from the where clause of an SQL-like query, and even calls to Web browsers. This is the basis of a system that provides bridges between the database and the Web technology.

The connections between path expressions and Datalog-like languages has been investigated in a number of papers (e.g., [AV97b, CM90a]).

A language and a system named Ozone, allowing us to access hybrid data combining semistructured and ODMG data as sketched here, has been developed at Stanford [LAW98a] on top of the O_2 system [Deu90].

5

Query Languages for XML

In this chapter, we discuss two query languages for XML. They bear a strong resemblance to query languages for semistructured data presented in Chapter 4 but were designed specifically for XML.

5.1 XML-QL

XML-QL combines XML syntax with query language techniques from the previous chapter. It uses path expressions and patterns to extract data from the input XML data; it has variables to which this data is bound; and finally it has templates which show how the output XML data is to be constructed. Both patterns and templates use the XML syntax. When restricted to relational-like data, XML-QL is as expressive as relational calculus or relational algebra; that is, XML-QL is relationally complete.

XML-QL assumes the semistructured data model from Chapter 2, in which data is represented as an edge-labeled graph. This does not always fit the XML data model, which is better described as a node-labeled graph. We have discussed in Chapter 3 the differences between the two models. Simple data like tree data is easily translated back and forth between the two models, and here the differences are not visible in XML-QL; they may become apparent, however, for more complex data with references.

We next give our first example in XML-QL. Don't be puzzled by minor differences in syntax. XML-QL is based on a where/construct syntax instead of the familiar select/from/where of SQL or OQL. In an UnQL style, the construct clause corresponds to select whereas the where combines the from and where parts of the query, that is, the ranging of the variables as well as some filtering.

Consider the following simple example retrieving all authors of books published by Morgan Kaufmann:

```
where <book>
        <publisher><name>Morgan Kaufmann</name></publisher>
        <title> $T </title>
        <author> $A </author>
      </book> in "www.a.b.c/bib.xml"
construct $A
```

Here $T and $A are variables, while

```
<book>
    <publisher><name>Morgan Kaufmann</name></publisher>
    <title> $T </title>
    <author> $A </author>
</book>
```

is a pattern. The query processor will match the pattern in all possible ways to the data and bind the variables $T, $A. For each such binding it will produce the result $A. A pattern only specifies what *should* be in the data, not what *shouldn't*. For example a <book> will match our pattern as long as it has a <publisher>, a <title>, and an <author> subelement with the right structures, no matter what other elements it might have.

A close analogy to patterns in Chapter 4 may be noticed here. The pattern above corresponds to

```
{book: { publisher: {name: "Morgan Kaufmann"},
         title: T,
         author A} }
```

This analogy is similar to that between XML data and ssd-expressions described in Chapter 3.

5.1.1 Constructing New XML Data

Many XML applications require queries to construct new XML data. In XML-QL, this is done by adding templates to the construct clause. Consider the following query:

```
where <book>
        <publisher> <name>Morgan Kaufmann </> </>
        <title> $T </>
        <author> $A </>
      </> in "www.a.b.c/bib.xml"
```

```
<book year="1991">
<!-- A good introductory text -->
<title> An Introduction to Parallel Algorithms and Architectures
</title>
<author> <lastname> Leighton </lastname> </author>
<publisher> <name> Morgan Kaufmann </name > </publisher>
  </book>

  <book year="1995">
    <title> Active Database Systems  </title>
    <author> <lastname> Ceri </lastname> </author>
    <author> <lastname> Widom </lastname> </author>
    <publisher> <name> Morgan Kaufmann </name > </publisher>
  </book>
```

Figure 5.1 Simple XML data.

```
construct <result>
            <author> $A </>
            <title>  $T </>
        </>
```

In this query we have introduced an abbreviation `</>` as the closing tag for the nearest unclosed tag. Thus `<publisher> <name> Morgan Kaufmann </> </>` is an abbreviation for

```
<publisher> <name> Morgan Kaufmann </name> </publisher>.
```

The query constructs one element of the form

```
<result> <author> . . . </author>
         <title>  . . . </title> </result>
```

for each binding of the variables `$A`, `$T`. To see a concrete example, consider the data in Figure 5.1. The result is shown in Figure 5.2.

The result in Figure 5.2 is not a correct XML document, however: it lacks a root element. It is easy to modify the query to add the root element, say, `<answer>`. . .`</answer>`:

```
<answer>
  where <book>
            <publisher> <name>Morgan Kaufmann </> </>
            <title>  $T </>
            <author> $A </>
        </> in "www.a.b.c/bib.xml"
```

```
<result>
   <author> <lastname> Leighton </lastname> </author>
   <title> An Introduction to Parallel Algorithms and Architecture
   </title>
</result>

<result>
   <author> <lastname> Ceri </lastname> </author>
   <title> Active Database Systems </title>
</result>

<result>
   <author> <lastname> Widom </lastname> </author>
   <title> Active Database Systems </title>
</result>
```

Figure 5.2 Query result.

```
construct <result>
               <author> $A </>
               <title>  $T </>
            </>
</answer>
```

5.1.2 Processing Optional Elements with Nested Queries

A key difference between XML and relational data is the frequency of optional elements. For example the <price> tag in <book> may be optional. Suppose we want all book titles and, where available, we want the prices too. The following query is *not* correct with respect to our specification:

```
where <book> <title> $T </title> <price> $p </price>
      </book> in "www.a.b.c/bib.xml",
construct <result> <booktitle> $T </booktitle>
                   <bookprice> $P </bookprice>
         </result>
```

It is incorrect since the pattern insists that a <price> be present; hence, books without a price are not reported. XML-QL lets us easily deal with optional parts through *nested queries*, as in the query below:

```
where <book> $B </book> in "www.a.b.c/bib.xml",
      <title> $T </title> in $B
```

```
construct <result> <booktitle> $T </booktitle>
                   where <price> $P </price> in $B
                   construct <bookprice> $P </bookprice>
           </result>
```

On the right-hand side of in we may have either a URL (denoting an XML document) or a variable (denoting a fragment of an XML document). The second where . . . construct query is called a *nested query*. For each binding of the pattern `<price>$P</price>`, it generates an element of the form `<bookprice>$P</bookprice>`. If no price is found, then no bookprice is generated, but the book is still part of the result. The result of this query has the form

```
<result> <booktitle> . . . </booktitle> </result>
<result> <booktitle> . . . </booktitle>
         <bookprice> . . . </bookprice>
</result>
<result> <booktitle> . . . </booktitle>
         <bookprice> . . . </bookprice>
</result>
<result> <booktitle> . . . </booktitle> </result>
<result> <booktitle> . . . </booktitle>
         <bookprice> . . . </bookprice>
</result>
. . .
```

5.1.3 Grouping with Nested Queries

Another distinction between relational data and XML is nesting and grouping. For example, a bibliography database will have one element for each book, with all authors grouped in that element. Suppose we want to retrieve all authors, and for each of them find all titles he/she published. That is, we want to regroup the data. This can be done in XML-QL with subqueries:

```
where <book> <author > $A </> </> in "www.a.b.c/bib.xml",
construct <result>
          <author> $A </>
          where  <book> <author> $A </author>
                        <title> $T </title>
                 </book> in  "www.a.b.c/bib.xml",
          construct <title> $T </>
          </>
```

5.1.4 Binding Elements and Contents

Variables in XML-QL are bound to nodes in the semistructured data model (i.e., to oids or atomic values). In terms of XML, this means that variables are bound to element content, not to elements. XML-QL has syntactic sugar that allows us to bind to elements. For example, consider the following query:

```
where <book> <publisher> <name> Morgan Kaufmann
                         </name> </publisher>
      </book>
      element_as $B in "abc.xml"
construct $B
```

The variable $B is bound to the element <book> . . . </book>. This is just syntactic sugar. The XML-QL processor will translate the query into

```
where <book> $T </book> in "abc.xml",
      <publisher> <name> Morgan Kaufmann
                  </name> </publisher> in $T
construct <book> $T </book>
```

Similarly, the construct content_as binds a variable to an element's content. For example:

```
where <book> <publisher> <name> Morgan Kaufmann
                         </name> </publisher>
      </book> content_as $C in "abc.xml"
construct <result> $C </result>
```

is just syntactic sugar for

```
where <book> $C </book> in "abc.xml",
      <publisher> <name> Morgan Kaufmann
                  </name> </publisher> in $C
construct <result> $C </result>
```

5.1.5 Querying Attributes

Querying attributes in XML is straightforward. The following query finds all book titles in French:

```
where <book language="French">
          <title> </>  element_as $T
      </> in "abc.xml"
construct $T
```

while the following reports all languages in our database:

```
where <book language=$L> </> in "abc.xml"
construct <result> $L </result>
```

Notice that an attribute value from the input now becomes an element value in the output. The converse is also possible.

5.1.6 Joining Elements by Value

We can express "joins" by using the same variable in two matchings. For example, the following query retrieves all authors who have published at least two books:

```
where <book> <author> $A </author> </book>
        content_as $B1 in "abc.xml",
      <book> <author> $A </author> </book>
        content_as $B2 in "abc.xml",
      B1 != B2
construct <result> $A </result>
```

5.1.7 Tag Variables

Sometimes XML documents use distinct tags to refer to variants of the same concepts. In our bibliography example, both tags <author> and <editor> denote person elements. In an object-oriented system, we would model this as a superclass person with two subclasses author and editor. XML, however, does not have inheritance. To circumvent that, XML-QL uses tag variables, much like the label variables in Section 4.5. For example, the following query finds all publications published in 1995 in which Smith is either an author or an editor:

```
where <$P> <title> $T </title>
          <year> 1995 </>
          <$E> Smith </>
      </> in "www.a.b.c/bib.xml",
      $E in {author, editor}
construct <$P> <title> $T </title>
              <$E> Smith </>
          </>
```

There are two tag variables here: $P is bound to a top-level tag (e.g., book, article, etc.), while $E is bound to author and editor only.

5.1.8 Regular Path Expressions

Consider the following DTD that defines the self-recursive element part:

```
<!ELEMENT part (name, brand, part*)>
<!ELEMENT name  (PCDATA)>
<!ELEMENT brand (PCDATA)>
```

Any part element can contain other nested part elements to an arbitrary depth. To query such a structure, XML-QL provides regular path expressions, which can specify element paths of arbitrary depth. For example, the following query produces the name of every part element that contains a brand element equal to "Ford", regardless of the nesting level at which $R occurs:

```
where <part*> <name> $R </> <brand> Ford </> </>
      in "www.a.b.c/bib.xml"
construct <result> $R </>
```

Here part* is a regular path expression and matches any sequence of edges, all of which are labeled part. The pattern

```
<part*> <name> $R </> <brand> Ford </> </>
```

is equivalent to the union of the following infinite sequence of patterns:

```
<name> $R </> <brand> Ford </>
<part> <name> $R </> <brand> Ford </> </>
<part> <part> <name> $R </> <brand> Ford </> </> </>
<part> <part> <part> <name> $R </> <brand> Ford </> </> </> </>
. . .
```

A note of caution. We have seen regular expressions in DTDs in Chapter 3. These are not to be confused with regular expressions in XML-QL. The former are "horizontal"; that is, they specify which tags are allowed to occur on the same level in the XML tree. In XML-QL, regular expressions like <part*> are "vertical"; that is, they traverse the XML tree vertically.

The wild card $ matches any tag and can appear wherever a tag is permitted. For example, this query is like the one above, but matches any sequence of elements, not just parts:

```
where <$*> <name>$r</> <brand>Ford</> </>
      in "www.a.b.c/bib.xml"
construct <result>$r</>
```

We abbreviate $* by *. As in Chapter 4, a period denotes concatenation of regular expressions; hence, the pattern

```
<*.brand> Ford </>
```

matches the brand Ford at any depth in the XML graph.

In other respects, XML-QL's path patterns follow exactly the syntax of regular expressions for paths in Chapter 4: alternation (|), concatenation (.), and Kleene-star (*). Also allowed are (+) and (?). A more complex use of regular expressions is illustrated in

```
where <part+.(subpart|component.piece)>$r</>
      in "www.a.b.c/parts.xml"
construct <result> $r</>
```

5.1.9 Order

So far we have assumed the semistructured data model of Chapter 2. This is sufficient for most applications. XML's data model, however, is ordered, and for some applications the order is vital. XML-QL has two distinct semantics, one for unordered data and one for ordered data, and requires distinct query processors for the two models.

For the ordered data model, patterns in the where clause are still interpreted as unordered. For example, the pattern

```
<a> <b> $X </b> <c> $Y </c> </a>
```

will match both the XML data

```
<a> <b> 1 </b> <c> 2 </c> </a>
```

and the data

```
<a> <c> 2 </c> <b> 1 </b> </a>
```

Variable bindings in the where clause are now ordered. Consider the XML data

```
<a> <b> 1 </b>
    <c> 2 </c>
    <b> 3 </b>
    <c> 4 </c>
</a>
```

and the pattern <a> <b> $X </b> <c> $Y </c> </a>. The variables will be bound in the following order:

```
$X       $Y
 1        2
 1        4
 3        2
 3        4
```

Note that, for the purpose of the order, it matters how we write the pattern. If we change the pattern definition to

$$< a > < c > \$Y < /c > < b > \$X < /b > < /a >$$

then we get a different binding order (sorted by $Y first, then by $X).

In more complex cases, when the data graph has shared subgraphs, two bindings may be in different orders due to different paths to those nodes. In conjunction with regular expressions, this may lead to infinite results. To avoid this problem, XML-QL has the following semantics. First, the XML graph is preprocessed and its vertices enumerated. It is not specified how this enumeration is done. In the case of an XML document, the enumeration should coincide with the order in which the elements occur in the XML document. During query evaluation, variable bindings are ordered by their node numbers, and duplicate bindings are eliminated. This ensures that the answer is always finite. Although complex at a first glance, the definition in essence states that the query preserves the order of the input graph.

Index variables are also supported. For example, the patterns

```
<a[$I]>  . . .  </>
<$X[$J]> . . .  </>
```

bind $I or $J to an integer 0, 1, 2, . . . that represents the index in the total order of the edges. For example, the following query retrieves all persons whose last name precedes the first name:

```
where <person> $P </> in "www.a.b.c/people.xml",
      <firstname[$I]> $X </> in $P,
      <lastname[$J]>  $Y </> in $P,
      $J < $I
construct <person> $P </>
```

An optional ORDER-BY clause specifies element order in the output. For example, the following query retrieves publication titles ordered by year and month:

```
where <pub>   $P </> in "www.a.b.c/bib.xml",
      <title> $T </> in $P,
```

```
      <year> $Y </> in $P
      <month> $Z </> in $P
order-by $Y,$Z
construct <result> $T </>
```

For a more complex example, the following query reverses the order of all authors in a publication:

```
where <pub> $P </> in "www.a.b.c/bib.xml"
construct <pub> where <author[$I]> $A </> in $P
               order-by $I descending
               construct <author> $A </>

               where <$E> $V </> in $P,
                     $E != "author"
               construct <$E> $V </>
         </pub>
```

5.2 XSL

XSL is a current W3C proposal for an XML extensible stylesheet language (hence, XSL). Its primary role is to allow users to write transformations from XML to HTML, thus describing the presentation of the XML document. As a transformation language, however, it can also serve in data applications, hence our interest here. Unlike XML-QL, XSL is not relationally complete. It does not have joins, and in general, the transformations it can express are limited. However, its data model accurately corresponds to XML's, and all XML constructs are addressed in the XSL language.

The data model for XSL is an ordered tree. References and links must be dealt with separately.

An XSL program is a set of *template rules*. Each rule consists of a pattern and a template, roughly corresponding to the where and construct clauses in XML-QL. The computation model differs from XML-QL's and from other query languages discussed in this book. XSL starts from the root element and tries to apply a pattern to that node. If it succeeds, it executes the corresponding template. The latter usually instructs XSL to produce some XML result and to apply the templates recursively, on the node's children. Here the same process is repeated. Thus, an XSL program is like a recursive function (we shall discuss such functions in Chapter 6), while XML-QL applies the pattern/template rule only at the top level.

Consider the following simple XML bibliography document:

```
<bib> <book>   <title>  t1 </title>
                <author> a1 </author>
                <author> a2 </author>
        </book>
        <paper> <title>  t2 </title>
                <author> a3 </author>
                <author> a4 </author>
        </paper>
        <book>   <title>  t3 </title>
                <author> a5 </author>
                <author> a6 </author>
                <author> a7 </author>
        </book>
</bib>
```

The following XSL program returns all book titles:

```
<xsl:template>
    <xsl:apply-templates/>
</xsl:template>
<xsl:template match="/bib/*/title">
    <result>
        <xsl:value-of/>
    </result>
</xsl:template>
```

Each of the two <xsl:template> constructs defines a template rule. Consider the second rule: its match attribute defines the pattern, and its content defines the template. When the match attribute is missing (like in the first rule), the template matches any node. Path expressions in XSL follow the Unix directory/subdirectory syntax. Here, /bib/*/title means any <title> element inside any element inside a <bib> element. The expression <result> <xsl:value-of/> </result> is the template. It says that a <result> element is to be emitted and its content is the "value of" the current node. The result will have the form

One or more?

```
<result> t1 </result>
<result> t2 </result>
<result> t3 </result>
```

Let us inspect more closely how XSL works. It starts from the root `<bib>` . . . `</bib>` and tries to match some pattern to the root node. In this case, the first template matches. Thus, XSL evaluates its body, `<xsl:apply-templates/>`. This determines the whole program to be applied to all the children, that is, to the three `<book>` . . . `</book>` elements. Again, only the first rule matches, so we end up applying the program to `<title>` and `<author>` elements. Finally, the second template will match the `<title>` element. Here XSL generates a `<result>` . . . `</result>` element. Its content is the value of the current node, that is, the title string. The construct `<xsl:value-of/>` returns the string value of the current node.

The above query can be expressed equivalently in XML-QL:

```
where <bib> <book> <title> $T </> </> </> in input
construct <result> $T </result>
```

We describe XSL patterns first, then XSL template rules. Patterns are path expressions, like in the following examples:

bib	matches a bib element
*	matches any element
/	matches the root
/bib	matches a bib element immediately after root
bib/paper	matches a paper following a bib
bib//paper	matches a paper following a bib at any depth
//paper	matches a paper at any depth
paper | book	matches a paper or a book
@language	matches a language attribute
bib/book/@language	the language attribute of a book

To understand patterns we need to discuss XSL's data model. It consists of a tree with a unique root node denoting the whole document. This is *different* from the topmost element of the XML document. The root node is matched by / only, and has a unique element child that is the topmost element—in our example, `<bib>`. In other words, in the XSL data model there is an additional root node sitting on top of the regular root. The reason for introducing this additional node is that comments and processing instructions are part of XSL's data model, and they may occur before or after the top element, as in

```
<!-- this is comment 1 -->
<!-- this is comment 2 -->
<bib> . . . </bib>
<!-- this is comment 3 -->
```

In this case the root has four children: three comments and the <bib> element.

So far all patterns are linear. We can express nonlinear patterns in XSL through *qualifiers*, which are enclosed in [. . .]. For example paper[year] matches a paper element that has a year subelement. This is different from paper/year, since the latter matches the year element (if it is inside a paper element). Qualifiers can be combined with boolean connectors, as in

```
bib/paper[year and publisher/name and @language]
```

matching a paper element in bib but only if it has a year subelement, a publisher subelement with a name, and a @language attribute.

Interestingly, XSL does not use variables. On the one hand, this allows for concise programs, but on the other hand it limits its expressive power; for example, XSL cannot express joins.

We now turn to XSL templates rules, whose general form is

```
<xsl:template match="pattern">
    template
</xsl:template>
```

The XSL processor prepends each pattern with a //; hence, in our example above we can simplify the pattern /bib/*/title to title (since we know that the root is bib and titles occur two levels below). The template contains a mixture of XML text to be generated and XSL instructions. The latter are identified by the fact that their element names start with xsl: (i.e., they belong to the XSL namespace). These instructions always refer to the current node and usually access its tag name, its attributes, and its contents (including its children).

We have seen the <xsl:value-of> instruction, which evaluates to the string value of the current node. If the node is not atomic, its value is the string concatenation of values of its children. Another useful instruction is <xsl:element name=" . . . ">, which creates a new element with name " . . . ". Hence:

```
<xsl:template match="A">
   <xsl:element name="B">
      <xsl:value-of/>
   <xsl:element/>
</xsl:template>
```

[handwritten: element is not very useful here ..]

is equivalent to

```
<xsl:template match="A">
   <B><xsl:value-of/></B>
</xsl:template>
```

An example when <xsl:element> is truly useful is the following, which copies all top-level elements from the input file:

```
<xsl:template match="*">
   <xsl:element name="name()">
      <xsl:value-of/>
   </xsl:element>
</xsl:template>
```

[handwritten: TO see no we open use? ... (pattern)]

Here name() returns the name of the current node, which we use as the name of the output node.

We end this section with an XSL example illustrating a translation of XML to HTML. Considering our bibliography example, the XSL query of Figure 5.3 would produce the output in Figure 5.4.

To start, note that the only template matching the root node is the first template (match="/"). This creates an HTML document consisting of a title and a body that is filled by recursively processing the templates. The latter triggers the template with the pattern "bib", which creates the table body, then calls the program recursively on the subelements (in our example <book>, <paper>, and <book>). Each time, only the template with the "book|paper" pattern matches; this creates a table row and applies the program recursively to the title children first, then to the author children. Finally the templates with patterns "title" and "author" match, and they will create an entry in the table. The resulting HTML document is shown in Figure 5.4. Readers familiar with HTML will recognize an HTML table here.

```
<xsl:template match="/">
  <HTML>
    <HEAD>
      <TITLE>Bibliography Entries</TITLE>
    </HEAD>
    <BODY>
      <xsl:apply-templates/>
    </BODY>
  </HTML>
</xsl:template>
<xsl:template match="title">
  <TD>
     <xsl:value-of/>
  </TD>
</xsl:template>
<xsl:template match="author">
  <TD>
     <xsl:value-of/>
  </TD>
</xsl:template>
<xsl:template match="book">
  <TR>
     <xsl:apply-templates select="title"/>
     <xsl:apply-templates select="author"/>
  </TR>
</xsl:template>

<xsl:template match="bib">
  <TABLE>
    <TBODY>
       <xsl:apply-templates/>
    </TBODY>
  </TABLE>
</xsl:template>
```

Figure 5.3 An XSL query producing HTML data.

```
<HTML>
  <HEAD>
    <TITLE>Bibliography Entries</TITLE>
  </HEAD>
  <BODY>
    <TABLE>
      <TBODY>
        <TR><TD> t1 </TD> <TD> a1 </TD> <TD> a2 </TD> </TR>
        <TR><TD> t2 </TD> <TD> a3 </TD> <TD> a4 </TD> </TR>
        <TR><TD> t3 </TD> <TD> a5 </TD> <TD> a6 </TD> <TD> a7 </TD> </TR>
      </TBODY>
    </TABLE>
  </BODY>
</HTML>
```

Figure 5.4 Result of translating XML to HTML.

5.3 BIBLIOGRAPHIC REMARKS

The language XML-QL is described in [DFF⁺98, DFF⁺99]. XSL's official source is the W3C Web page. At the time of writing, it was not an approved standard yet, and the latest document was [XSL98]. Microsoft's Internet Explorer version 5.0 implements XSL. A programmer's manual is [Hom99].

Another language for XML is XMAS, designed in the context of an XML-based mediation system called MIX [BGL⁺99].

6

Interpretation and Advanced Features

T<small>HE FEATURES FOUND</small> in the query language in Chapter 4 form the basis of query languages for semistructured data. There have been many proposals to go beyond. The consensus for a query language is that the language should be *declarative* (an ill-defined notion), be the basis of potential optimization (an aspect that is clearly technology dependent), and have some esthetic (a parameter not easy to measure). We will not resolve here the choice of a query language for semistructured data—the jury is still out on this issue. We will not even settle the issue of precisely what expressive power it should have, since we lack a well-accepted yardstick such as relational calculus. In this chapter, we limit ourselves to describing the relationship between the semistructured query languages we have seen in Chapter 4 and more conventional notions of query languages and programming languages. In particular, we shall investigate the relationship with relational query languages, languages that create objects, structural recursion, and graph rewriting.

This comparison will suggest several things. First, it will give us some partial answers to what the expressive power of semistructured query languages should be. Second, it will suggest some extensions to the languages we saw in Chapter 4 that will allow more complex transformations of the input data. Third, it will sharpen our notion of semantics for these languages, especially for the more advanced features. Finally, it will suggest certain implementation strategies (more on that in later chapters).

This chapter presents some technically involved material. Readers interested in an overview of semistructured data may wish to skip it in a first reading of the book.

6.1   FIRST-ORDER INTERPRETATION

The relational model comes equipped with the formal foundation of first-order logic. Indeed, we can query relational databases using *relational calculus* and evaluate the answer by transforming the query into a *relational algebra* query. The query language used in practice, SQL, has at its core a reasonably elegant combination of calculus and algebraic features. The semantics of the core of SQL can thus be cleanly formalized in first-order logical terms. It is therefore interesting to consider an interpretation of a portion of the query language for semistructured data that roughly corresponds to the core of SQL, in first-order terms. We do this briefly next.

It is easy to model the data graph as a finite relational structure. The structure is many-sorted. Besides the type **oid** for identifiers, there is one sort **dom** for atomic values and labels. (To simplify, we assume there is a single sort of atomic values, say, *string*.) The sets **dom** and **oid** are assumed to be countably infinite and disjoint. A data graph is then an instance over the following schema:

```
ref ( source: oid, label: dom, destination: oid )
val ( obj: oid,    value: dom )
```

More precisely, $ref(o_1, l, o_2)$ indicates that o_1, o_2 are oids, with o, a complex object, and that there is an edge labeled l from o_1 to o_2; and $val(o, v)$ means that o is atomic and has value v. The structure also contains one or more constants denoting the oid for each root of persistence. (For instance, *db* denotes the root object for the bibliography in Figure 6.1.) Finally, an instance must also obey the following constraints:

1. *atomic/complex* No oid occurs in the first column of both *ref* and *val*.
2. *reachability* Every object is reachable from some root; that is, for each object o, there is a directed path from r to o for some root of persistence r.
3. *key* The *oid* attribute is a key in relation *val*.
4. *value* The *value* attribute is a key in relation *val* (optional).

The first condition is technical, and its removal would not seriously affect the model. It allows us to assume that, by definition, objects occurring in the first column of *val* are atomic and all other objects are complex. (An object occurring in the third column of *ref* and not in any other column is therefore an empty complex object.)

The second condition is in the ODMG spirit of persistence by reachability. An object that becomes unreachable (and thus cannot be accessed by queries) is simply garbage collected.

The third condition should be clear: each object has at most one value.

The last condition, when enforced, allows us to blur the distinction between an atomic value and an atomic object. An equivalent alternative from a query viewpoint would be to have **dom** (the set of atomic values) be a subset of **oid**. We will see an example where this condition simplifies querying.

Figure 6.1(a) shows a data graph with labels. The corresponding relational structure is given in Figure 6.1(b).

We can now consider first-order logic over this structure. This allows us to express certain queries. Consider, for example, the following query, in our core query language:

```
select author: X
from biblio.book Y,
     Y.author X
where "Database Systems" in Y.title
```

We can describe the set of objects X that contribute to the result by

$$\{X \mid \exists Y, Z, V, W(\textit{ref}(\textit{db}, \texttt{"biblio"}, W) \wedge$$
$$\textit{ref}(W, \texttt{"book"}, Y) \wedge$$
$$\textit{ref}(Y, \texttt{"author"}, X) \wedge$$
$$\textit{ref}(Y, \texttt{"title"}, V) \wedge$$
$$\textit{val}(V, \texttt{"Database Systems"}))\}$$

While this describes a set of vertices in our data graph, it is not yet a query that produces semistructured data, that is, a new data graph. Let us assume the existence of a new particular node, say, ans (for answer), that will denote the result. This may be a new root of persistence. Figure 6.1 shows this new node, ans with author edges connecting to existing nodes. The result of the query is the graph whose root is ans and that contains all nodes accessible from ans.

To construct this graph, we can invoke a Datalog program to augment the *ref* relation with new author edges. Datalog is such a simple language that the semantics of Datalog queries in the following examples should be clear even to readers exposed for the first time to that language.[1]

---

1. Datalog can be viewed as Horn clauses without function symbols or as a small fragment of Prolog without function symbols.

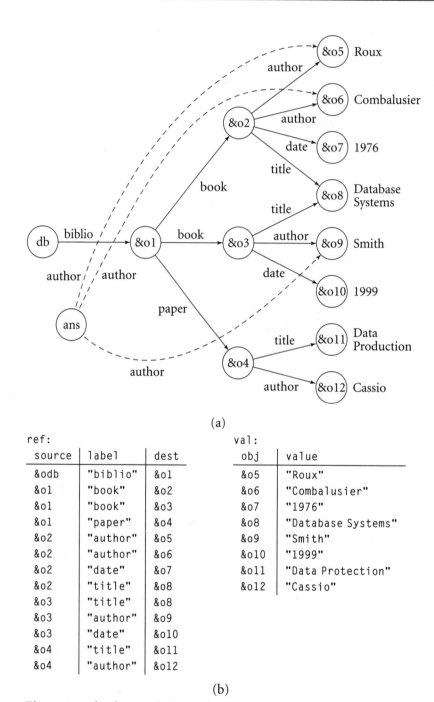

(a)

ref:

source	label	dest
&odb	"biblio"	&o1
&o1	"book"	&o2
&o1	"book"	&o3
&o1	"paper"	&o4
&o2	"author"	&o5
&o2	"author"	&o6
&o2	"date"	&o7
&o2	"title"	&o8
&o3	"title"	&o8
&o3	"author"	&o9
&o3	"date"	&o10
&o4	"title"	&o11
&o4	"author"	&o12

val:

obj	value
&o5	"Roux"
&o6	"Combalusier"
&o7	"1976"
&o8	"Database Systems"
&o9	"Smith"
&o10	"1999"
&o11	"Data Protection"
&o12	"Cassio"

(b)

Figure 6.1 A database with object identities: (a) data graph with labels; (b) corresponding relational structure.

$$ref(ans, \texttt{"author"}, X) \leftarrow ref(db, \texttt{"biblio"}, W),$$
$$ref(W, \texttt{"book"}, Y),$$
$$ref(Y, \texttt{"author"}, X),$$
$$ref(Y, \texttt{"title"}, V),$$
$$val(V, \texttt{"Database Systems"})$$

This Datalog program consists of a single *rule*. The rule's head is *ref*(*ans*, "author",*X*), while the rule's body is the conjunction of the five predicates on the right of the "←" sign. The interpretation of this rule is the following: for every binding of the variables W, Y, X, V that makes the body true in the current datagraph, the tuple (*ans*, "author", X) is inserted in the *ref* relation.

Note that the extended graph satisfies the condition of reachability with two roots of persistence, namely, db and ans. Observe that the program shows how to *append* edges to *ref* to construct the answer. We could have written a Datalog program to generate a new *ref'* relation just for the answer. But the *ref* and *ref'* graphs would share vertices and the specification of the mapping from *ref* to *ref'* would be somewhat messy.

We can also take care of certain regular path expressions in Datalog. For example,

```
select title: X
from   biblio.paper.section.(title | paragraph.heading) X
```

is expressed with the Datalog program

$$ref(ans, \texttt{"title"}, X) \leftarrow section(Y), ref(Y, \texttt{"title"}, X)$$
$$ref(ans, \texttt{"title"}, X) \leftarrow section(Y), ref(Y, \texttt{"paragraph"}, Z),$$
$$ref(Z, \texttt{"heading"}, X)$$
$$section(Y) \leftarrow ref(db, \texttt{"biblio"}, W),$$
$$ref(W, \texttt{"paper"}, V),$$
$$ref(V, \texttt{"section"}, Y)$$

The two queries above could also be expressed in first-order logic, but clearly we are fast reaching the limits of first-order logic. It is not obvious how we construct more than one new node, and the Kleene closure in path expressions is certainly not specifiable in first-order logic, that is, without the use of recursion in our Datalog programs. Indeed, we cannot even verify in first-order logic that the instance satisfies the (*reachability*) condition. For regular expressions on labels or data, we need to exploit some form of recursion. For instance,

```
select part: Y
from    product X, X.(subpart)* Y
```

is expressed with the Datalog program

$$ref(\mathit{ans}, \texttt{"part"}, Y) \leftarrow q(Y)$$
$$q(Y) \leftarrow ref(\mathit{db}, \texttt{"product"}, Y)$$
$$q(Y) \leftarrow q(Z), ref(Z, \texttt{"subpart"}, Y)$$

The form of recursion that is used here is very limited. For instance, for a given X, the recursion bears on the single variable Y and is therefore some form of monadic recursion. The potential for optimization is very high.

6.2   OBJECT CREATION

A useful feature of a language based on objects is the creation of new objects, for example, the *new* provided by ODMG. Even within a query language, it is convenient to create new objects. Indeed, we already encountered quite a few queries that were creating new nodes. Some languages have been considered that provide the means to create new objects explicitly. A convenient notation originating from logic is the use of special syntax to *name* these new objects.

Consider a simple semistructured query that returns the equivalent of a *set* of rows, for example:

```
select row: {title: T, year: Y}
from biblio.book X,
     X.title T,
     X.year Y
```

In order to produce a result, we need to create a new object for each {title: T, year: Y} row produced by this query. We do this by writing a Datalog program that generates object identifiers such as $f(o_1), f(o_2), \ldots$ where $o_1, o_2, \ldots$ are existing identifiers. In effect, we can think of these new identifiers simply as names that are the concatenation of a new tag f with an existing name (identifier) of an object. The tag f—or more properly, the function that tags object identifiers with the name f—is called a *Skolem* function. Here is an example of how we can augment Datalog programs with Skolem functions to answer the query above:

$$ref(ans, \texttt{"row"}, f(X)) \leftarrow ref(db, \texttt{"biblio"}, B),$$
$$ref(B, \texttt{"book"}, X)$$
$$ref(f(X), \texttt{"title"}, T) \leftarrow ref(X, \texttt{"title"}, T)$$
$$ref(f(X), \texttt{"year"}, Y) \leftarrow ref(X, \texttt{"year"}, Y)$$

Assuming that every book has a title and a year, the Datalog program returns the same answer as the query.

To see another example, consider the following two queries that return information about reports found in two distinct databases:

```
select row: {num: N, title: Y}
where {number: N, title: Y} in db1.report

select row: {num: N, postscript: P}
where {num: N, postscript: P} in db2.myrep
```

Suppose we want to perform the fusion of these results based on report num(ber); that is, we want to provide for each report num(ber) all data found about this report. Thus we are combining data based on some value stored in the databases rather than on object identities. We may want to do this if db1 and db2 are from two physically distinct databases. The object identities in the two databases are disjoint. We assume here that *ref* and *val* are obtained by taking the union of the respective tables in the two databases. We still specify the query with Datalog rules that use a Skolem functor *rep* and the num(ber) to create the new objects that are needed for the query:

$$ref(ans, \texttt{"row"}, rep(N)) \leftarrow ref(db1, \texttt{"report"}, X),$$
$$ref(X, \texttt{"number"}, Y),$$
$$val(Y, N)$$
$$ref(ans, \texttt{"row"}, rep(N)) \leftarrow ref(db2, \texttt{"myrep"}, X),$$
$$ref(X, \texttt{"num"}, Y),$$
$$val(Y, N)$$
$$ref(rep(N), \texttt{"title"}, T) \leftarrow val(Y, N),$$
$$ref(X, \texttt{"number"}, Y),$$
$$ref(X, \texttt{"title"}, T)$$
$$ref(rep(N), \texttt{"postscript"}, P) \leftarrow val(Y, N),$$
$$ref(X, \texttt{"num"}, Y),$$
$$ref(X, \texttt{"postscript"}, P)$$

The first two rules generate the desired objects. Only one object is generated for each distinct report number. Note that if a report, say, report 122, is listed both in *db1* and *db2*, then the created object *rep*(122) will have both title and postscript fields. This program would have been much simpler if we had assumed that both *db1* and *db2* were in the *same* database. We could, for example, use *rep(Y)* as a Skolem name for the newly created objects because of condition (*value*).

The following rules may be used to add a number attribute to each report:

$$ref(rep(N), \text{"number"}, num(N)) \leftarrow ref(db1, \text{"report"}, X),$$
$$ref(X, \text{"number"}, Y),$$
$$val(Y, N)$$

$$val(num(N), N) \leftarrow ref(db1, \text{"report"}, X),$$
$$ref(X, \text{"number"}, Y),$$
$$val(Y, N)$$

$$ref(rep(N), \text{"number"}, num(N)) \leftarrow ref(db2, \text{"myrep"}, X),$$
$$ref(X, \text{"num"}, Y),$$
$$val(Y, N)$$

$$val(num(N), N) \leftarrow ref(db2, \text{"myrep"}, X),$$
$$ref(X, \text{"num"}, Y),$$
$$val(Y, N)$$

The query above is typical of fusion queries that are required across databases. We should remark that the query is also expressible in our core language, but involves nested selects and unions:

```
select report:{ number: N,
            ( select title: T
              where {number: N,  title T} in db1.report),
            ( select postscript: P
              where {num:N,  postscript: P} in db2.myrep) }
where N in db1.report.number union  db2.myrep.num
```

Another interesting notion that we want to mention here is the *rest variable*. It allows importing fields from an object without advanced knowledge of what fields there are. To continue with the previous example, suppose we want to import all fields from *db1* and not simply the title. Instead of the first nested query in the select clause, we would use the query

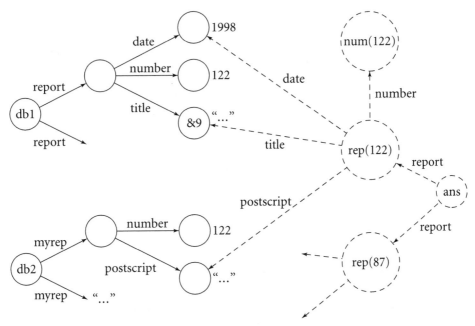

Figure 6.2 Merging databases.

```
select rest
where {number: N; rest} in db1.report
```

Observe that the same effect can be obtained using label variables:

```
select L: V
where {number: N, L: V} in db1.report
```

Thus we obtain the result of Figure 6.2 even if the rules did not mention the label *date*. We should remark that it is also straightforward to modify our Datalog program to perform the same operation, again by using a variable in the label position in the ref tuples.

Remark 6.2.1 Within this framework, it becomes easy to consider the limits of computability over graph data at least in the context of a graph database containing a unique unordered atomic domain.

We can say that a language is *complete* (in this context) if it expresses exactly the set of functions mapping semistructured databases to semistructured databases that are computable and generic. Here "generic" means that for each database I, each query q, and automorphisms μ on **dom** and **oid**, if J is a result to query

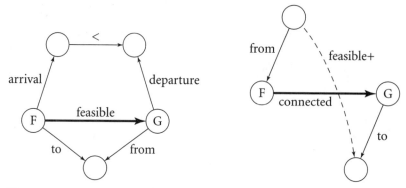

Figure 6.3 A query in GraphLog.

q on input I, then $\mu(J)$ is a result to query q on input $\mu(I)$. One can then define languages complete in that sense for such structures. For instance, the language IQL is a rule-based language with object creation that can be shown to be complete.

In the case of atomic domains with particular structures such as the integer, and with coercion between these domains, the notion becomes less clear. □

6.3   GRAPHICAL LANGUAGES

Graphical languages in the style of QBE are rather popular for the relational model. In the case of a graph model, the use of graphical queries seems even more appropriate. The patterns that we use in queries are indeed "visual." We will not develop this aspect here but only illustrate it with an example from a pioneering language for graph data, which was based on Datalog extended with powerful path expressions and expressed through the use of graphical interfaces, namely, GraphLog.

Consider the GraphLog query of Figure 6.3. It consists of two graphs. The first defines the predicate *feasible(F,G)* that holds if flight F arrives in some airport before flight G departs from the same airport. The second defines when two airports are connected, that is, when there is a sequence of feasible flights connecting them. To see the connection with our first-order interpretation of queries given earlier, and to underscore the elegance of this approach, here is the corresponding Datalog program:

$$ref(F, \text{"feasible"}, G) \leftarrow ref(F, \text{"to"}, X),$$
$$ref(G, \text{"from"}, X),$$
$$ref(F, \text{"arrival"}, A),$$
$$ref(F, \text{"departure"}, D),$$
$$val(A, I), val(D, J), I < J$$
$$ref(X, \text{"feasible+"}, Y) \leftarrow ref(X, \text{"feasible"}, Y)$$
$$ref(X, \text{"feasible+"}, Y) \leftarrow ref(X, \text{"feasible"}, Z),$$
$$ref(Z, \text{"feasible+"}, Y)$$
$$ref(F, \text{"connected"}, G) \leftarrow ref(X, \text{"from"}, F),$$
$$ref(G, \text{"to"}, Y),$$
$$ref(X, \text{"feasible+"}, Y)$$

6.4 STRUCTURAL RECURSION

Sometimes applications require complex transformations on semistructured data, which involve deep traversal of the data followed by the reconstruction of a entirely new graph. Such transformations could be expressed in Datalog, but an interesting alternative is given by structural recursion. It turns out that in most applications we only need a particular form of recursion on semistructured data—hence the term *structural recursion*—which is much simpler to implement than arbitrary recursive functions. Structural recursion for semistructured data was first introduced in the context of the UnQL query language and has an interesting connection to XSL.

We start by considering only trees. We then have another look at the XSL language in the light of structural recursion. We finally consider structural recursion on arbitrary semistructured data, that is, on graphs.

6.4.1 Structural Recursion on Trees

Recall our syntax for tree data. For example, the data in Figure 6.1 is written as

```
{biblio: { book:   { author: "Roux", author: "Combalusier",
                     date: 1976 },
           book:   { author: "Smith",
                     date: 1999, title: "Database Systems"},
           paper:  { title: "Data Protection",
```

```
                        author: "Cassio"}}}
```

Recall that {. . .} is a set notation. For example, t1 = {author: "Roux", author: "Combalusier", date: 1976} is a set with three elements. Given two trees t1, t2, it makes sense to define their *union*, t1 union t2. For example, by taking t2 = { author: "Smith", date: 1999, title "Database Systems"} we have

```
t1 union t2 = {author: "Roux", author: "Combalusier",
               date: 1976, author: "Smith", date: 1999,
               title: "Database Systems"}
```

Assume that we want to find all integers in the database t. This can be computed by the following recursive function f1, which uses pattern matching:

```
f1(v)         = if isInt(v) then {result: v} else {}
f1({})        = {}
f1({l: t})    = f1(t)
f1(t1 union t2) = f1(t1) union f1(t2)
```

The first line defines f1 on atomic values, the other three on complex values. The function calls itself recursively until it hits a leaf, where it returns either {result: v} or {}. Here {} denotes a graph with a single node (which is not a value) and with no outgoing edges. In the most complex case, when the tree has a root with more than one outgoing edge, there are several ways we can split it as t1 union t2, but all choices lead to the same result. On our bibliography data example, f1 returns {result: 1976, result: 1999}.

The particular functional combinators used to define the recursive function f1 are an instance of *structural recursion*.

We can express transformations with structural recursion. For example, the function f2 copies the OEM tree and converts all integers to strings:

```
f2(v)         = if isInt(v) then int2String(v) else v
f2({})        = {}
f2({l: t})    = {l: f2(t)}
f2(t1 union t2) = f2(t1) union f2(t2)
```

It is interesting to note that f2 makes changes "arbitrarily deeply" in the data. By comparison the select-from-where formalism can only *retrieve* data at arbitrary depths (by using regular expressions), but cannot reconstruct the data above the changed portion. In general, structural recursion is strictly more powerful than the select-from-where formalism, but less powerful than Datalog.

We can define several mutually recursive functions. For example, assuming a bibliography database consisting of publications like papers, books, and so on, the function f3 below changes strings to integers but only in books, leaving papers or other kinds of publications unchanged:

```
f3(v)           = v
f3({})          = {}
f3({l: t})      = if l = book then {book: g3(t)} else {l: f3(t)}
f3(t1 union t2) = f3(t1) union f3(t2)

g3(v)           = if isInt(v) then Int2String(v) else v
g3({})          = {}
g3({l: t})      = {l: g3(t)}
g3(t1 union t2) = g3(t1) union g3(t2)
```

It is easy to express regular path expressions with structural recursion. For example, consider:

```
select answer: X
from *.paper.((section.subsection) | paragraph) X
```

can be expressed as three mutually recursive functions:

```
f4(v)           = {}
f4({})          = {}
f4({l: t})      = if l = paper then f4(t) union g4(t)
                    else f4(t)
f4(t1 union t2) = f4(t1) union f4(t2)

g4(v)           = {}
g4({})          = {}
g4({l: t})      = if l = section then h4(t)
                    else if l = paragraph then {answer: t}
                       else {}
g4(t1 union t2) = g4(t1) union g4(t2)

h4(v)           = {}
h4({})          = {}
h4({l: t})      = if l = subsection then {answer: t} else {}
h4(t1 union t2) = h4(t1) union h4(t2)
```

To summarize, structural recursion allows us to define recursive functions following a certain strict pattern. The function, say, f, has to be defined by four cases, covering atomic values, {}, {1: t}, and t1 union t2, respectively. For the {} and t1 union t2 cases, f must return {} and f(t1) union f(t2), respectively. In practice, a user would never have to write these two cases; we always include them, for clarity purposes. The only really interesting case is {1: t}, where the function may call itself recursively on t (and any of the other mutually recursive functions), and the user has the choice of how to combine the recursive results.

We end this section by describing a surprising property of structural recursion: we can often combine two successive structural recursion transformations on a datagraph into a single transformation and optimize it in the process. Consider a bibliography database t like Figure 6.1, and consider the following two computations in sequence:

1. Compute a *view* t' in which all integers in books are replaced by strings: t'= f3(t) with f3 defined above.
2. Retrieve all integers in the view: t''= f1(t'), with f1 defined above.

By doing some simple algebraic manipulations on f1, f3, and g3, we observe that one can compute t'' in a single pass on the original data, namely, as f1'(t), where:

```
f1'(v)         = if isInt(v) then {result: v} else {}
f1'({})        = {}
f1'({1: t})    = if 1 = book then {} else f1'(t)
f1'(t1 union t2) = f1'(t1) union f1'(t2)
```

Note that f1' can be much more efficient than f3, g3, and f1 combined because it does not traverse the subtrees underneath book labels.

6.4.2 XSL and Structural Recursion

We have described XSL in Chapter 5 and discussed that its computation model is different from that of other query languages considered here. In fact, its computation model is precisely that of structural recursion. Consider the XSL program below:

```
<xsl:template>
    <xsl:apply-templates/>
</xsl:template>
<xsl:template match="a">
    <A>
        <xsl:apply-templates/>
    </A>
```

```
</xsl:template>
<xsl:template match="b">
    <B>
        <xsl:apply-templates/>
    </B>
</xsl:template>
<xsl:template match="c">
    <C>
        <xsl:value-of/>
    </C>
</xsl:template>
```

Recall that the first template is necessary to get us started and to keep us going until we find an <a> element or a <b> element. The program assumes the input data to be a tree with internal nodes labeled either <a> or <b> and leaves labeled <c>, and transforms it into an isomorphic tree with capitalized tags. Any other tag will be deleted. For example, an XML data like

```
<a> <e> <b> <c>1</c> <c>2</c> </b> <a> <c>3</c> </a> </e> </a>
```

is transformed into

```
<A>        <B> <C>1</C> <C>2</C> </B> <A> <C>3</C> </A>        </A>
```

   The program can be expressed by the following recursive function:

```
f(v)     = v
f({})    = {}
f({l:t}) = if l = "c" then {""C:t}
           else if l = "b" then {"B":f(t)}
           else if l = "a" then {"A":f(t)}
           else f(t)
f(t1 union t2) = f(t1) union f(t2)
```

This is a structural recursion function in which the third line reflects the patterns in the XSL template rules. Note that the rules are reflected in the reversed order; this is the semantics in XSL, and its rationale is to allow us to put the "default" rule first. Most XSL programs in practice (and all described in this book) can be expressed as one recursive function.

   We have seen useful applications of structural recursion with two or more recursive functions. There is a corresponding feature in XSL called *processing mode*. Each template rule may have an optional attribute mode, whose value is a string, for example, <xsl:template mode="f" match="a"> or <xsl:template mode="g">. The <xsl:apply-patterns> construct is also allowed to have a mode attribute. In that case, only the templates with that mode are applied; otherwise only the templates without a mode attribute are applied.

However, there are differences between XSL and structural recursion. First, XSL works only on trees, while structural recursion works on arbitrary graphs, as we shall discuss next. Even so, all structural recursion programs are guaranteed to terminate (even on graphs with cycles), while in XSL we can easily write a nonterminating program, even on trees! For that, consider the program above extended with the following rule:

```
<xsl:template match="e">
   <xsl:apply-patterns select="/">
</xsl:template>
```

The select attribute instructs <xsl:apply-patterns> on which node to apply the program recursively; in this case, we selected the root. From there, the other XSL rules will continue the recursion forward, thus entering an infinite loop!

So far we have illustrated structural recursion on trees only. While in general, when a recursive function is applied to a cyclic graph, it runs into an infinite loop, structural recursive functions can be computed on cyclic data too. How this is done is best illustrated on a variation of the OEM data model, based on bisimulation. This data model was used originally in UnQL.

6.4.3 Bisimulation in Semistructured Data

We make the following variation on the OEM data model presented in Chapter 2. The new data model is still a graph but nodes do not have oids; that is, sometimes we are allowed to split nodes or merge nodes without changing the data's semantics.

To justify this, consider the two graphs in Figure 6.4. Do they denote the same data? They are written as ssd-expressions as follows:

```
t1 = { book: { author: "Smith",
               author: "Smith",
               title: "Database Systems"}}
t2 = { book: { author: "Smith",
               title: "Database Systems"}}
```

In the first tree the inner set has the element author:"Smith" occurring twice, hence t1 becomes t2 after "duplicate elimination." In the remainder of this section we will always assume duplicate elimination. This is similar in spirit to the relational data model, where a table is a set, and duplicate elimination is always

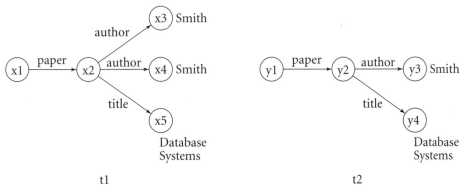

Figure 6.4 Two databases.

assumed.[2] Note that duplicate elimination makes no sense with oids: of the two, which "Smith" nodes should we eliminate?

Duplicate elimination has to be done for subtrees first, before moving up to surrounding trees. For example, consider

```
{ person: { name: "John",
            phone: 8774,
            phone: 8774},
  person: { name: "Sue",
            office: A471}
  person: { name: "John",
            name: "John",
            phone: 8774}}
```

Working from leaves up to the root, we eliminate in the first stage the duplicate phone and duplicate name. At this point the first and last person become equal; hence, in the second stage we can eliminate one of them.

When we have cycles, duplicate elimination seems less obvious: consider for example the three databases in Figure 6.5. We could easily argue that the two publications in t2 are equal, since their graphs are isomorphic. But you can even argue that the two publications in t3 are equal: both have references as their single outgoing label and, assuming that the two publications are equal,

---

2. In practice, duplicate elimination is done in a controlled fashion, both for efficiency reasons and to accommodate aggregate operators like count, sum, and so on.

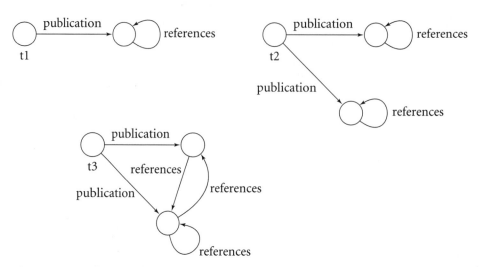

Figure 6.5 Databases with cycles.

their `references` labels lead to equal objects. This suggests defining equality recursively and, hence, performing duplicate elimination recursively also.

Given an object, we consider the infinite unfoldings of the data reachable from that object. For example, the three graphs in Figure 6.5 will be unfolded as in Figure 6.6. Although infinite, any unfolding has the special property that the number of its distinct subtrees is finite; an infinite tree with this property is called a *rational* or *regular* tree. Without being formal, we can say that two objects are equal if we can prove, recursively, that their two unfolded, infinite trees are equal.

For example, consider the two linear subtrees in t2 (Figure 6.6). Although there is no bottom to start the recursion, we note that there is no contradiction in assuming that all pairs of nodes (x1,y1), (x2, y2), (x3, y3), . . . are equal. Hence objects x1 and y1 are equal, and we can eliminate one of them: t2 becomes equal to t1.

In more complicated cases, like t3 in Figure 6.6, we need to combine duplicate elimination with equality testing. Here we observe that each nonroot node x is equal, after duplicate elimination, with an infinite chain $x \rightarrow x2 \rightarrow x3 \rightarrow \ldots$ where each edge is labeled `references`. Then, in x's parent we can eliminate one of its two children. This suggests a recursive, "bottom-up" duplicate elimination procedure. This is, of course, very informal, since there is no "bottom" to start at; we will give a more precise definition in a moment. Notice that after unfolding and duplicate elimination, the three databases t1, t2, t3 become equal.

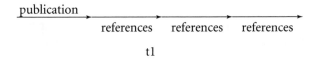

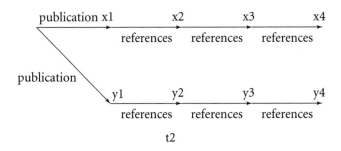

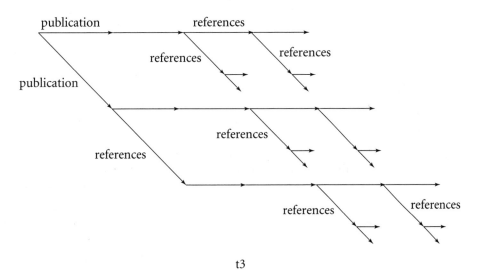

Figure 6.6 Cycle unfolding.

There exists an efficient and more systematic way to detect when two data graphs t1, t2 are equal, without unfolding them, by computing a *bisimulation* between the two graphs. A bisimulation is a binary relation between the nodes of the two graphs, in notation $x \sim y$, satisfying the four properties below. Here x, x' are nodes in t1 and y, y' are nodes in t2.

1. If x and y are the roots of t1, t2, then $x \sim y$.
2. If $x \sim y$ and one of x or y is the root in its graph, then the other one is the root as well.
3. If $x \sim y$ and (x, l, x') is an edge in t1, then there exists an edge (y, l, y') in t2, with the same label, such that $x' \sim y'$. Conversely, if $x \sim y$ and (y, l, y') is an edge in t2, then there exists an edge (x, l, x') in t1 such that $x' \sim y'$.
4. If $x \sim y$ and x is a leaf with value v in t1, then y is also a leaf with the same value v in t2. And conversely.

Define two graphs t1, t2 to be equal whenever there exists a bisimulation from t1 to t2. For example, t1, t2 in Figure 6.4 are equal because the following relation is a bisimulation:

$$x1 \sim y1, x2 \sim y2, x3 \sim y3, x4 \sim y3, x5 \sim y4$$

A graph is always bisimilar to its infinite unfolding; hence, this definition of equality corresponds to the informal one in terms of unfoldings and duplicate elimination.

There exists a simple and efficient way to compute a bisimulation between two graphs t1, t2 if one exists. Initialize a binary relation R to the set $\{(x, y) \mid x \in t1, y \in t2\}$. Then drop any pair (x, y) from R that fails to satisfy one of the conditions 2, 3, or 4. For example, if $(x, y) \in R$ and there exists an edge (x, l, x') in t1 such that there exists no edge with the same label (y, l, y') in t2 such that $(x', y') \in R$, then drop (x, y) from R. Repeat this until no more changes can be made to R. In the end, if the roots of t1, t2 are still in R, then t1, t2 are bisimilar. Note that if the graphs have n_1, n_2 nodes, respectively, then the algorithms makes at most $n_1 n_2$ iterations.[3]

To summarize, graphs are equal if they can be equated by unfolding and duplicate eliminations. The key concept for checking graph equality is bisimulation, and bisimulations can be efficiently computed.

---

3. Notice, however, that in this naive algorithm each iteration inspects all pairs of nodes in the two graphs, resulting in $O(n_1^2 n_2^2)$ steps. An efficient algorithm due to Paige and Tarjan [PT87] computes the bisimulation in $O((m_1 + m_2) \log(m_1 + m_2))$, where m_1, m_2 are the number of edges in each graph.

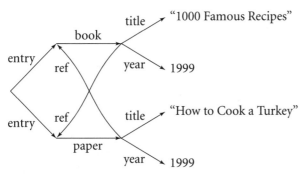

Figure 6.7 Another database with cycles.

6.4.4 Structural Recursion on Cyclic Data

Consider a bibliography database and the following function incrementing each year:

```
h(v)         = v
h({})        = {}
h({l: t})    = if l = year then {year: t+1} else {l: h(t)}
h(t1 union t2) = h(t1) union h(t2)
```

If the data were a tree, h simply copies it and increments the year values. But what happens if the data has cycles, like in Figure 6.7? A simple answer is that we unfold the database into a tree first, then apply h on this infinite tree. The result is a tree isomorphic to the original one; hence, when folded back, it results in an identical copy of the original graph with all years incremented by one. Of course, it is not clear how to implement folding back an infinite tree.

Before addressing implementation issues, let us take a closer look and consider the function f below, which increases only year values occurring under a book label and leaves the rest of the graph unchanged:

```
f(v)         = v
f({})        = {}
f({l: t})    = if l = book then {book: g(t)} else {l: f(t)}
f(t1 union t2) = f(t1) union f(t2)

g(v)         = v
g({})        = {}
g({l: t})    = if l = year then {year: t+1} else {l: g(t)}
g(t1 union t2) = g(t1) union g(t2)
```

For the data in Figure 6.7, it is not clear if we want the paper year incremented, since that can be reached either directly via

Root.entry.paper.year,

or

Root.entry.book.ref.paper.year

In the first case, it should be left untouched, but in the second, it should be incremented. The answer lies also in the database unfolding. Figure 6.8 shows the infinite unfolding and the result of applying f to it. Note that the result is still a rational tree; hence, it could be "folded" back into a finite graph, but it is not clear how this would be implemented.

A second approach is to rely on a *locality* property for structural recursion. Namely, structural recursion acts locally on each edge. There is no information passed from one edge to the next. For our functions f, g, this local action is illustrated in Figure 6.9. Each edge (x, l, y) is transformed by f,g into a local graph with two inputs, f(x), g(x), and two outputs f(y), g(y). The shape of the graph depends on whether l is book, or year, or anything else. The combined action on the graph t in Figure 6.7 is illustrated in Figure 6.10. It looks like two copies of t, except that the second copy has all years increased by one, and the book links of the first copy cross over to the second one. We have to perform a postprocessing that traverses the graph and computes the part accessible from the root; the rest has to be discarded (the two dotted edges are discarded). It is interesting to notice that the unfolding of the resulting graph is precisely the infinite tree in Figure 6.8.

So we can compute structural recursion either through infinite unfolding, or by performing local actions on each edge followed by a graph cleanup. In UnQL, however, the processor does not proceed in either of these two ways. Instead it evaluates structural recursion as any recursive function, by traversing the graph top-down. Starting with f(r), where r is t's root, it calls recursively f or g on other nodes. As it proceeds it "memoizes" each recursive call f(x) or g(x). Rather than doing the construction of the result when the recursion is unfolding, the processor does that construction eagerly, before entering any recursive call; this is possible due to the restricted form of recursion. Hence, when the computation reaches a call which has been already memoized, it stops, avoiding an infinite loop.

In summary, there are three equivalent ways to interpret structural recursion on graphs (with or without cycles): by doing tree unfolding, by doing parallel edge transformations followed by a cleanup, or by memoizing the recursive function's results.

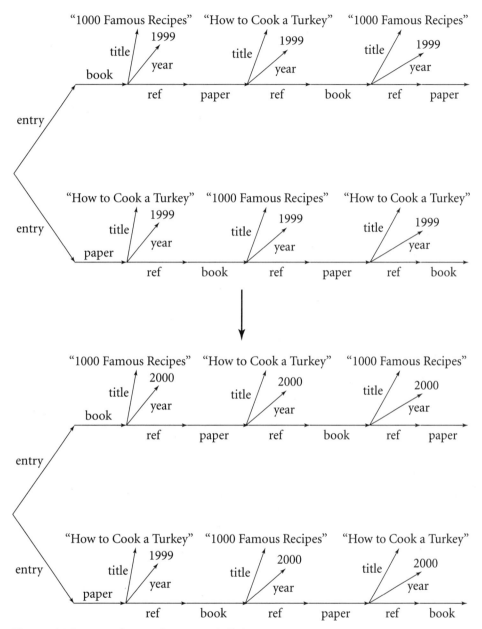

Figure 6.8 Structural recursion on an infinite tree.

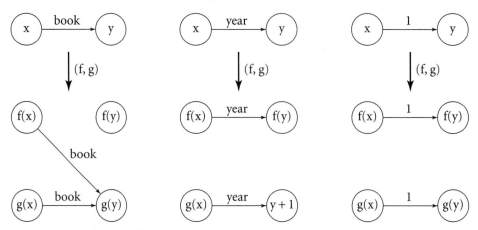

Figure 6.9 Local action for structural recursion.

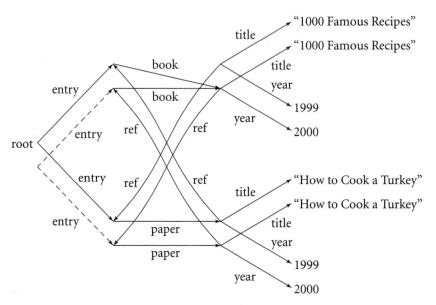

Figure 6.10 Result of applying structural recursion.

6.5 STRUQL

Strudel is a Web site management system, and is an interesting application of semistructured data. It is intended for Web sites with a rich structure and servicing a large amount of data. Starting from raw data, Strudel defines the entire Web site as a *view* over that data, expressed in a query language. For example, the raw data may be a bibliography database, while the Web site is a complex graph, describing both the interpage structure (Web pages and links between them) and intrapage structure. For each author we could have one home page plus several pages for their publications; there could be one page for each journal, and one for each conference, and so on. The query expresses in a declarative way how the Web site is constructed from the raw data. The semistructured data model is used both for raw input data and for the output Web site. We will describe the Strudel system in more detail in Chapter 10. Here we highlight some features of its query language, StruQL.

StruQL has two distinguishing features. It allows fine-grained control of the graph's construction, and it has block structure to facilitate writing large queries.

StruQL uses the syntax x -> a -> y to denote an edge labeled a from node x to node y. Assuming the bibliography database from Figure 6.1, the following query constructs a home page for each author with links to all their publications.

```
// Query Q0
where   Biblio(X), X -> _ -> P, P -> "author" -> A,
                   P -> L -> V, L in {"title", "year"}
create  HomePage(A), PubPage(P)
link    HomePage(A) -> "publication" -> PubPage(P),
        PubPage(P) -> "author" -> HomePage(A),
        PubPage(P) -> L -> V
```

The query has three clauses: The where clause is similar to the from and where clauses in Lorel; its purpose is to bind variables. The create clause specifies what new nodes to create, and the link clause describes the new edges to be created. Strudel enhances the OEM data model with *collections*: each collection is a set of nodes, with a name. For instance, here Biblio denotes a collection consisting only of the root node. Hence, the where clause looks for an edge from the root (X -> _ -> P), and for the author, title, year attributes of P. L is a label variable that can be bound to title or year only. New nodes are created with Skolem functions, in this case HomePage(A) and PubPage(P). It is easy to add edges between any nodes; here we have both an edge from HomePage(A) to PubPage(P), and another edge back. We can also have edges pointing back to the input graph, like title and year from PubPage(P).

When the output graph is complex, we can use a block structure. The following query constructs additional links for books:

```
// Query Q1---subblocks
where   Biblio(X), X -> K -> P, P -> "author" -> A,
                   P -> L -> V, L in {"title", "year"}
create HomePage(A), PubPage(P)
link    HomePage(A) -> "publication" -> PubPage(P),
        PubPage(P) -> "author" -> HomePage(A),
        PubPage(P) -> L -> V
   {  where   K = "book", P -> "publisher" -> Q
      create BookAuthors()
      link    BookAuthors() -> "entry" -> HomePage(A),
              PubPage(P) -> "publishedBy" -> Q
   }
```

The outer block is executed as before: for each binding of the variables X, K, P, A, L, satisfying the where conditions, the appropriate create and link actions are taken. For each such binding, if the where conditions in the subblock can be satisfied as well, then the create and link statements in the subblock are performed too. Note that the BookAuthors() node is created only if there exists at least one book in our database. If we want that node created anyway, we can move it to the outer block.

The block structure can always be flattened away. Query Q1 is equivalent to the union of Q1.a and Q1.b:

```
// Query Q1 rewritten

//    Q1.a
where   Biblio(X), X -> K -> P, P -> "author" -> A,
                   P -> L -> V, L in {"title", "year"}
create HomePage(A), PubPage(P)
link    HomePage(A) -> "publication" -> PubPage(P),
        PubPage(P) -> "author" -> HomePage(A),
        PubPage(P) -> L -> V

//    Q1.b
where   Biblio(X), X -> K -> P, P -> "author" -> A,
                   P -> L -> V, L in {"title", "year"},
        K = "book", P -> "publisher" -> Q
```

```
create BookAuthors()
link   BookAuthors() -> "entry" -> HomePage(A),
       PubPage(P) -> "publishedBy" -> Q
```

6.6 BIBLIOGRAPHIC REMARKS

Some theoretical issues related to object creation were considered in the context of the IQL language [AK89, AK98]. The logic-based perspective on object creation based on Skolem functions was first informally discussed in [Mai86] and refined in a number of proposals (e.g., [CW89, HY90, KLW93, KW89, KL89]).

Skolem functions were first introduced in semistructured data in the language MSL [PGMU95, PAGM96] and used for data integration in the Tsimmis project. MSL is a Datalog-style language allowing the manipulation of semistructured data. MSL also introduced "rest" variables. These are closely related to "functional updates" for record types in functional programming languages, described in the database language Machiavelli [OBB89].

The foundations of structural recursion on collection types (sets, bags, and lists) were first presented in [BTS91]. For semistructured data, structural recursion was first proposed in [BDS95]. Following that, [BDHS96] proposes the language UnQL and describes the optimization for compositions. In these works the term "structural recursion" applies to a more powerful form of recursion; the form considered here is termed *gext*.

The language GraphLog in [CM90b] was proposed by the database group at the University of Toronto. Fancier graphical interfaces to graph data were investigated by the same group, notably Hy+ [CEH+94]. A precursor for graphical query languages is QBE [Zlo77].

An efficient algorithm for bisimulation was given by Paige and Tarjan in [PT87]. A good introduction to bisimulation for process algebras can be found in [Mil89].

The Strudel system is available from [Str99]. It was first demonstrated in [FFK+97], and the query language described in [FFLS97]. The experience of using the Strudel system is reported in [FFK+98].

III

Types

7

Typing Semistructured Data

So far we have presented semistructured data as self-describing. There is no need for an a priori schema as in the relational or object-oriented data models. Even if such a schema were available, we "forget" it, thus potentially allowing arbitrary deviations from the schema. Most often, however, the data is not fully unstructured. It may have some structure, but that structure may not be explicitly stated, may be confined to only a portion of the data, may change without notice, or may simply be too complex to be described in terms of traditional database models. In previous chapters, we have chosen to ignore completely any structure that might exist.

Enterprise applications use schemas in a crucial way for efficient data processing, improved storage, and user guidance; schemas here may be relational, entity relationship, or object-oriented. To achieve similar goals in processing Web data, we need to be able to describe and exploit the underlying structure of the data. In this chapter we present techniques for describing a schema for semistructured data when one exists or when one can be found.

The idea of structuring or typing semistructured data is somewhat novel and certainly controversial. So far, we lack a well-accepted approach to typing. This is an area of much research activity. Many formalisms for describing structure have been proposed so far, and not all are fully explored. Here, we chose two of the simplest ones and describe them in some depth: one logic-based and one based on graph simulations. We also describe a connection between the two approaches. Then we mention some more advanced features proposed in schemas for semistructured data.

Schemas for semistructured data differ, however, from those for relational or object-oriented data. In a traditional database approach, types are always fixed prior to populating the database. Once the data is populated, its binary storage

121

cannot be interpreted without knowing the schema. With semistructured data we may specify the type *after* the database is populated. The type may often describe the structure only for a part of the data and, even then, do that with less precision. An important consequence is that a data instance may have more than one type. This leads to the possibility of *schema extraction*, that is, given one particular data instance, finding the most specific schema for it. In a different scenario we may deal with different data instances, but they are all generated automatically by a legacy system, say, as the result of a query. This leads to another interesting possibility: *schema inference*, that is, finding the most specific schema by analyzing the query, a process similar to type inference in programming languages.

Consider for instance the following query:

```
select row: {name: N, resume: R}
where {name: N, resume: R} in Person,
      {title: T, address.country: "France"} in R,
      contains(T, "SGML")
```

We can make no assumption on the input data. For instance, we cannot infer that person objects have a resume component with a title and address components. Due to the semantics of our query language, any of those components may be missing, and the result of the query becomes empty. But interestingly, we know something about the structure of the resulting piece of data. It consists of a collection of pairs, and the resume component for each element has a title component and an address with a country subcomponent. An application consuming results produced by this query may, and should, use such schema information in processing its data.

There are a number of motivations for considering structure:

1. *To optimize query evaluation.* Knowing the structure may guide the query processor to search only a small fragment of the data.
2. *To facilitate the task of integrating several data sources.* Once some structure is known for each source, we can choose an integrating structure and specify the conversions.
3. *To improve storage.* Besides pure storage space, better clustering may reduce the number of page fetches, thus improving query performance.
4. *To construct indexes.* Indexes are often associated to certain structures, for example, given a class *company* with an attribute *name* of type string, an index on company names.
5. *To describe the database content to users and facilitate query formulation.*
6. *To proscribe certain updates.* This is a classical usage of typing in databases that is certainly much less relevant for Web data applications.

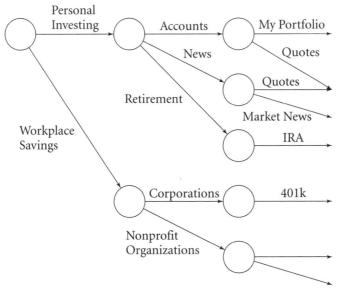

Figure 7.1 Example of a site map for a financial company.

7.1   WHAT IS TYPING GOOD FOR?

Before getting started on formalisms to specify types in semistructured data, we first come back to possible usages of types in our context. We will not consider the use of types as constraints here in more detail since this is a standard notion for the database world, and it is less relevant in a semistructured data context.

7.1.1 Browsing and Querying Data

Knowing some information is useful for browsing data. Most Web sites with a complex structure have some kind of *site map*. Figure 7.1 illustrates a fragment of a site map for a financial company's Web site. The map describes the site's top structure. For example, a user wishing to access his personal account can figure out that he has to follow the `"Personal Investing" "Accounts" "My Portfolio"` links to get there.

The Lore system uses a *data guide* to help users browse semistructured data. A portion of the data guide for the Stanford Database Group Web site is shown in Figure 7.2. By clicking, the user may expand or shrink the portion that is exposed.

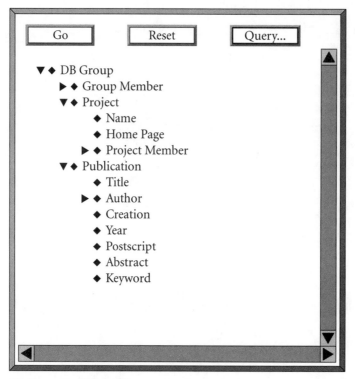

Figure 7.2 A data guide.

7.1.2 Optimizing Query Evaluation

Consider the following query, printing all titles of entries having a `zip` attribute with value "12345":

```
select X.title
from   biblio._ X
where  X.*.zip= "12345"
```

To evaluate this query we would have to scan all `biblio` objects X, recursively scan all their subobjects, searching for some `zip` attribute. Type information could help us by restricting the search. For example, we may know that only books contain a `zip` attribute, while other entries don't. Furthermore, the `zip` can only occur directly underneath an `address` attribute. (The type in Figure 7.3 could be interpreted as saying that.) Then, an optimizer would rewrite the query into

```
select X.title
from    biblio.book X
where   X.address.zip= "12345"
```

This query can be evaluated more efficiently than the previous one since we only have to look at book entries and, moreover, only have to search for zip in the address field.

7.1.3 Improving Storage

As we have noted in Section 6.1, we can store any data graph in a relational database, for instance, with the following schema:

```
ref ( source: oid, label: dom, destination: oid )
val ( obj: oid,    value: dom)
```

A problem with this schema is that it splits information in small pieces that may end up in many different pages on disk. For instance, consider bibliography data with type as described in Figure 7.3. The title, author names, and addresses may span several pages. However, if we have the type information and expect to have many book objects, we may decide to use a particular relation:

```
book( source: oid, title: string,
      firstname: string, lastname: string,
      street: string, city: string, zip: string)
```

Observe that this reduces storage needs since a book will be represented by a single record. Accessing the book requires a single record fetch. On the other hand, the physical organization should not preclude a book from having additional attributes, even additional authors; these are simply stored in ref (since the type is not strict here).

It is indeed common to use such relations in semistructured data applications. Consider, for example, the Web-catalog system,[1] a large system for mail orders. Products in the catalog may be thought of as OEM objects. But they do share some common properties such as name, identification number, price, availability, and so on. All this information is maintained in a relational database. Each product has other additional *individual* properties; for example, a PC has a processor field. In Web-catalog, for each object, these properties are stored as a list of property name (label) and value pairs.

---

1. http://www.ezecom.com/.

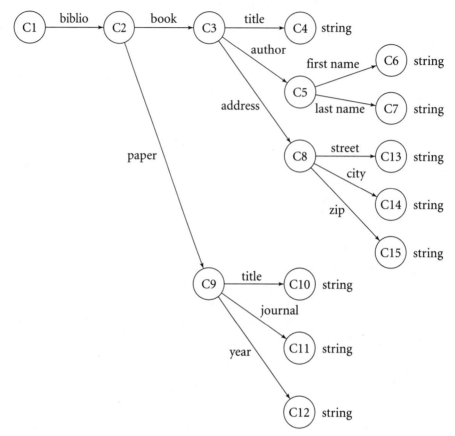

Figure 7.3 Partial description of the structure of a bibliography database.

7.2   ANALYZING THE PROBLEM

Assuming we know what a type is, a first dimension of the problem is, given a database and given a type, *does the database conform to this type?*

In our context, a database consists primarily in a set of objects and the typing also involves the classification of objects. So, another facet of the problem is, *which objects belong to each class?*

An important component of typing is therefore the description of the structure of each class and its relationships with other classes. Observe that this is quite close to standard type definitions in object databases. However, some aspects make the situation here radically different:

1. Classes are defined less precisely. As a consequence, objects may belong to several classes.
2. Some objects may not belong to any class (besides the default *object* class) or may have properties that do not pertain to any class.
3. The typing may be *approximate*. For example, we may accept in a class an object that does not quite conform to the specification of that class. This aspect is less understood than the other two, and we will ignore it.

From a formal viewpoint, a main consequence of the first point is that the classification is not a *partition* of the set of objects (as in an object database) but a covering of it. A consequence of the second is that the covering may be partial.

The fact that the same object may belong to several classes should be thought of as the object having several *roles*. Suppose, for instance, that data about people has been gathered from several independent sources containing information about soccer players, employees, car owners, stamp collectors, and movie freaks. The integrating OEM database will have an object per person with outgoing edges for each of these collections. If we attempt to classify objects too precisely by their structure, we may end up introducing classes such as *employees who own cars and loves movies, soccer players who collect stamps*, and so on. The covering would prevent us from having a combinatorial explosion of the number of classes. An employee who owns a car and goes to movies would simply be a member of two classes, *car-owner* and *movie-lover*.

We start by describing formalisms available for specifying structure. We do so in the context of OEM, which is, in some sense, a rather minimal, typeless model. Types become more complex when the data includes order, inheritance, various types of pointers, and other features found in object database models and some document standards such as XML. We discuss some of the approaches for these features, without attempting to give a definite answer.

7.3 SCHEMA FORMALISMS

We describe next formalisms for specifying structure.

7.3.1 Logic

We start by using first-order logic and Datalog to describe structure. An illustration of the kind of structure we wish to describe is in the following example.

Example 7.3.1 We want to specify three kinds of objects in the database:

- Root object(s) have
  - outgoing edges labeled *company* to company objects and *person* to person objects
- Person objects have
  - outgoing edges labeled *name* and *position* to string objects
  - outgoing edges labeled *worksfor* to company objects
  - incoming edges labeled *manager* and *employee* from company objects
- Company objects have
  - outgoing edges labeled *name* and *address* to string objects
  - outgoing edges labeled *manager* and *employee* to person objects
  - incoming edges labeled *worksfor* from person objects

□

Before we can express this in first-order logic, we need to explain more precisely the intended meaning of such a description. Take a simpler example in which we want to define a class c as having outgoing a-edges to string objects and incoming b-edges from c'-objects. What do we actually mean? There are several choices:

- *If.* If an object has a-edges to strings and b-edges from c'-objects, then it is a c-object, that is,

$$\forall X, Y, Z(ref(X, a, Y) \land string(Y) \land c'(Z) \land ref(Z, b, X) \rightarrow c(X))$$

Formulas like this often occur when describing structure, and we rewrite it to the equivalent

$$(\exists Y, Z(ref(X, a, Y) \land string(Y) \land c'(Z) \land ref(Z, b, X))) \rightarrow c(X)$$

where the free variable X is assumed to be universally quantified.

- *Only-if.* Any c-object has some a-edge to strings and some b-edge from c'-objects:

$$(\exists Y, Z(ref(X, a, Y) \land string(Y) \land c'(Z) \land ref(Z, b, X))) \leftarrow c(X)$$

Combining the two, we can obtain an "if and only if" definition:

$$(\exists Y, Z(ref(X, a, Y) \land string(Y) \land c'(Z) \land ref(Z, b, X))) \leftrightarrow c(X)$$

- *Consequence.* We don't define the class c but describe consequences of belonging to that class. For example, for c-objects, outgoing a-edges are to string objects and incoming b-edges from c'-objects; moreover, c-objects do not have other edges than the a- and b-edges:

$$c(X) \wedge ref(Z, b, X) \rightarrow c'(Z)$$
$$c(X) \wedge ref(X, a, Y) \rightarrow string(Y)$$
$$c(X) \wedge ref(X, L, Y) \wedge L \neq a \wedge L \neq b \rightarrow false$$

The latter is a negative consequence, leading to a contradiction when it is satisfied. Listing consequences defines a class indirectly: all objects not violating the consequences could belong to that class.

We used here first-order logic as a syntax for typing. A typing T consists of a set of formulas involving extensional predicates,[2] for example, *ref*, *string* and intensional (implicit) unary predicates, one per class. Given a data graph D and a typing T, our two questions of interest are restated now in terms of logic:

1. Does D satisfy T, noted $D \models T$, that is, is there a model of T that coincides with D over the extensional predicates?
2. If $D \models T$, what is the classification that is induced?

Thus, first-order logic leads to very general typings, probably too general for what is needed in semistructured data; it could also lead to undecidability or intractability. In practice, however, we never need very complex types, but types that can be expressed in restricted logic formalisms. The study of restricted and tractable logics is not a novel topic. For instance, *description logics* have been proposed for knowledge representation. We consider next an approach based on a rule-based language (Datalog), and in the following section one based on graph theoretic concepts.

7.3.2 Datalog

First, we will use Datalog rules with a fixpoint semantics. We will see how this corresponds to the formal notion of typing previously introduced.

Datalog allows us to state that if a conjunction of facts holds, then some new fact can be derived. Considering Example 7.3.1, we could define a typing by the following set P_0 of rules:

---

2. The second extensional predicate string is used in place of val. If we have in the database a fact such as val(o_4, "Versailles"), we only need to know from a typing viewpoint that o_4 is an atomic and that *string* is its sort. This information would be given in the extensional relation string.

```
r(X) :- ref(X,person,Y), p(Y),  ref(X,company,Z), c(Z)
p(X) :- c(Y), ref(Y,manager,X), c(Z), ref(Z,employee,X),
        ref(X,worksfor,U), c(U),
        ref(X,name,N), string(N), ref(X,position,P), string(P)
c(X) :- p(Z), ref(Z,worksfor,X), p(Z), ref(Z,worksfor,X),
        ref(X,manager,M), p(M), ref(X,employee,E), p(E),
        ref(X,name,N), string(N), ref(X,address,A), string(A)
```

why repeated twice.type [handwritten annotation]

The intensional predicates r, p, and c stand for root, person, and company, respectively. The extensional predicates ref and string come directly from our relational representation of data graphs.

The traditional interpretation of Datalog rules is that of *if* conditions. For example the first rule reads that if X has outgoing edges labeled person and company to objects satisfying predicates p and c, then X satisfies predicate r. For the moment, let us assume the *if* interpretation of the rules. We will revise this shortly.

Now suppose the data graph D consists of the following objects:

```
&o1 {company: &o2{name: &o5 "O2",
                  address: &o6 "Versailles",
                  manager: &o3,
                  employee: &o3, employee: &o4 },
     person:  &o3{name: &o7 "Francois",
                  position: &o8 "CEO",
                  worksfor: &o2 },
     person:  &o4{name: &o9 "Lucien",
                  position: &o10 "programmer",
                  worksfor: &o2 }
    }
```

Let us consider first the standard interpretation of Datalog. We start from an empty set of facts and see what can be derived. In that case, nothing. In other words, the empty set of facts is the least fixpoint for this program. In English, we failed to type any object. This is indeed the case because every rule has a right-hand side that contains at least one intensional predicate; since initially these are empty, no new facts are ever derived. This is not surprising since our goal "to type the largest set of objects" clearly leads to the *greatest* fixpoint.

In this alternative semantics for Datalog programs, we start from the instance D that contains all our knowledge:

- e.g., ref(&o1,company,&o2), ref(&o2,name,&o5), etc.
- e.g., string(&o5), string(&o6), etc.

and we apply a greatest-fixpoint semantics. From a semantic viewpoint, the desired model M is the greatest fixpoint of P_0 containing D. More precisely, it is an instance M that coincides with D on the extensional predicates and such that each typing fact in M can be derived from facts in M using one rule in P_0, and it is the greatest such instance.

From a computational viewpoint, M can be obtained as follows. Start from J_0 containing D and all possible typing facts, that is, each $c(o)$ such that o is an object and c a class. From J_0 derive J_1 consisting of D together with the facts that can be derived using J_0. In a similar manner, derive J_2 from J_1, then J_3 from J_2, and so on. This is iterated until a fixpoint is reached. In our example, the fixpoint is reached at the second stage:

- $J_0 = D \cup \{r(\&o_1), r(\&o_2), r(\&o_3), r(\&o_4), p(\&o_1), p(\&o_2), p(\&o_3), p(\&o_4),$
  $c(\&o_1), c(\&o_2), c(\&o_3), c(\&o_4)\}$;
- $M = J_2 = J_1 = D \cup \{r(\&o_1), c(\&o_2), p(\&o_3), p(\&o_4)\}$.

We correctly managed to type all objects.

We can revisit our assumption that Datalog rules be interpreted as *if* conditions. Consider the *if* conditions associated to the first Datalog rules in P:

$$r(X) \leftarrow (\exists Y, \exists Z(ref(X, person, Y) \land p(Y) \land ref(X, company, Z) \land c(Z)))$$

and similarly for the other two rules. What is the maximal model for them? It turns out it is J_0, which includes *every* typing fact. Of course this is not what we want. Consider some fact in the result M, for instance, $c(\&o_2)$. Since it is in the fixpoint, this means that there is a rule that allows us to derive it. In other words, the fact that $c(\&o_2)$ is derived implies that the body of the third rule holds for some values of Y, Z, M, E, N, A. In general, facts about c imply that the following rule holds:

$(*) \ \forall X(c(X) \rightarrow \exists Y, Z, M, E, N, A$

  $p(Z) \land ref(Z, worksfor, X) \land$

  $ref(X, manager, M) \land p(M) \land ref(X, employee, E) \land p(E) \land$

  $ref(X, name, N) \land string(N) \land ref(X, address, A) \land string(A)))$

This shows that the greatest-fixpoint semantics that we use here is connected to the *only-if* interpretation of Datalog rules.

A short digression in the world of Datalog and fixpoint semantics will illustrate the logical foundations of this *only-if* interpretation. Consider a Datalog program P. Let Γ_P denote the corresponding set of *only-if* formulas, that is, the formulas obtained as $(*)$ above. Then the greatest fixpoint of P is the maximal model of Γ_P. This is not surprising. It is a well-known fact that the least fixpoint of P is the minimal model of the set of *if* formulas corresponding to P.

To summarize, we consider typings expressed as Datalog rules with a certain form. They enable us to define classes by specifying what incoming and/or outgoing edges are *required*. With such restricted rules we cannot prohibit objects from having additional edges; for example, a Person object may have an edge best-friend. If such descriptions are needed, we could write more complex Datalog rules. For example, the following rule states that the only outgoing edges allowed from Person are worksfor, name, and position:

```
fail()  :- p(X), ref(X,L,Y),
           L != worksfor, L != name, L!= position
```

The fail() condition in the head is equivalent to an empty head and leads to a contradiction if the body is satisfied. Of course, for such Datalog rules the existence of a greatest fixpoint is not guaranteed anymore.

To conclude this section, we consider the use of some a priori knowledge. For instance, suppose also that we happen to know that $\&o_2$ is a *c*-object. This can be easily incorporated as a rule:

```
c(&o2) :-
```

The framework also allows us to easily incorporate such added information:

```
r(&o9) :-                       % &o9 is the root
       :- r(X), r(Y), X!=Y  % no other object is a root
       :- c(X), c'(X),       % an object cannot belong
                              % to both c and c'
```

7.3.3 Simulation

A different approach to describing structure is based on *simulation*. Simulation (together with bisimulation, discussed in Section 6.4.3) has been extensively studied in other areas of computer science.

Consider the data instance in Figure 7.4(a). After a short inspection we can see that the data consists of two major kinds of objects: two Company objects &c1, &c2 and three Person objects &p1, &p2, &p3. They seem to have a fairly regular structure except for the Person's descriptions (shown with dotted lines). An easy way to describe the data is to list what subobjects are allowed where. For instance, a Company can have name, url, address, manager, and employee edges. Not all these edges are required in every object, but we will ignore this for a moment. Similarly Person objects have (at most) worksfor, name, phone, manager, position, and description. The description edge is rather interesting. It leads to objects of a class Any, which can have any labels leading to other objects of type Any. An underscore means "any labels." This information is concisely described by the graph in Figure 7.4(b), which, in addition to Person and Company classes, also defines a Root class and a string class. We call such a graph a *schema graph*. Its semantics is that it simply lists all permitted labels. For example, a Person object is not allowed to have an address edge. The classification induced by the schema graph is given in Figure 7.5.

Our definition of a schema graph is the same as that for a data graph with the following minor changes. Labels can now be alternations (like name | address) or underscore; atomic values are type names, like string, int, float. We call the oids of complex objects *classes*, like Person, Company. As with any data graph, a schema graph has a designated root object.

We address next the two questions of interest: Does a given database conform to a given schema graph? And, if yes, then which objects (in the data graph) belong to which classes (in the schema graph)? Both questions require a careful inspection.

The answers to both lie in the mathematical notion of simulation. We review its definition next. A (binary) *relation* on sets S, T is a subset of the cartesian product $S \times T$. If R is such a relation, we follow mathematical convention xRy for $(x, y) \in R$. Given a directed, labeled graph (V, E), each edge label l induces a binary relation $[l]$ on V, V. Thus we write $x[l]y$ whenever there is an l-labeled edge from x to y. This is simply an abbreviated notation for $ref(x, l, y)$ used earlier. We shall assume that edge labels are drawn from some prescribed set L.

Definition 7.3.1 Given graphs $G_1 = (V_1, E_1)$, $G_2 = (V_2, E_2)$, a relation R on V_1, V_2 is a *simulation* if it satisfies

$$\forall l \in L \; \forall x_1, y_1 \in V_1 \; \forall x_2 \in V_2(x_1[l]y_1 \wedge x_1 R x_2 \Rightarrow \exists y_2 \in V_2(y_1 R y_2 \wedge x_2[l]y_2)) \quad \square$$

This is something of a mouthful, but it states a simple property: Every edge in G_1 must have a "corresponding" edge in G_2 under the simulation. The condition is best visualized by Figure 7.6. The condition for R to be a simulation is that whenever we see the edge pattern given by the solid lines, we can find a vertex y_2 that completes the diagram with dotted lines. We may want to check that the formula in Definition 7.3.1 states precisely this condition. We say that the edge $x_1[l]y_1$ is simulated by the edge $x_2[l]y_2$. It is also interesting to observe that a relation R is a bisimulation (Section 6.4.3) if it is a simulation and the reverse R^{-1} (defined as $yR^{-1}x \Leftrightarrow xRy$) is also a simulation.

We now define a simulation between a semistructured data instance (OEM) and a schema graph by making the following changes in the previous definition. First we allow an edge $x_1[l]y_1$ in the OEM data to be simulated by some edge

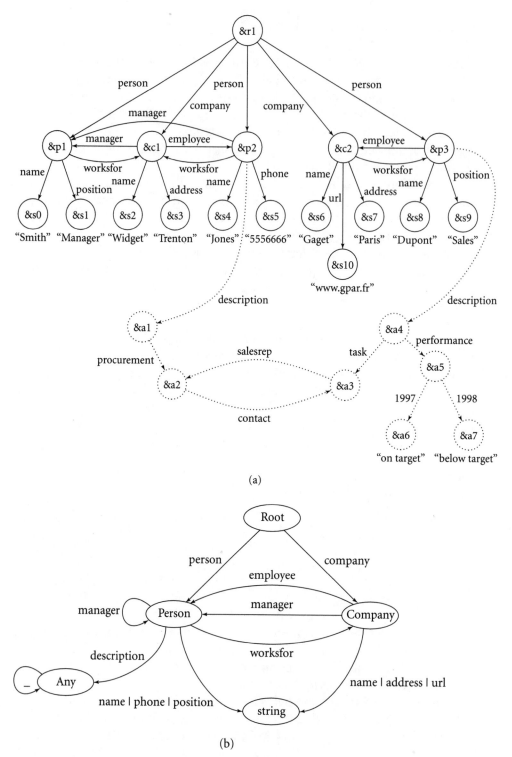

Figure 7.4 (a) Data graph, and (b) schema graph.

Data node	Schema node
&r1	Root
&c1,&c2	Company
&p1,&p2,&p3	Person
&s0,&s1,&s2,&s3,&s4,&s5,	string
&s6,&s7,&s8,&s9,&s10	
&a1,&a2,&a3,&a4,	
&a5,&a6,&a7	Any

Figure 7.5 Classification for the data graph and schema graph in Figure 7.4.

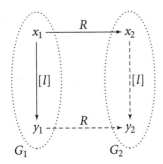

Figure 7.6 Diagram of simulation.

$x_2[l']y_2$ when l' is a wild card (_) or an alternation containing the label l. Second, we require the following:

- The roots must be in the simulation: rRr', where r, r' are the roots of the OEM data and schema graph, respectively. We say that the simulation is *rooted*.
- Whenever xRy, if y is an atomic type (like string, int), then x must be an atomic node too and have a value of that type. We say the simulation is *typed*.

Returning to our example, we can see that the relation R defined by Figure 7.5 is indeed a simulation.

To check that, we have to consider every oid o and class c for which oRc, and every outgoing edge from o. We illustrate with the oid &p1, the class Person, and the edge worksfor from &p1 to &c1. Checking the simulation condition, we find an edge worksfor from Person to Company, and indeed the pair (&c1, Company) is in R. In addition, the simulation is rooted (because the pair (&r1,

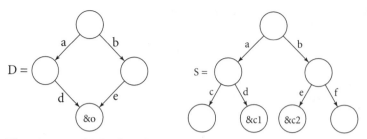

Figure 7.7 Multiple classification for an object.

Root) is in the table), and it is typed (because all nodes (&s0, &s1, ...,&s10) simulated by string have atomic values of type string).

This answers our first question: When does a data graph D conform to a schema graph S? When there exists a rooted, typed simulation between the data and the schema.

Turning to the second question, the guiding principle is that oid o should belong to class c if oRc. An interesting remark is that, in this way, a rooted simulation R will always classify all objects. This is because in the OEM data every node is reachable by some path from the root, and that R is rooted. However, the classification need not be unique. In Figure 7.7, &o is classified both in &c1 and in &c2.

In general, we may have more than one simulation R between some data and a schema graph. For example, consider the data and the schema in Figure 7.8. Object &o could be classified as either &b1, or &b2, or both, resulting in three different rooted, typed simulations.

At this point we state a simple property for simulation. We shall write $G_1 \preceq_R G_2$ whenever R is a simulation from G_1 to G_2.

Fact If $G_1 \preceq_{R_1} G_2$ and $G_1 \preceq_{R_2} G_2$ then $G_1 \preceq_{R_1 \cup R_2} G_2$.

This result, while simple, is extremely useful (it also holds for rooted and typed simulations), since it allows us to conclude that for any data graph D conforming to some schema graph S, there is always a *maximal* simulation from D to S. This answers our second question: an object o belongs to some class c if oRc, where R is the maximal simulation between the OEM data and the schema graph.

It is common in managing heterogeneous databases to want to "retrofit" a schema to some existing data. The existence of a maximal simulation provides—

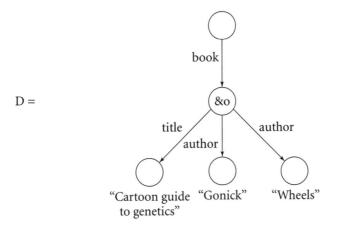

D =

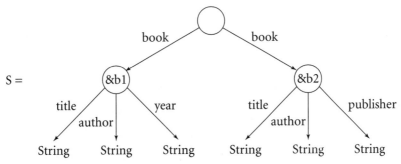

S =

Figure 7.8 Ambiguity in classification.

in this rather simple context—a guarantee that there is always a "best fit" between data and schema.

Maximal simulations can be computed in a similar way to maximal Datalog fixpoints. Given a data graph D and schema graph S, start with the relation R_0 classifying every object o in every class c (that is oR_0c for any o, c). Next compute R_1 from R_0 to be the set of pairs (o, c) that do not violate the simulation condition with respect to R_0; that is, oR_1c if every edge $o[l]o'$ in D is simulated by some edge $c[l']c'$ in S with $o'R_0c'$, and if c is labeled with an atomic type, then o is an atomic value of that type. Similarly construct R_2 from R_1, and so on. Stop when a fixpoint is reached. This process always terminates since the relations $R_0, R_1, R_2, \ldots$ get smaller and smaller. We note here, however, that more efficient algorithms are known for computing maximal simulations.

We conclude this section with an interesting application of simulations.

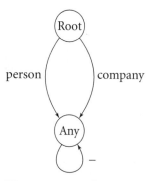

Figure 7.9 A schema graph.

Comparing schemas

In practice we often learn more about the data over time. Initially we may know very little about the structure and describe it with a general schema, but later refine some of the classes. Referring to the data in Figure 7.4(a), assume that we initially had for it the schema S' in Figure 7.9. This schema tells us very little: there is a root node whose only outgoing edges allowed are person and company. Beyond that, any structure is allowed, that is, any edges are allowed, to any kinds of objects. Later we learn more about the data and derive the schema S in Figure 7.4(b). This raises an interesting question: *Do all databases conforming to schema S also conform to schema S'?* In this case we say that S is a refinement of S', or that S' subsumes S.

To answer this question, we use another simple fact about simulations.

Fact If $G_1 \preceq_R G_2$ and $G_2 \preceq_{R'} G_3$, then $G_1 \preceq_{R \circ R'} G_3$.
Here we use $R \circ R'$ for the *composition* of two relations: $x(R \circ R')z \Leftrightarrow (\exists y, (xRy) \wedge (yR'z))$.

This gives the answer: to check that S is a refinement of S', simply check if there exists a rooted, typed simulation[3] from S to S'. Indeed, whenever some data graph D conforms to S, the fact above guarantees that D also conforms to S'. In our example, the simulation is given by Figure 7.10.

---

3. It is obvious how to extend the notion of simulation between schema graphs S and S'. For example, an edge labeled name | address is simulated by an edge labeled name | address | url or by an edge labeled _, but not by an edge labeled name.

Node in S	Node in S'
Root	Root
Person	Any
Company	Any
string	Any
Any	Any

Figure 7.10 A simulation between two schemas.

7.3.4   Comparison between Datalog Rules and Simulation

Datalog rules define a class by saying what minimum incoming and outgoing edges are *required*. Schema graphs (simulation) define classes by saying what outgoing edges are *permitted*. These two seem dual to each other. In this section we make the duality precise.

We have to be careful in comparing the two, since Datalog rules are much more flexible and powerful than simulations. They can express added information about the data and can check both incoming and outgoing edges. In order to facilitate the comparison, here we will restrict Datalog rules to check only outgoing edges.

We define first *dual schema graphs:* these are like schema graphs, but list all required edges rather than the allowed edges. For example, consider the dual schema graph in Figure 7.11 defining classes Root, Person, and Company. An object o is in class Person if it has at least one attribute name of type string and one attribute worksfor whose value is an object in class Company. Similarly an object is in class Company if it has at least one name of type string and one manager in class Person. The semantics of dual schema graphs can also be described in terms of simulation relation R, but now in the reversed direction, from S to D. Referring to the data D in Figure 7.4(a) and schema S in Figure 7.11, the simulation is defined as in Figure 7.12.

Consider first the node Root in S, and assume that for some data object X, (Root, X) is in R. The simulation condition requires that each edge from Root has some corresponding edge from X. Since there are two edges from Root, this condition is

$$Root(X) \rightarrow (\exists Y, Z(ref(X, person, Y) \wedge Person(Y) \wedge$$
$$ref(X, company, Z) \wedge Company(Z)))$$

This is an *only-if* kind of condition, which, based on our earlier discussion, can be written as the following Datalog rule with greatest-fixpoint semantics:

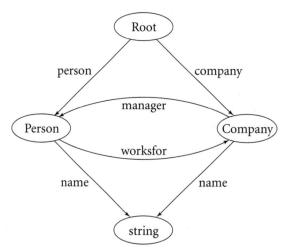

Figure 7.11 A dual schema graph for the data in
Figure 7.4(a).

```
Root(X)   :-   ref(X,person,Y), Person(Y),
               ref(X,company,Z), Company(Z)
```

Proceeding similarly for the other two classes, we arrive at the following set of
Datalog rules:

```
Root(X)      :-   ref(X,person,Y), Person(Y),
                  ref(X,company,Z), Company(Z)
Person(X)    :-   ref(X,name,N), string(N),
                  ref(X,worksfor,Y), Company(Y)
Company(X)   :-   ref(X,name,N), string(N),
                  ref(X,manager,Y), Person(Y)
```

The connection between this Datalog program and simulation is remarkably
tight: any model for the Datalog program[4] corresponds to a simulation, and vice
versa. More generally, Datalog typing rules correspond precisely to dual schema
graphs, and vice versa.

A consequence of this connection is that it potentially provides an efficient
algorithm to compute the greatest fixpoint for Datalog schemas, by using some
algorithm for simulation. Of course this algorithm cannot be applied to *any*
Datalog program, but only to those having the particular form corresponding

---

4. To be precise, the model has to be for the *only-if* formulas.

Schema node	Data node
Root	&r
Person	&p1
Company	&c1
Person	&p2
Company	&c2
Person	&p3
string	&so
...	...
string	&so

Figure 7.12 A simulation between a schema and a data.

to simulation. It is not clear what relationship this has to general optimization techniques developed for Datalog programs.

Finally, we remark that the connection can be pushed beyond the simple framework of classes defined by outgoing edges. For example, in schema graphs (and dual schema graphs), we can use a label $-l$ on some edge to denote the fact that its condition is about an incoming edge, rather than an outgoing edge. The definition of a simulation can be extended accordingly.

7.4   EXTRACTING SCHEMAS FROM DATA

What sets apart schemas for semistructured data from traditional schemas is the fact that a given semistructured data instance can have more than one schema. This raises the following intriguing possibility: Given a semistructured data instance for which we do not have any a priori knowledge, compute automatically some schema for it; of course, given several possible answers, we want the schema that best describes the structure of that particular data. We call this problem *schema extraction*. In this section we illustrate schema extraction both for schema graphs and Datalog typings. We shall use the data instance in Figure 7.13 as an illustration throughout this section.

7.4.1   Data Guides

Data guides were originally introduced in the Lore project as a concise and accurate summary of a given data graph. Before addressing the schema extraction problem, let us recall the original motivation first. Consider the data graph in Figure 7.13. In order to derive a summary of that graph, we begin by examining

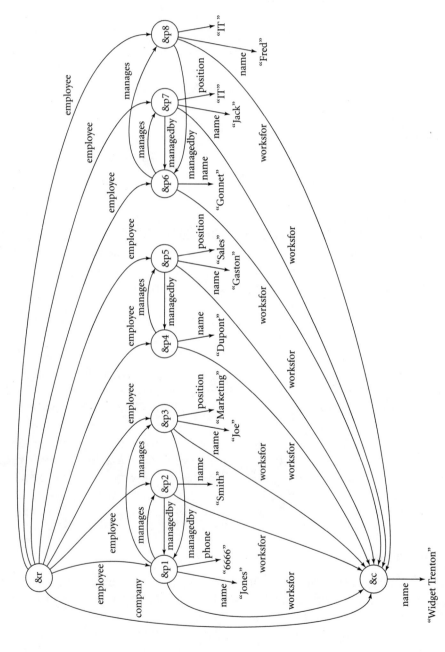

Figure 7.13 An example of OEM data.

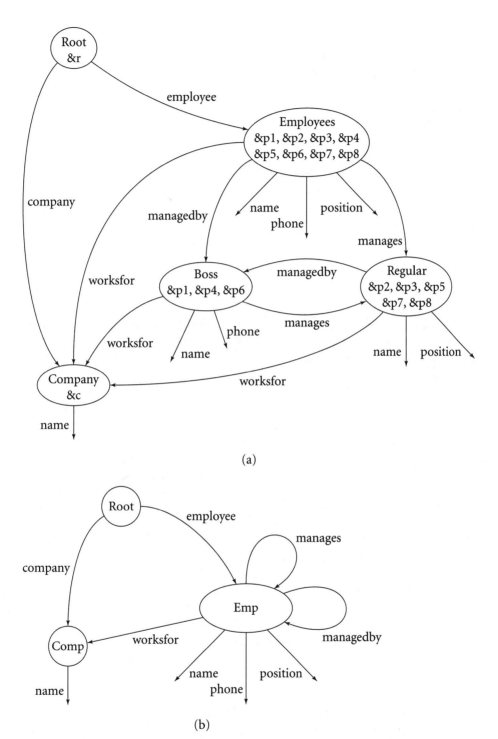

Figure 7.14 (a) A data guide, and (b) a schema graph. All atomic objects are labeled string.

all possible paths in the data, starting from the root &r. Some of them are (in no particular order).

```
employee
employee.name
employee.manages
employee.manages.managedby
employee.manages.managedby.manages
employee.manages.managedby.manages.managedby
company
company.name
employee.worksfor
employee.worksfor.name
...
```

The list is infinite, since we have cycles in the data, but it forms a regular language.

Our goal is to construct a new OEM graph that is a finite description of this list of paths; this will be the *data guide*. Moreover, we are looking for the following two properties to be fulfilled in the data guide.

- *Accurate.* Every path in the data occurs in the data guide, and every path in the data guide occurs in the data.
- *Concise.* Every path in the data guide occurs exactly once.

We proceed as follows. Obviously the data guide will have a root node; call it Root. Next we examine one by one each path in the list, and add new nodes to the data guide, as needed:

- employee: There are eight such paths in the data, reaching &p1, &p2, &p3, &p4, &p5, &p6, &p7, &p8; we create a new node in the data guide, call it Employees, and connect Root and Employees with an edge labeled employee.
- employee.name: All these paths in the data lead to atomic values of type string; hence, we create a node called string and connect Employees and string with an edge labeled name.
- employee.manages: We create a new node (call it Regular) and connect Employees and Regular by an edge labeled manages; note that in the data, these paths lead to &p2, &p3, &p5, &p7, &p8.
- employee.manages.managedby: We create a new node called Boss and connect Regular and Boss by an edge labeled managedby; in the data these paths lead to &p1, &p4, &p6.

- `employee.manages.managedby.manages`: Here we observe that the set of data nodes reached by these paths is `&p2`, `&p3`, `&p5`, `&p7`, `p8`, which we have seen before (the `Regular` node); rather than creating a new node, we connect `Boss` and `Regular` with an edge labeled `manages`.

- `employee.manages.managedby.manages.managedby`: Again this leads to the set `&p1`, `&p4`, `&p6`, which corresponds to `Boss`. Moreover, we already have an edge labeled `managedby` from `Regular` to `Boss`; hence, we do not create any new nodes or edges.

- `company`: We create a new node called `Company` and a corresponding new edge.

- We continue examining paths until no new nodes and no new edges are created.

The resulting data guide is illustrated in Figure 7.14(a).

The data guide summarizes the data in a concise way. For example, if the data increased to hundreds of companies and thousands of employees, the data guide would have stayed the same. This construction of the data guide resembles the technique to transform a nondeterministic finite state automaton into a deterministic one and entails taking the power set of the set of states.

The nodes in a data guide define classes of nodes in the data. In fact, our construction went the other way around, creating data guide nodes for sets of data nodes. The classification is not unique: for example, the node `&p1` belongs both to `Boss` and to `Employee`. Interestingly, the data guide identified two subclasses of `Employee`: the `Boss` subclass and the `Regular` subclass. This is certainly meaningful for many data instances, but it also poses the danger of a combinatorial explosion in the size of the data guide; in a pathological worst case we may end up creating a node in the data guide for every subset of nodes in the semistructured data. Note that here we are using the term *subclass* to denote a subset, and not in the object-oriented meaning of the term.

We now return to our original problem: given the data in Figure 7.13, find the most specific schema graph. Now the answer is simple: it is the data guide! To see this, start with the observation that the data guide is indeed a schema graph, and that the given data conforms to it. The latter is easily checked; Figure 7.15 provides us with a simulation.

Now we argue that the data guide is the *most specific* schema graph for that data. Precisely:

- The data guide is a deterministic schema graph.[5]

---

5. A schema graph is deterministic if at each node its outgoing edges have distinct labels.

Node in data graph	Node in data guide
&r	Root
&p1, &p2, &p3, &p4, &p5, &p6, &p7 &,p8	Employee
&p1, &p4, &p6	Boss
&p2, &p3, &p5, &p7, &p8	Regular
&c	Company

Figure 7.15 Simulation between a data graph and a data guide.

Node in data guide	Node in schema graph
Root	Root
Employee	Emp
Boss	Emp
Regular	Emp
Company	Comp

Figure 7.16 Simulation from the data guide to the schema graph.

■ Any other deterministic schema graph to which our data conforms subsumes the data guide.

We illustrate the last point. Consider another schema for the given semistructured data instance; such a schema is illustrated in Figure 7.14(b). Obviously the data guide is more specific because it distinguishes between Boss and Regular employees. We can also verify that formally by providing a simulation from the data guide to the schema graph (Figure 7.16).

In fact, this still holds when we replace the schema in Figure 7.14(b) with any other deterministic schema S: from the simulation $D \preceq S$ we can construct in a systematic way a simulation $G \preceq S$, where G is a data guide.

We conclude this section with some observations about the data guide:

■ *Deterministic vs. nondeterministic.* The finite state automaton in the example is deterministic, but there is no reason for this to be. In some cases, a nondeterministic automaton may be much more compact. (Recall that building the deterministic equivalent of an automaton may introduce an exponential expansion.) An example of a nondeterministic automaton viewed as a data graph is given in Figure 7.17. Note that the employee component of the root now has two possible structures, therefore, the nondeterminism. In Chapter 8 we shall see how nondeterminism can be exploited to construct indexes.

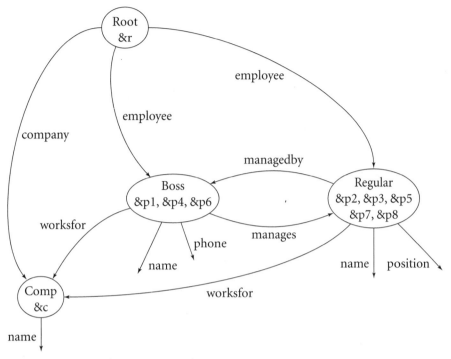

Figure 7.17 A nondeterministic schema.

- *Accuracy.* We already said that we are often willing to live with structural information that is approximate. We may prefer, instead of the data guide, an automaton that is only an approximation of the set of paths (probably a superset so that no correct path is ignored) but is much smaller.
- *Inverse edges.* As discussed earlier, it is possible to also consider paths by following edges backward. It suffices to abstractly reverse such edges and think of label l, say, as $-l$. Clearly, this enlarges the language.
- *If and only if.* As before, we may require that every path from v be a word in the language, and we may also require that each word in the language denote a path from v. The data guide insists on this *if and only if*.

7.4.2 Extracting Datalog Rules from Data

We now address the data extraction problem for the other kind of schema formalisms: Datalog rules. Recall that a Datalog typing defines classes by enumerating their required edges. As before, we have a semistructured data instance and want to extract automatically the most specific typing given by a set of Datalog rules.

We illustrate this process on the OEM data in Figure 7.13. For readability purposes we will restrict our search to Datalog rules constraining only the outgoing edges; incoming edges can be dealt with similarly. As a starting point we create one intensional predicate for each complex value object in the data. That is, we create the following predicates:

```
pred_r, pred_c, pred_p1, pred_p2, pred_p3, pred_p4,
           pred_p5, pred_p6, pred_p7, pred_p8
```

corresponding to the objects &r, &c, &p1, &p2, &p3, &p4, &p5, &p6, &p7, &p8. Next we write a set of Datalog rules defining each predicate based exactly on the outgoing edges of its corresponding object:

```
pred_r(X)   :- ref(X, company, Y), pred_c(Y),
               ref(X, employee, Z1), pred_p1(Z1),
               ...
               ref(X, employee, Z8), pred_p8(Z8),
pred_c(X)   :- ref(X,name,N), string(N)
pred_p1(X) :- ref(X,worksfor,Y), pred_c(Y), ref(X,name,N),
               string(N), ref(X,phone,P), string(P),
               ref(X,manages,Z), pred_p2(Z), ref(X,manages,U),
               pred_p3(U)
pred_p2(X) :- ref(X,worksfor,Y), pred_c(Y),
               ref(X,name,N), string(N),
               ref(X,managedby,Z), pred_p1(Z)
pred_p3(X) :- ...
...
```

We could argue that this type is "most specific," since it describes the data "exactly." However, it is also useless since it is much too large: it defines one predicate for each object in the database. To reduce the number of predicates, we attempt to identify equivalent ones. For that we compute the largest fixpoint of the Datalog program on the given data. Recall that this is computed by initializing each predicate with the set of all objects (a model that we denoted with J_0 in Section 7.3.2), then iteratively applying the Datalog rules computing successive models $J_1, J_2, \ldots$ until a fixpoint is reached. In our example, J_1 classifies the objects as shown in Figure 7.18.

The first entry is obvious: only &r has the outgoing edges company and employee required by pred_r. The next predicate, prec_c, only requires a name edge; all objects &c, &p1, &p2, &p3, . . . have that. The other entries are similar.

Object	Predicate
&r	pred_r
&c, &p1, &p2, &p3, &p4, &p5, &p6, &p7, &p8	pred_c
&p1	pred_p1
&p2, &p3, &p5, &p7, &p8	pred_p2
&p3, &p5, &p7, &p8	pred_p3
&p1, &p4, &p6	pred_p4
&p3, &p5, &p7, &p8	pred_p5
&p1, &p4, &p6	pred_p6
&p3, &p5, &p7, &p8	pred_p7
&p3,p &5, &p7, &p8	pred_p8

Figure 7.18 Extents of predicates after one iteration.

Object	Predicate
&r	pred_r
&c, &p1, &p2, &p3, &p4, &p5, &p6, &p7, &p8	pred_c
&p1	pred_p1
&p2, &p3	pred_p2
&p3	pred_p3
&p1, &p4, &p6	pred_p4
&p3, &p5, &p7, &p8	pred_p5
&p1, &p4, &p6	pred_p6
&p3, &p5, &p7, &p8	pred_p7
&p3, &p5, &p7, &p8	pred_p8

Figure 7.19 Extents of predicates after two iterations.

Next we compute J_2 by using the facts in J_1, and we obtain Figure 7.19.

Object &p5 is no longer in pred_p2 (because of the condition ref (X,managedby,Z), pred_p1(Z) in the body of pred_p2); for the same reason it is removed from pred_p3 too. Other removals happen for similar reasons. At this point we have reached a fixpoint, since $J_3 = J_2$.

Some predicates are populated by exactly the same set of objects. Define an equivalence relation between the predicates $p \equiv p'$ iff p and p' are populated by the same set of objects. We have pred_p4 $\equiv$ pred_p6 and pred_p5 $\equiv$ pred_p7 $\equiv$ pred_p8. We reduce the number of predicates by replacing equivalent predicates with a single predicate. To complete our example, we also change their names into more suggestive ones,[6] obtaining the following Datalog rules:

```
Root(X)      :- ref(X,company,Y), Company(Y), ref(X,employee,Z1),
                Boss1(Z1), ref(X,employee,Z2), Boss2(Z2)
                ref(X,employee,U1), Regular1(U1), ...,
                ref(X,employee,U3), Regular3(U3)
Company(X)   :- ref(X,name,N), string(N)
Boss1(X)     :- ref(X,worksfor,Y), Company(Y),
                ref(X,name,N), string(N), ref(X,phone,P),
                string(P), ref(X,manages,Z), Regular1(Z),
                ref(X,manages,U), Regular2(U)
Boss2(X)     :- ref(X,worksfor,Y), Company(Y),
                ref(X,name,N), string(N), ref(X,phone,P),
                string(P), ref(X,manages,Z), Regular3(Z)
Regular1(X):- ref(X,worksfor,Y), Company(Y),
                ref(X,name,N), string(N),
                ref(X,managedby,Z), Boss1(Z)
Regular2(X):- ref(X,worksfor,Y), Company(Y),
                ref(X,name,N), string(N), ref(X,position,P),
                string(P), ref(X,managedby,Z), Boss1(Z)
Regular3(X):- ref(X,worksfor,Y), Company(Y),
                ref(X,name,N), string(N), ref(X,position,P),
                string(P), ref(X,managedby,Z), Boss2(Z)
```

The Datalog rules are best visualized in Figure 7.20, where it is represented as a dual schema graph.

Connection to simulation

Given our previous discussion comparing Datalog typing rules with simulation, the above set of rules can also be extracted from the data using algorithms for computing simulation, as follows. Start by computing the largest (rooted and typed) simulation R between the semistructured data D and itself. Such a simulation exists, since the identity relation $\{(o, o)|o$ an object in $D\}$ is obviously a rooted and typed simulation. Define two objects o and o' to be equivalent if both (o, o') and (o', o) belong to R. Construct a new data graph whose objects are the

---

6. We rename as follows: pred_r to Root, pred_c to Company, pred_p1 to Boss1, pred_p4 and pred_p6 to Boss2, and the others to Regular1, Regular2, Regular3, respectively.

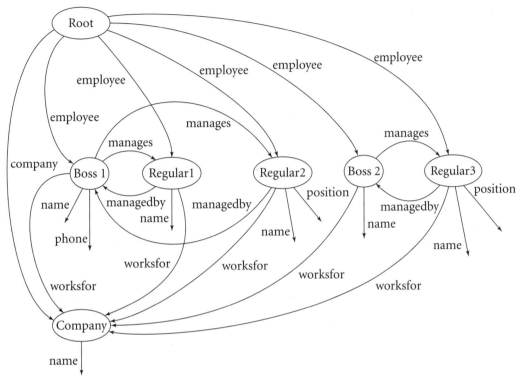

Figure 7.20 Illustration for the most specific Datalog program.

equivalence classes $[o]$, $[o']$, . . . , and for which we have an edge labeled l from $[o]$ to $[o']$ iff there is such an edge from o to o' in the data. The resulting graph corresponds exactly to the extracted set of Datalog rules (i.e., it is the associated dual schema graph).

7.5 INFERRING SCHEMAS FROM QUERIES

Some semistructured data instances are created by legacy systems or are the result of queries. In these cases it may make sense to derive the structure from the query that generated the data, rather than produce the data, then extract the schema from the data.

To illustrate this we use StruQL (Section 6.5) in order to construct more complex graphs. The following StruQL query takes a bibliography file and constructs a home page for every author:

```
where   bib -> L -> X, X -> "author" -> A, X -> "title" -> T,
        X -> "year" -> Y
create Root(), HomePage(A), YearEntry(A,Y), PaperEntry(X)
link    Root() -> "person" -> HomePage(A),
        HomePage(A) -> "year" -> YearEntry(A,Y),
        YearYentry(A,Y) -> "paper" -> PaperEntry(X),
        PaperEntry(X) -> "title" -> T,
        PaperEntry(X) -> "author" -> HomePage(A),
        PaperEntry(X) -> "year" -> Y
```

A possible result of this query is shown in Figure 7.21(a).

It is easy to infer a schema graph directly from the StruQL query. The schema will have one class for each Skolem function, and one edge for each line in the link clause. This is illustrated in Figure 7.21(b). We may try to prove that this schema, S, is indeed a correctly inferred schema in the following way. For any input data D, let D' be the result of this query applied to D. Then D' conforms to S.

Schema inference from queries is similar in spirit to type inference in programming languages. Polymorphic languages, like ML, have the property that each program has a unique most general type, and efficient type inference algorithms exist that infer the most general type. For semistructured data, the most general type need not exist or may be impossible to infer. Consider the following example:

```
where   /* some complex conditions on X, Y */
create Root(), F(X), F(Y), G(X), H(Y)
link    Root() -> "A" -> F(X),   F(X) -> "C" -> G(X),
        Root() -> "B" -> F(Y),   F(X) -> "D" -> H(Y)
```

Applying the same construction as above, we reach the following schema:

```
Root: { A : F,  B : F}
F: {C : G,  D : H}
```

This may not necessarily be the most general one. Indeed, assume that, after examining the complex conditions binding X and Y, we conclude that the two variables will never be bound to the same object in any input data instance. For example, the conditions might be

```
X -> "price" -> P, P > 50,   Y -> "price" -> Q, Q < 20
```

and we know that each object in all our instances has at most one price edge. Then the following tighter schema will describe all instances produced by the query:

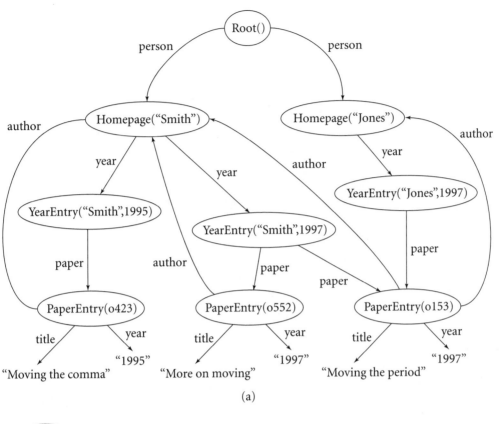

(a)

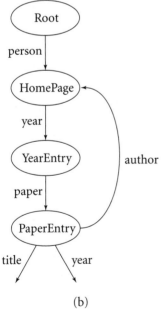

(b)

Figure 7.21 (a) Data instance resulting from a query and (b) schema graph inferred from the query.

```
Root { A : F1 { C : G}, B : F2 {D : H}}
```

That is, the schema forbids any object to have both a C and a D edge. This is tighter, but we cannot be sure that all output conform to that schema unless we check that the bindings of X and Y are disjoint for all data instances. Checking this condition is undecidable in general. In practice, however, it often suffices to settle for an approximation like the first schema.

7.6   SHARING, MULTIPLICITY, AND ORDER

We have examined flexible and powerful ways of typing data. It is now time to reexamine standard data models in view of this typing. We discuss here sharing, controlling attribute multiplicities, and order. Of course, all these features complicate our typing formalisms, and it is no longer clear how to do schema extraction as well as schema inference.

7.6.1 Sharing

Let us first consider the relational model. More precisely, consider a binary relation r with two attributes a, b of type integer. Such data can be trivially represented as OEM. For example,

```
I { tuple: o1 { a: o2(5), b: o3(6) }
    tuple: o4 { a: o5(5), b: o6(7) } }
```

seems to suggest the type

```
type r =  { tuple: v1 { a: v2(string), b: v3(string) } }
```

Clearly, I is of type r. Unfortunately, the following slight variant I' is also of type r:

```
I' { tuple: o1 { a: o2(5), b: o3(6) },
     tuple: o4 { a: o2(5), b: o6(7) } }
```

where the only difference is that the two tuples share a subobject.

It is sometimes important to be able to distinguish between shared and unshared components. Indeed, it seems useful to be able to locally prohibit sharing as in the relational model. This can be syntactically achieved as follows. We will assume that the type r above does not allow sharing. So, from this new definition, I is of type r and I' is not. On the other hand, I' is of the following type r' that allows sharing (of the a field only):

```
type r = { tuple : v1 { a : &v2, b : v3(string) } }
     v2(string)
```

In some sense, we can view the *a* component has being an object component, and an object can be shared. On the other hand, the *b* component is a value component, or more precisely an unsharable object.

The ability to control sharing is a versatile tool for typing. We illustrate here an interesting example. We use the symbol "&" to denote allowed sharing. We also use the keyword OR to denote alternative structures.

Example 7.6.1 We can define

```
type t = { a: t , b: t } OR string
```

This defines all binary trees (without sharing). On the other hand, the type

```
type t = { a: &t , b: &t } OR string
```

defines a graph of *t* objects that are either strings or have *a*, *b* components that are *t* objects.   □

The following example illustrates the typing of ODMG data.

Example 7.6.2 Consider the following type:

```
type r = { person: &p }
type p = { name: string, firstname: string,  friend: &p }
```

An instance of it is

```
I { person o1, person o2, person o3 }
o1 { name: "smith", firstname: "john", friend: &o3 }
o2 { name: "smith", firstname: "sue" }
o2 { name: "doe", firstname: "bob", friend: &o1, friend: &o3 }
```

□

It should be noted that by combining the "&" construct with other typing features such as disjunctive type, we can indeed obtain a generic type for all ODMG data.

7.6.2 Attribute Multiplicity

Neither Datalog typings nor simulations allow us to control the multiplicity of a certain attribute. For example, we can either allow or require the presence of some title attribute. In practice we may want to say that title is a unique attribute;

that is, its cardinality is 1. More generally, we may want to control the multiplicity of any attribute. This leads us to an alternative technique of describing structure as a regular expression. For example, the following defines a schema for `paper` objects:

```
type p  = {(author:string)+, title:string, (year:int)?}
```

An object o is of type p if it has at least one `author`, exactly one `title`, an optional `year` attribute, and nothing else.

A more complex example is

```
type b = {( paper: {  (author:string)+,
                      title:string,
                      (year:int)? }
          | book:  {  (author:string)+,
                      title:string,
                      publisher:string,
                      (edition:int)*      })*}
```

An object of type b may have an arbitrary number of `paper` and/or `book` outgoing edges. Each `paper` edge leads to a node with `author(s)`, `title` edges, and an optional `year` attribute. Similarly, constraints are imposed on the node reached via a `book` edge.

This is reminiscent of DTDs (discussed in Chapter 3), but there are two key differences. First, the order of the attributes doesn't matter. Second, DTDs blur the distinction between types and label names. For example, the following cannot be expressed as a DTD:

```
type Bib = {(proceedings: {paper:conference-paper} |
             journal:     {paper:journal-paper})*}
type journal-paper    = { (author:string)+,
                          title:string, journal:string}
type conference-paper = { (author:string)+,
                          title:string, conference:string}
```

Here there are two possible types below a `paper` edge, namely, `conference-paper` and `journal-paper`. In a DTD, we are forced to accept the same structure under all `paper` tags.

7.6.3 Order

In some instances we want to say that the order of the subobjects in a complex object is imposed. This is not possible in our generic OEM model, but it is easy to extend the model to allow two kinds of complex objects: unordered (as before) and ordered (in which the subobjects form a list rather than a set).

We extend now the type syntax with a list notation [...], whose meaning is that objects of that type will have their subobjects ordered. For example:

```
type Company =
   {(person:
      {name:string, assignments:Assign, (phone:string)?})*}
type Assign   =
   [(assignment:
      {name:string, year:string, (kind:string)*})]
```

Here `Assign` is a list rather than a set. An instance would be

```
c1 { person:
      {name: "Dupont",
       assignments:
        [assignment: {name: "prototype design",
                      year: 1994,
                      kind: "low priority"},
          assignment: {name: "production design",
                       year: 1997,
                       kind: "high priority"}],
       phone: "2345"},
     person: {...}}}
```

7.7   PATH CONSTRAINTS

In structured databases, the schema serves two purposes. First, it describes the *structure* or type of the data; second, it describes certain *constraints*. In relational databases, for example, the type of a relation describes the structure of the tuples (the field names and their types), while the constraints include assertions about keys and inclusion dependencies. In object-oriented databases the story is essentially the same, with some additional complications. The type of an object is described by its class, which is typically defined in the syntax of some object-oriented language, while the constraints are imposed by the database management system or by the programmer. The boundary between what is a type and what is a constraint is not always well-defined and depends on the formulation of the type system. As a practical distinction, the fact that a program does not violate the type of a database can usually be checked statically by analysis of the code of the program, while constraints are usually checked dynamically when the database is updated.

We shall discuss here constraints on semistructured data. First, we briefly review the forms in which constraints are expressed in relational and object-oriented databases and describe the state of play in XML.

7.7.1 Constraints in Relational Databases

Figure 7.22 shows a fragment of a typical relational schema definition. The structure of the `Departments` relation would be described by a type such as

```
set(tuple(DeptId:integer, DName:char(10)))
```

in a language that supports set and tuple types. However, the relational declaration tells us more than the types. First, it tells us that there is a named component of the database, `Departments`, which has this type. This is often called an *extent*. Second, it imposes a key constraint so that no two tuples have the same `DeptId` field. In the `Employees` relation we see the addition of a foreign key constraint: any `DeptId` field that occurs in the `Employees` relation must also occur in the `Departments` relation.

7.7.2 Constraints in Object-Oriented Databases

Figure 7.23 shows an ODMG schema. To see the connection between this and an object-oriented type system, strike out lines A1, A3, P1, and P3, and change the `relationship` to `attribute` in lines A2 and P2. We are left with something that closely resembles a type/class declaration. In fact, it is a declaration that can be expressed directly in a language such as C++ with type templates.

```
create table Employees
   ( EmpId: integer, EmpName: char(30),
     DeptId: integer, ...
     primary key(EmpId),
     foreign key(DeptId) references Departments )

create table Departments(
    DeptID: integer, DName: char(10),
    ...
    primary key(DeptId)
)
```

Figure 7.22 A relational schema.

```
interface Publication
    extent publication                    // line P1
    { attribute String title;
      attribute Date date;
      relationship set<Author> auth        // line P2
         inverse  Author::pub;             // line P3
    }

interface Author
    extent author                         // line A1
    { attribute String name;
      attribute String address;
      relationship set<Publication> pub    // line A2
         inverse  Publication::auth        // line A3
    }
```

Figure 7.23 An ODMG schema.

The added lines impose some additional structure and constraints:

1. The extent declarations define two persistent variables publication and author whose types are, respectively, set<Publication> and set<Author>.
2. Whenever an instance of Author is created, it is inserted automatically into the author set. Similarly, whenever an instance of Publication is created, it is inserted into the publication set.
3. For any publication p, the set p.auth is a subset of the set author. Note that this constraint is guaranteed by our previous condition on object creation. Similarly for any author a, the set a.pub is a subset of publication.
4. For any publication p, and for any author a in p.auth, p is a member of a.pub.
5. For any author a, and for any publication p in a.pub, a is a member of p.auth.

Conditions in 3 are called *inclusion constraints*, and conditions 4 and 5 are, naturally, called *inverse relationships*. Note that these constraints are independent of each other. None of them is a result of any subset of the others. How do we formulate such constraints in some generic fashion? This is an area in which our semistructured model for data gives us some ideas and in turn suggests how constraints may be exploited in semistructured data.

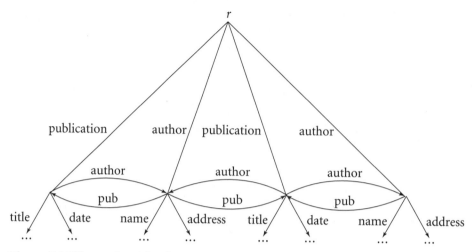

Figure 7.24 Illustration of path constraints on semistructured data.

7.7.3 Path Constraints in Semistructured Data

Figure 7.24 shows a semistructured graph representation of a database described by the object-oriented schema in Figure 7.23. Of course, there is nothing semistructured about the graph, since it describes a perfectly regular structure. However, we shall now ignore the structure imposed by the types and focus on the constraints.

A simple inclusion constraint is expressed as follows. Any vertex that is reached from the root by following an `author` edge followed by a `pub` edge can also be reached from the root by following a `publication` edge. In terms of path expressions, the set of nodes given by the path expression `author.pub` is a subset of the set of nodes given by the path expression `publication`. Treating the edge labels as binary predicates on the vertices, the constraint is

$$\forall p(\exists a(\texttt{author}(r, a) \land \texttt{pub}(a, p)) \rightarrow \texttt{publication}(r, p))$$

Here and in the following, r denotes the root of the graph data. More generally, an inclusion constraint will state that the set of vertices reachable along path α is a subset of the set of vertices reachable along the path β. To express this, we introduce the additional notation $\alpha(x, y)$ to assert the existence of a path α from x to y. Our constraint is now expressed as $\forall p(\texttt{author.pub}(r, p) \rightarrow \texttt{publication}(r, p))$. The general form of an inclusion constraint is

$$\text{(inclusion constraint)} \quad \forall x(\alpha(r, x) \rightarrow \beta(r, x))$$

```
// query Q1
select row: P2
from   r.publication P1,
       r.publication P2,
       P1.auth A
where "Database Systems" in P1.title and
      A in P2.auth


// query Q2
select row: P'
from   r.publication P,
       P.auth A,
       A.pub P'
where "Database Systems" in P.title
```
Figure 7.25 Equivalent queries.

which is simply a logical reformulation of the containment predicate $\alpha \subseteq \beta$ in which we interpret α and β as path expressions rather than predicates.

Constraints of this form cannot express inverse relationships. In the database in Figure 7.24, an example of an inverse relationship is

$$\forall p(\text{publication}(r, p) \rightarrow \forall a(\text{auth}(p, a) \rightarrow \text{pub}(a, p)))$$

The general form of this constraint is

(inverse relationship) $\forall x(\alpha(r, x) \rightarrow \forall y(\beta(x, y) \rightarrow \gamma(y, x)))$

which says that if you traverse an α path from the root to an object x, and from there you can reach an object y via a β path, then x is reachable from y via a γ path.

Constraints are important not only because they provide some form of semantic integrity. They are also important in query optimization. This holds true both for structured and semistructured data. As an example, consider the queries in Figure 7.25. The query plan implicit in the first one requires two iterations over publication—with P1, P2—whereas the second requests only one iteration over this potentially very large set—with P.

Now it can be seen informally that with the inverse and inclusion constraints described above, the two queries are equivalent. Thus, if query Q1 is requested, we may use a query plan that iterates only once over the set of publications. We should emphasize that this is just a glance at the optimization issue. Setting up the formal machinery to derive these optimizations from the constraints is beyond the scope of this book.

7.7.4 The Constraint Inference Problem

If we know that certain constraints hold, it is sometimes possible to infer the existence of other constraints. A rather obvious example is the following. Suppose we know that

$$\forall x(\texttt{author.pub}(r, x) \rightarrow \texttt{publication}(r, x))$$
$$\forall x(\texttt{publication.auth}(r, x) \rightarrow \texttt{author}(r, x))$$

It then follows that

$$\forall x(\texttt{author.pub.auth}(r, x) \rightarrow \texttt{author}(r, x))$$

More generally, given constraints $C_1, \ldots, C_n$, we can infer that another constraint C holds. What we mean by this is that whenever a data graph satisfies constraints $C_1, \ldots, C_n$, it will also satisfy C. Clearly, knowing the answer to such questions will be of further help in optimization and also in constraint checking. Database management systems generally check that constraints continue to hold when the database is updated, and this checking can be costly. If we know that $C_1, \ldots, C_n$ imply C, then there is no need to check C after an update, given that we have checked $C_1, \ldots, C_n$.

We shall briefly summarize what is known about the constraint inference problem. We already introduced *inclusion constraints*. We also consider *path constraints* that generalize the inverse relationships already introduced:

$$(\text{path constraint}) \qquad \forall x(\alpha(r, x) \rightarrow \forall y(\beta(x, y) \rightarrow \gamma(x, y)))$$

Such constraints also have a practical use. They arise notably when we embed one semistructured database in another. Note that inclusion constraints are now a special case of path constraints (make α the empty path in a path constraint).

For inclusion constraints, the inference problem is decidable. Moreover, we can generalize this result to the case when α and β are *regular* path expressions. This result is useful for optimizing Web queries that involve the structure of URLs.

For path constraints, an apparently mild generalization of inclusion constraints, the inference problem is undecidable. However, there are various ways of limiting path constraints in order to take account of the forms that occur in practice. Under such limitations, the problem becomes decidable.

A final twist on the problem occurs when we reintroduce types. Note that, even though we used typed databases to introduce constraints, our description

```
<elementType id = "Author">
  <attribute name = "Name"/>
  <attribute name = "Pub" range = "#Publication"/>
  ...
</elementType>

<elementType id = "Publication">
  <attribute name = "Title"/>
  <attribute name = "Auth" range = "#Author"/>
  <attribute name = "Pub_date" range = "#Date"/>
  ...
</elementType>
```

Figure 7.26 An example of XML-Data.

of constraints relies only on data graphs (i.e., only on semistructured representations). It turns out that certain decidable path constraint inference problems become undecidable when types are imposed. Thus, type systems may not always be an advantage in reasoning about constraints.

7.7.5 Constraints in XML

There are a number of proposals for type systems for constraining the structure of XML documents. At present they are just type systems; they do not impose constraints in the sense we have described above. Figure 7.26 shows an example of the use of XML-Data to describe the type of data. Note that the type is expressed in XML itself. In XML-Data the range assertion constrains the type of the associated element; it does not tell us anything about the location of the data. In this sense XML-Data is constraining the data in the same way that it is constrained in Figure 7.23

It is easy to imagine inverse and inclusion constraints being added to XML-Data in much the same way that they have been expressed in object-oriented data definition languages. Apart from XML-Link, which can express simple co-reference constraints, there is nothing in the current proposals for inclusion or path constraints. However, several proposals emphasize the importance of constraints as the next step in the development of type systems for XML. Whether constraints will be introduced independently of these type systems or will be embedded in them remains an open question.

7.8 BIBLIOGRAPHIC REMARKS

The first schemas for semistructured data were introduced in [NUWC96], which predated data guides, and [BDFS97], which introduced graph schemas. Applications of graph schemas to query optimization are described in [FS98]. Data guides are presented in [GW97], and unary Datalog rules for typing semistructured data were introduced in [NAM97].

A very elegant and powerful typing language for semistructured data is introduced in YAT [CDSS98]. The language allows us to type very precisely or to be very liberal. Indeed, the same data may be typed with various degrees of precisions in YAT. Complexity issues for various typing constructs, ranging from very simple to very powerful, are studied in [BM99].

Simulation is discussed in [HHK95], where an efficient algorithm for computing simulation is presented. An efficient algorithm for bisimulation was previously known from [PT87].

Type inference is well studied in programming languages (see any standard textbook, e.g., [Mit96]).

Schemas and constraints have been intensively studied in object-oriented systems and query languages [AK89, Deu90, OHMS92, Cat94].

Inclusion constraints for regular path expressions were studied in [AV97a]. General path constraints were described in [BFW98, BFW99]; the second of these discusses the interference of type and path constraints.

There are many proposals for schemas for XML: XML-Data [LJM$^+$], SOX [FMM98], RDF [RDF99], DCD [DCD99].

An approach to typing semistructured data based on description logic is proposed in [CGL98].

In this book we have only paid lip service to the connection between semistructured data and dynamic type systems, which have been studied and implemented in programming languages for over 15 years. A closer examination of the connection might well bear fruit. Dynamic types were introduced in Luca Cardelli's Amber language [Car86], in which we can mix dynamic and static (conventional) types. It supports conversion between the two and allows dynamic inspection of types and values. It thus mixes a semistructured structured representation of data.

IV

Systems

8

Query Processing

THERE IS A WELL-DEVELOPED TECHNOLOGY for designing stores and query processors/optimizers for managing structured data. Such a tradition does not exist for semistructured data. Therefore, the material of this chapter is more speculative than would be a discussion on query processing for, say, the relational model. We try here to highlight issues that will have an important impact on performance and to exploit connections with traditional query optimization.

8.1 ARCHITECTURE

Web data forces a shift in the data processing systems architecture. Traditional database systems use a client/server architecture[1] (see Figure 1.1). The data server is responsible for storing and maintaining the data, the metadata, indexes, and data statistics. The application running on the client side sends queries to the server, which evaluates it and returns answers. Thus, most of the technology at the server site focuses on query optimization, query evaluation, and storage-related issues (clustering, indexes, etc.). The connection between the client and the server is usually tight, and the two modules are provided by the same vendor.

The need to make data more widely available over the network has given rise to two new architectures: data warehouses and mediators. In a data warehouse (Figure 8.1), there is a new layer between the client and the data source(s)

---

1. A more recent variation is the *three-tier* architecture, consisting of client, application server, and data server. Clients are now "thin," consisting most of the time of a browser. The fact that the application software is centralized simplifies maintenance.

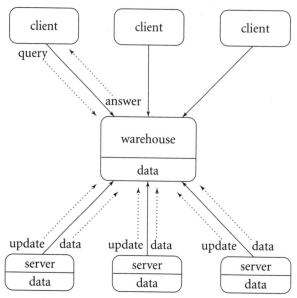

Figure 8.1 A data warehouse architecture.

(servers), called the *data warehouse*, which stores data from several sources. Such an architecture serves both for data integration and for decoupling decision support queries from production systems. Two new technologies are needed in a data warehouse: efficient data loading and incremental update maintenance.

Mediator systems (Figure 8.2) constitute a radically different architecture. They are used in data integration where data freshness is critical, or where it is impossible or difficult to load the entire data from the sources. In this architecture no data is actually stored at all in the middle tier. Instead, when clients ask queries, the mediator simply forwards them to the appropriate source(s). This architecture is particularly attractive for integrating data from sources on the Web, since in most cases we cannot download the entire data source, and we cannot expect to be notified when updates occur. The technology here differs quite radically from traditional data servers, since it involves more algebraic manipulations on the queries than data processing. First, the mediator has to decide which sources contribute to the given query; this can be nontrivial when the mediator integrates data from tens or hundreds of sources (as in the Information Manifold). Second, once the relevant sources are identified, the mediator performs a source-to-source query transformation, a process sometimes called *query rewriting*. When data from two or more sources is to be extracted, then the

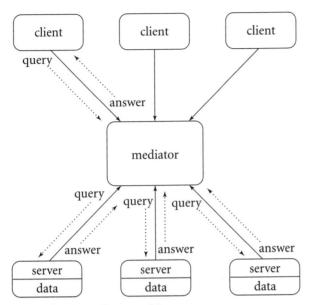

Figure 8.2 A mediator architecture.

mediator needs to produce a global execution plan, determining in which order to query the sources.

Our concern here is with systems for processing Web data. Web applications deploy both data warehouse and mediator architectures, in hybrid systems. Let us illustrate this with an example. We want to build an application for comparison car shopping in New Jersey. Our data sources are

- several local car dealers' Web sites
- the National Highway Traffic Safety Administration (NHTSA) site offering crash test data for most car models[2]
- several national car review sites

We want to provide an integrated view to the users, listing for each car all dealerships selling that car together with their availabilities and asking prices, NHTSA's ratings for that car (if available), and all available reviews. A "user" here can be a human user who needs to browse the integrated data or some other application that needs access to the data through queries.

___

2. The site is at http://www.nhtsa.dot.gov.

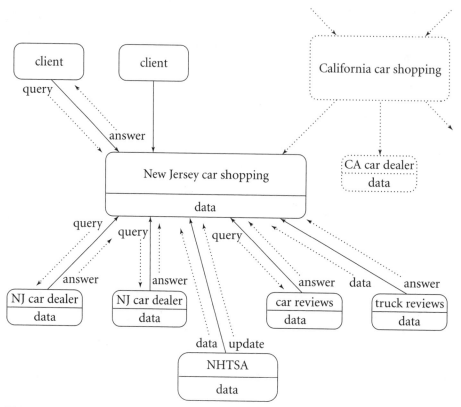

Figure 8.3 A complex, multitier architecture.

For up-to-date information on prices and availability, we use a mediator to integrate the dealers' sources. We decide to warehouse the NHTSA data, since it is large, slow to access at its original site, and changes rarely. For the reviews, we use a hybrid architecture: we copy locally some reviews and leave others on their sites. For each review site we make this decision based on a number of factors: whether the data from that site can be downloaded, whether it changes often, and whether it is a trustworthy source of information (if not, probably few users will request reviews from that site and we don't warehouse it). The resulting architecture for our Web application is depicted in Figure 8.3. Updates can be detected by using an internet difference engine like AIDE (http://www.research.att.com/~douglis/aide).

Continuing the example, assume that we decide to start a similar Web application in California. The new applications may use the NHTSA and review data from the New Jersey site (thus exploiting the existing integration of these sources), but replace the dealership data with information for Californian dealers. The result is a *multitier* system. Such a system has to deploy a mixed bag of technologies: traditional data servers, data warehouses, and mediator systems.

8.2   SEMISTRUCTURED DATA SERVERS

Query processing in semistructured data servers resembles query processing in relational or object databases. It features the same main components:

1. a parser that generates a query plan,
2. an optimizer that rewrites the query plan taking into account access structures and knowledge about the data, the system, and the application
3. an engine that evaluates the optimized query plan.

We describe an example of such a system, namely, the Lore system, in Chapter 9. We will see that it involves standard operators found in database systems such as *scan*; it also uses indexes specific to semistructured data. We postpone to that chapter a description of the algebraic evaluation of queries over semistructured data.

What sets semistructured data servers apart from relational and object-oriented servers is the lack of typing. This affects mostly the way the data is stored and indexed. Relational and object-oriented storage managers group objects according to their types and store large collections of homogeneous objects in efficient ways; this is no longer possible in semistructured data. Similarly, indexes in traditional systems are intimately associated to type information.

Another distinction from traditional data processing is the inherently distributed nature of Web data. Some techniques developed for distributed query processing in relational databases can be transferred to our context. Again, the lack of typing information requires some specialized techniques.

We discuss here storage, indexes, and distributed evaluation.

8.2.1   Storage

We analyze storage along two dimensions:

- *Storage back end.* The back end can be a plain text file, a relational database, or an object-oriented database. We examine each of these three alternatives below. A fourth alternative, a specialized object repository, is discussed in Chapter 9, in the context of the Lore system.
- *Type information.* The storage may exploit partial typing information, or it can be oblivious to types. Type information, when available, can be used to improve the storage.

We examine next how semistructured data can be stored in each of the three back ends.

Text files

Consider XML data. The simplest way to store it is in a text file (see Figure 8.4(a)); this is indeed the way XML data is understood and how it is often stored. This simple approach presents the advantage that the subobjects composing an object are naturally grouped together. For instance the `age`, `profession`, `hobby`, and `cellular` subobjects of the first `person` are stored physically close to each other and to the `person` object. On the other hand, this may artificially impose a level of granularity (the XML document) that may be inappropriate for many applications. For instance, suppose the granularity level is the XML document. To update a beeper number, we may have to check out an entire document. In a distributed environment, this is expensive in terms of communications and also may prevent others from simultaneously accessing the document if locks are used. Similarly, if a catalog is composed of a large collection of items, we should be able to access/modify an item without accessing the entire collection. We will favor approaches that focus on a smaller granularity. However, we shall return to the idea of storing a portion of semistructured data as text since it is not always a bad idea.

Relational databases

Alternatively, we could store any semistructured data in tables. It is tempting to use a database system since these systems provide a number of useful features such as the management of secondary storage, concurrency control, recovery, version, and so on. However, it is not so easy to manage semistructured data in existing database systems. Let us see why.

We assume that we have no typing information about the semistructured data; the data can be an arbitrary graph. We can store it in two tables `Ref(src, label, dst)` and `Val(oid, value)`. Figure 8.4(b) illustrates these two tables for the XML instance in Figure 8.4(a). The first table stores all edge information; the second stores values. A simple query like

```
select X
from family.person.hobby X
```

will be translated into an SQL query

```
select v.value
from Ref r1, Ref r2, Ref r3, Val v
where r1.src = "root" AND r1.label = "family"
```

```
<family id="o1">
  <person id="p1"> <name> Joan </name>
          <age>  36 </age>
          <profession> database administrator </profession>
          <hobby> gardening </hobby>
          <cellular> 555-6234 </cellular>
  </person>
  <person id="p2"> <name> John </name>
          <age> 38 </age>
          <profession>systems administrator </profession>
          <beeper> 555-3322 </beeper>
  </person>
</family>
```

(a)

Ref

src	label	dst
"root"	"family"	"o1"
"o1"	"person"	"p1"
"o1"	"person"	"p2"
"p1"	"name"	"p11"
"p1"	"age"	"p12"
"p1"	"profession"	"p13"
"p1"	"hobby"	"p14"
"p1"	"cellular"	"p15"
"p2"	"name"	"p21"
"p2"	"age"	"p22"
"p2"	"profession"	"p23"
"p2"	"beeper"	"p24"

Val

oid	value
"p11"	"Joan"
"p12"	36
"p13"	"database administrator"
"p14"	"gardening"
"p15"	"555-6234"
"p21"	"John"
"p22"	38
"p23"	"systems administrator"
"p24"	"555-3322"

(b)

Figure 8.4 (a) A text file and (b) a relational store.

```
AND r1.dst = r2.src AND r2.label = "person"
AND r2.dst = r3.src AND r3.label = "hobby"
AND r3.dst = v.oid
```

This is a four-way join. It can be very inefficient, but an index on the label column can improve the efficiency to acceptable levels.

This relational schema is actually incorrect, since values of different types are mixed in the value column of Val; strings like "Joan" are mixed with integers like 36. More correctly, we would have a separate table for every atomic type:

src	label	dst	flag	valString	valInt	valDate
"root"	"family"	"o1"	0	null	null	null
"o1"	"person"	"p1"	0	null	null	null
"o1"	"person"	"p2"	0	null	null	null
"p1"	"name"	"p11"	1	"Joan"	null	null
"p1"	"age"	"p12"	2	null	36	null
"p1"	"profession"	"p13"	1	"dba"	null	null
"p1"	"hobby"	"p14"	1	"gardening"	null	null
"p1"	"cellular"	"p15"	1	"555-6234"	null	null
"p2"	"name"	"p21"	1	"John"	null	null
"p2"	"age"	"p22"	2	null	38	null
"p2"	"profession"	"p23"	1	"sa"	null	null
"p2"	"beeper"	"p24"	1	"555-3322"	null	null

where flag = 0 means no value

= 1 means string

= 2 means int

= 3 means date

Figure 8.5 Inline representation of values.

ValInt, ValString, ValDate, and so on. Queries become even more complex, since now they need to take the union over all possible atomic types.

An optimization that reduces the number of joins by one is to inline the values in the Ref relation. This is illustrated in Figure 8.5. A flag indicates whether the destination node has a value: 0 means "no," 1 means "yes, an integer," 2 means "yes, a string," and so on.

While simple, this storage method has a few drawbacks. One, as we have seen, is that even simple queries are translated into a relatively large number of joins. A more severe source of inefficiency is that it goes against the basic assumptions used by relational database systems in organizing their data on disk. These systems save on storage costs by knowing in advance the structure of tables and the type of the entries in these tables. They also cluster data on disk pages by grouping tuples from the same relation in a page. This together with fast access methods (hash tables or B-trees) for indexes guarantees good performances for common queries.

Both these optimizations, however, fail on semistructured data due to lack of typing information. First, we need to store the schema information (the label field in Ref) as well as the data. Even if we assume a compressed form, this is

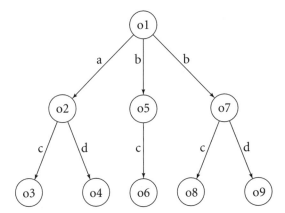

Figure 8.6 Some semistructured data.

still costly since for each (label, subelement) relationship, we need to store some information about the label. Second, consider clustering. Even if we assume that the underlying relational system provides us with full control of the clustering of tuples, the lack of typing information makes it difficult to cluster data properly. We illustrate this next.

Consider the semistructured data in Figure 8.6. The ternary relation Ref extends over two pages as in Figure 8.7(a). This example highlights the issue: it tends to spread the objects on disk in an uncontrolled manner, resulting in too many page fetches to answer queries. For example, to find the b-children of the root:

```
select X
from b X
```

we need two page accesses to obtain the two results o5, o7.

Suppose that the data model distinguishes between two kinds of links (component and reference) as, for example, in XML, where the component links describe subelements and the reference links are IDREFs. When distributing objects on disk, we have a choice of possible strategies. We may use a depth-first clustering, or we may prefer a breadth-first clustering. This depends on the queries that will be asked, and again this is adding difficulties. Because of path expressions the possible traversal of data is richer than, say, in the relational model.

The example above assumed a depth-first traversal. Each object description tends to be grouped in a page. But because of page size, this is possible only for the most nested data. Objects at higher levels tend to be spread across several

o1	a	o2		o5	c	o6
o2	c	o3		o1	b	o7
o2	d	o4		o7	c	o8
o1	b	o5		o7	d	o9

(a)

o1	a	o2		o2	d	o4
o1	b	o5		o5	c	o6
o1	b	o7		o7	c	o8
o2	c	o3		o7	d	o9

(b)

Figure 8.7 Two possible page layouts for data in Figure 8.6

pages. So, for instance, object o2 lies entirely within the first page, while o1 is spread across two pages.

In a breadth-first traversal the objects may be clustered as in Figure 8.7(b). This attempts to store all top-level information of each in the same place, but tends to separate objects from their deeper-nested components. For example, a simple query like

```
select X
from a.d X
```

requires two disk accesses because the root object o1 is on a different page than its o4 component.

Object-oriented databases

Virtually all today's commercial XML data servers use an object-oriented system as a back end. Unlike the method presented before, these systems use the typing information given by the DTD to derive the storage schema.

There is a canonical way to derive a class hierarchy from a given DTD. To illustrate, consider the DTD below:

```
<!ELEMENT company  (employee)*>
<!ELEMENT employee (name, address, project*, (phone|email))>
<!ELEMENT name     (#PCDATA)>
<!ELEMENT address  (city, country)>
<!ELEMENT city     (#PCDATA)>
<!ELEMENT country  (#PCDATA)>
<!ELEMENT project  (name, deadline)>
<!ELEMENT phone    (#PCDATA)>
<!ELEMENT email    (#PCDATA)>
<!ELEMENT deadline (#PCDATA)>
```

We could store such XML data in the following class:

```
class Company  public type set(Employee)
class Employee public type tuple(name:string,
                                 address:Address,
                                 projects: list(Project),
                                 pe: PE)
class Address  public type tuple(city:string, country:string),
class Project  public type tuple(name:string, deadline:string),
class PE       public type union (phone: int, email: string)
```

The guiding principle is that each element becomes a class: for example, company, employee, address become the classes Company, Employee, Address. Tags that are #PCDATA can be inlined as string (or as some other base type, like int); for instance, there is no Name class, but instead it is replaced everywhere with string. The interesting part is how to deal with regular expressions. Consider employee, with the regular expression

```
(name, address, project*, (phone|email))
```

Obviously it corresponds to a tuple for the Employee class, with four components. The first two (name, address) are clear. The third (project*) is a list because of the Kleene-star, while for the last we introduce a new class PE to capture the union type.[3]

Let us call this the *structured* approach to storage. Observe that the structure depends on the power of the underlying data model. In particular, the object model naturally captures the ordering (with the *list* constructor) and nesting of collections.

The structured storage allows the system to optimize both storage and query processing. For instance, the access to the *l*-subobjects of a given object may be in constant time, whereas for the unstructured storage, it may require a scan of the (label, subobject) list. On the other hand, loading data may be more expensive if its typing is not known in advance since it may require the creation of new data structures. Also, if the type evolves (e.g., the DTD changes), this leads to expensive schema updates. In general, the structured approach is preferable in a stable environment when the types are known ahead of time and not changing much. To illustrate: for a catalog of books in an electronic bookstore, a structured

---

3. We assume here a union type that carries information about *which* component (phone or email) has been defined. Union types in C and C++ do not have this property. In Java, which does not support union types, they have to be simulated through interfaces or subclasses.

storage would be more appropriate; in a repository allowing searches for books to buy over the entire Web, unstructured storage may be preferable. (Although in that latter case, a structured view over the books, giving for instance, the titles, authors, vendors' names, and prices, may in turn prove useful.)

Assuming we know the DTD, it is not clear whether a relational or object-oriented back end would be preferable. In some sense the object-oriented model is closer to the semistructured one and can deal easier with nested collections and order (lists); by contrast, these need to be simulated in a relational system, by enlarging the number of tables and/or the number of attributes. But with fast joins, a relational system may still provide decent performance. Still, object databases may provide better clustering for the elements and thus would lead to much fewer page fetches. Performance studies are needed to settle the issue.

One source of inefficiency in object databases is the fragmentation of the schema and data. New classes and objects need to be created for regular expressions, for example, to introduce union types for the | operator. More fragmentation comes from the fact that small XML elements may end up being represented with unnecessarily many objects (one for each component). This can be alleviated by storing relatively small objects as text. In our example above, we could store an address as an XML text:

```
class Employee public type tuple(name:string,
                address:string,
                projects: list(Project),
                pe: PE)
```

with values of the form <city> . . . </city> <country> . . . </country>. The address needs to be parsed at runtime in order to extract the city and country components.

We end this section with two remarks.

Self-organizing storage

We can imagine that a system would try to optimize storage based on data it maintains and the most frequently asked queries. A system may, for instance, detect (by analyzing the data) that thousands of objects have a name, an address, a social security number, that among those many have an email and a picture, and that access by name is often performed. Performance can be improved if we use a relation with

- these five attributes (with the first three compulsory)

■ a last attribute, say, *misc*, to point to the remaining information for each of these objects
■ an index by name

Using statistical information both on the data and on the queries can dramatically improve storage performance.

Hybrid storage

From the previous discussion it follows that we essentially split the storage in two parts:

■ a structured storage following more or less the typing of the semistructured data (based on the needs and the capabilities of the supporting data model)
■ an unstructured storage that uses no typing information

The system would attempt to exploit all typing information (either explicitly given by the user or extracted from the data) in order to store as much as possible in the structured storage; the rest will be stored in the unstructured (*overflow*) part.

8.2.2 Indexing

Indexes for semistructured data cannot exploit type information as do indexes for relational and object-oriented data. For example, an index for relational data may be associated to the phone column of the Employee table; the index is typically a B-tree retrieving all rows in Employee with a given value in the phone field. The typing information is essential since this gives us the table (Employee), the column (phone), and the type of the atomic values in that column (for example, string). Since semistructured data lacks types, indexes need to cope with two problems: mixed atomic values (e.g., some phone numbers are strings, others are integers) and path expression queries. We defer the first issue (coercion between types) to Chapter 9, where we describe it in the context of the Lore system. Here we are concerned with indexes for path expressions.

Consider the following query:

```
select X
from   part._*.supplier.name X
```

It requires us to traverse the data from the root and return all nodes X reachable by a path matching the given regular path expression. The issue is how to design a data structure (index) that allows the system to answer regular path expressions without traversing the whole graph. We will describe such indexes next. However,

keep in mind that this is only a simplification of the problem. In practice we need
to mix that with indexing values, for example, to answer queries like

```
select X
from   part._*.supplier: {name: X, address: "Philadelphia"}
```

in which we might be able to exploit an index on values to narrow our search to
parts of the database that contain the string "Philadelphia".

There are two dimensions to the index problem:

- *Tree vs. graph data.* Tree-shaped semistructured data is easier to index than
  data that is an arbitrary graph. XML data is a tree, in its first approximation.
  But more complex applications require graph data.
- *Restricted vs. full regular expressions.* Indexes supporting only restricted
  forms of regular path expressions may be more efficient. In practice complex regular expressions are rarely encountered.

We start by describing indexes for tree data, since this covers the case of
XML. We use the data in Figure 8.8 as a running example. The data consists
of a collection of parts and subparts, with the latter recursively nested. Other
information consists of names, suppliers, and so on. The figure omits the atomic
values on the leaves. While the corresponding XML document could be quite
accurately described by a DTD, we will not exploit this in the index structures.
As queries we consider the following regular path expressions:

(R1)	part.name
(R2)	part.supplier.name
(R3)	_*.supplier.name
(R4)	part._*.subpart.name

A simple index for XML

We assume that the data is unordered. The index will also be a tree that summarizes path information. Each node in the index tree is a hash table. The root index
node contains all labels found at the root data node (part and subpart in our example). Figure 8.9 illustrates the index for our example. In general the index will
have one node for every sequence of labels leading to a nonleaf node in the data.
For instance, node h5 corresponds to the sequence part.subpart.supplier.
The height of the index tree equals that of the data tree. Each entry in each hash
table contains a list of pointers to the corresponding nodes in the data tree; for
example, the name entry in h5 contains a list of pointers to the three leaf nodes
accessible by the path part.subpart.supplier in the data. (These lists are not

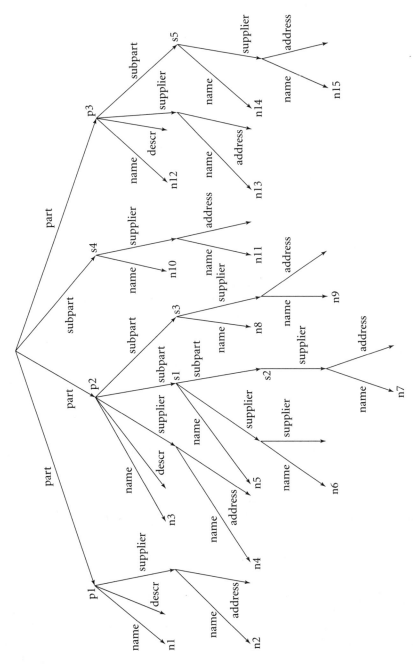

Figure 8.8 Some tree semistructured data; leaf values are omitted.

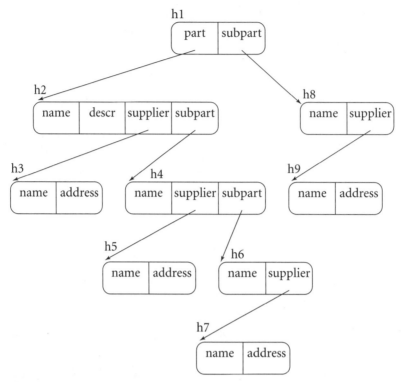

Figure 8.9 A simple index for tree-shaped semistructured data.

shown in the figure.) The XSet project at Berkeley constructs XML indexes based on this idea.

Query evaluation proceeds in a straightforward fashion. To evaluate R1 above, we would look for part in the root hash table h1, follow the link to table h2, then look for name. The entry there consists of the list of nodes (not shown in the figure), which is exactly our result. Query R2 proceeds similarly.

Regular path expressions can also be evaluated, although much less efficiently. Consider R4 first. Following part leads us to h2. From here we have to traverse all nodes in the index (this corresponds to _* in the regular expression), then continue with the path subpart.name. Thus, we explore the entire subtree dominated by h2. Still, this may be more efficient than traversing the entire data, especially if the index is small and fits in main memory, while the data is large and resides on disk. The leading wild card in query R3 forces us to consider all nodes in the index tree, resulting in an less efficient computation than for R4. Of course, evaluation of queries with leading wild cards can be further improved by indexing the index itself. Such an addional index would help us retrieve all hash tables that contain a `supplier` entry, and we can continue a normal search from there.

A region algebra

A number of powerful techniques have been developed for indexing *structured text databases*. These are large text documents, annotated with tags. For example, a text may be annotated with `<section>`, `<subsection>`, `<paragraph>`, and `<page>` tags. Elements defined by tags may overlap: a `<section>` tag may overlap with that defined by a `<page>` tag. XML documents are special cases of structured text, in which any two elements are either disjoint, or one is included in the other.

All indexing techniques for structured text rely in an essential way on the document being ordered; this assumption limits their applicability to semistructured data. Thus, for our discussion we assume that the data is given as an XML text file, and that we have access to the implicit ordering in the file. In addition these techniques only work with restricted forms of regular path expressions.

A *region* is just a (contiguous) segment of text in the file. A *region set* is a set of regions such that any two regions are either disjoint, or one is included in the other. For example, the text enclosed between a `<section>` tag and a `</section>` tag is a region. The set of all section regions is a region set (and sections are allowed to be nested within other sections). In our tree representation of the data, each node defines a region, and each set of nodes defines a region set. We will identify from now on regions with nodes in the data tree. For example, the node p2 is viewed as the region consisting of the text under the node p2. Similarly, the set { p2, s2, s1 } is a region set with three regions. Of special interest for us are region sets that correspond to an XML tag. For example in Figure 8.8, part defines the region set { p1, p2, p3 }, while subpart defines the region set { s1, s2, s3, s4, s5 }.

A region is represented by a pair (x, y) consisting of the start and the end position of the region in the text file. A region set is represented by an ordered tree in which each node corresponds to a region. In this tree a node $r = (x, y)$ is an ancestor of $r' = (x', y')$ if $x \leq x' \leq y' \leq y$; in this case we write $r' \subseteq r$. Similarly, r is to the left of r' if $x \leq y < x' \leq y'$. For example, the region set subpart consisting of { s1, s2, s3, s4, s5 } is represented as in Figure 8.10. Note that the tree for the region set preserves the "ancestor-descendent" and "left-right" relationships of the data tree.

A *region algebra* is an algebra on the region sets of a structured document. Several such algebras have been considered for manipulating structured text documents. Here we only illustrate a few operators. Given two region sets s1,

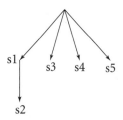

Figure 8.10 Tree representation of the *subpart* region set.

s2, each operator op in the algebra defines a new region set s1 op s2. Operators only construct new sets, but never new regions (the universe of regions is fixed to be the set of nodes in the data tree). We illustrate some operators below:

- s1 intersect s2 $\stackrel{\text{def}}{=}$ $\{r \mid r \in s1, r \in s2\}$.
- s1 included s2 $\stackrel{\text{def}}{=}$ $\{r \mid r \in s1, \exists r' \in s2, r \subseteq r'\}$.
- s1 including s2 $\stackrel{\text{def}}{=}$ $\{r \mid r \in s1, \exists r' \in s2, r \supseteq r'\}$.
- s1 parent s2 $\stackrel{\text{def}}{=}$ $\{r \mid r \in s1, \exists r' \in s2, r \text{ is a parent of } r'\}$.
- s1 child s2 $\stackrel{\text{def}}{=}$ $\{r \mid r \in s1, \exists r' \in s2, r \text{ is a child of } r'\}$.

Here "child of" and "parent of" refer to the data tree. To see an example, the expression subpart included part denotes the region set of all subparts included in some part, that is, { s1, s2, s3, s5 } (subpart s4 is not included in any part). This is of course different from part including subpart, which returns all parts having at least one subpart: { p2, p3 }. Another example is name child part, which returns all part names: { n1, n3, n12 }. This is different from name included part, which returns, in addition, all subpart names, supplier names, and so on.

Given the tree representation of a region set described above, each region operator can be efficiently evaluated by traversing the two trees simultaneously in a process similar to a merge join. We illustrate this for s1 included s2, and we assume that s1 (and similarly s2) is a set of disjoint regions. Then both input trees degenerate into ordered lists of pairs (x,y); the output region set will also be a degenerate tree (i.e., an ordered list). At each step the algorithm examines two such pairs: (x1, y1) from s1 and (x2, y2) from s2. Initially both (x1,y1) and (x2,y2) are the first elements of the two lists. The algorithm proceeds as follows:

- If $x1 < x2$, then advance in s1.
- If $y1 > y2$, then advance in s2.
- Otherwise add the region (x1,y1) to the result and advance in s1.

We may check that this indeed computes s1 included s2. It is easy to extend this algorithm to the case when s1 and s2 have nested regions (i.e., are represented by nonlinear trees).

Note that the algorithm above performs a linear scan. When one of the two lists is much shorter than the other, this algorithm can be improved. For instance, if s1 consists of a single region (x,y), then we can do a binary search in s2 to determine whether to include (x,y) in the result.

We can now illustrate how to use region algebra operators to answer regular path expressions. The four examples correspond to the following expressions:

```
part.name              name child (part child root)
part.supplier.name     name child (supplier child (part child
                       root))
_*.supplier.name       name child supplier
part._*.subpart.name   name child (subpart included (part child
                       root))
```

Note that only restricted forms of regular path expressions can be translated into region algebra operators; namely, expressions of the form $R_1.R_2 \ldots R_n$, where each R_i is either a label constant or the Kleene closure _*.

Interestingly, the region algebra allows us to answer more complex queries than regular path expressions. For example, the query

```
select X
from _*.subpart: {name: X, _*.supplier.address: "Philadelphia"}
```

translates into the following region algebra expression:

```
name child (subpart includes (supplier parent (address
 intersect "Philadelphia")))
```

Here "Philadelphia" denotes a region set consisting of all regions corresponding to the word "Philadelphia" in the text; such a region set can be computed dynamically using a full text index.

In summary, region algebras can provide a powerful technique for querying semistructured data, but with two limitations: the data must be an ordered tree, and regular expressions must be restricted. The first limitation is the more severe.

Beyond trees: indexes for arbitrary semistructured data

In practice the data is often not a tree. It may be a directed acyclic graph (DAG) or, more generally, an arbitrary graph. It is not immediately obvious how to generalize the tree index to such data. We will illustrate on the data in Figure 8.11.

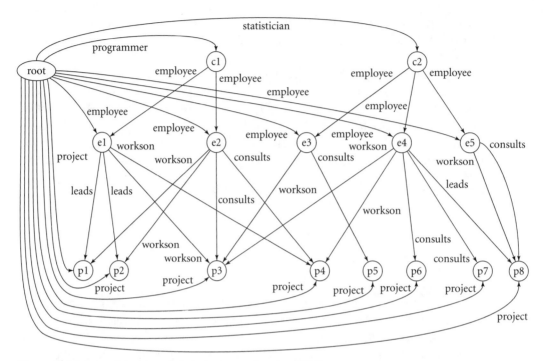

Figure 8.11 A semistructured data instance that is a DAG.

The data represents employees and projects in a company. Employees are of two kinds (programmers and statisticians) and have three kinds of links to projects: `leads`, `workson`, and `consults`. The data is a DAG. In practice, projects would have links back to employees, thus introducing cycles in the data. Cycles are not essential for our illustration, and we omit them to avoid further clutter.

We need an "index graph"—a reduced graph that summarizes all paths from the root in the data graph. Consider the node p1. The paths from `root` to p1 are labeled with the following five sequences:

```
project
employee.leads
employee.workson
programmer.employee.leads
programmer.employee.workson
```

Consider now the node p2: the paths from `root` to p2 happen to be labeled by exactly the same five sequences. We say that p1 and p2 are language-equivalent. The significance of this equivalence is that for any path expression query, either both p1, p2 are in the answer, or none is. Hence, an index graph may collapse these two nodes into a single one.

The general construction is as follows. For each node x in the data graph, let

$$L_x \overset{\text{def}}{=} \{w \mid \exists \text{ a path from the root to } x \text{ labeled } w\}$$

The set L_x may be infinite when the graph has cycles; however, it is always a regular set. Given two nodes x, y, we say that they are *language-equivalent*, in notation $x \equiv y$, if $L_x = L_y$. We construct the index I by taking the nodes to be the equivalence classes for $\equiv$. We use $[x]$ to denote the equivalence class of x. The edges in I are defined as follows. There will be an edge from class $[x]$ to class $[y]$ labeled a whenever there exists nodes $x' \in [x], y' \in [y]$ that are connected by an edge labeled a. Figure 8.12 illustrates the index for our example data. We have the following equivalences:

$$e1 \equiv e2$$
$$e3 \equiv e4 \equiv e5$$
$$p1 \equiv p2$$
$$p3 \equiv p4$$
$$p5 \equiv p6 \equiv p7$$

The index can be implemented as we discussed for tree data. Each node is a hash table containing one entry for each label at that node. In addition each index node has an *extent:* a list of pointers to all data nodes in the corresponding equivalence class. For example, the extent of node h4 is the list [e1, e2].

Path expression queries are computed as for tree data. We compute the query on the index and obtain a set of index nodes; next we compute the union of all extents. To illustrate, consider the path expression query

```
select X
from statistician.employee.(leads|consults): X
```

Computed on the index graph, this query returns the nodes h8, h9. Their extents are [p5, p6, p7] and [p8], respectively; hence, the query's result is the set p5, p6, p7, p8. Arbitrary regular expression queries can be computed this way.

The index graph is never larger than the data. In practice, however, it may be much smaller, and it is especially efficient when it can be stored in main memory. Constructing the index is, however, a problem. Checking whether two nodes x, y are language-equivalent ($x \equiv y$) is expensive.[4] A practical alternative is to

---

4. In general, this requires checking whether two regular path expressions L_x, L_y denote the same set and are PSPACE complete.

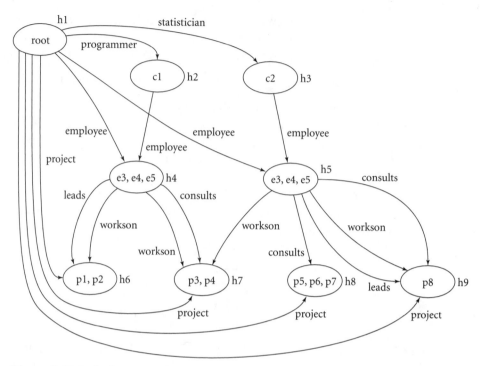

Figure 8.12 An index.

settle for an approximation: we check whether x, y are bisimilar in the reversed graph. We have discussed bisimulation in Section 6.4.3; here we use it as a relation between the reverse graph (i.e., in which all edges have their direction reversed) and itself. Adapting that definition, we say that $\approx$ is a bismulation on the reversed graph if the following two conditions hold:

- If $x \approx y$ and x is the root, then y is the root; conversely if y is the root, then x is the root.
- If $x \approx y$ and there exists an edge $x' \xrightarrow{a} x$, then there exists an edge $y' \xrightarrow{a} y$, and $x' \approx y'$; conversely, if there exists an edge $y' \xrightarrow{a} y$, then there exists an edge $x' \xrightarrow{a} x$, and $x' \approx y'$.

For any graph there exists a maximal bisimulation relation on the reversed graph, which can be efficiently computed; we will denote it with $\approx$. The following property is easy to check:

$$\forall x, y, x \approx y \implies x \equiv y$$

This property ensures that we can construct the index as before and use $\approx$ equivalence classes rather than $\equiv$ equivalence classes. The price we may have to pay is that the resulting index can be, in theory, larger (since we may have more equivalence classes). In practice, however, this rarely happens; for example, on the data in Figure 8.11, $\equiv$ and $\approx$ are identical, and the resulting index is shown in Figure 8.12.

An alternative to bisimulation is to compute the data guide of the semistructured data graph. We have described in Section 7.4.1 how to construct the data guide and mentioned that it can be used as an index. For our example data, the data guide is shown in Figure 8.13. The extents in the data guide are no longer disjoint, due to the requirement of having unique labels at each node. For example, root has a single project edge; its destination must be a node whose extent consists of all project objects, hence is different from all other nodes in the data guide. Query processing proceeds as before. The only difference is that, in general, the size of the index is no longer necessarily less than the data size.[5] Data guides may not be suitable as indexes when the data is irregular and has many cycles.

8.2.3 Distributed Evaluation

Web data is inherently distributed. If Web data follows the same patterns as Web documents, then we should expect links to become prevalent. A link is a reference in some document to an element in some other document possibly residing at a different site. XML has two accompanying standards dealing with links. XPointer is a small query language that allows us to describe the target of a link declaratively; for example, we may define a link to refer to the "third child of the object with identifier o3525 at the URL www.a.b.c/f.xml." XLink is a standard defining how different kinds of links are to be interpreted by applications.

We analyze distributed evaluation in two scenarios:

- Some schema information is known, which tells us how the data is distributed. Then query evaluation can use some of the techniques from distributed relational databases like semijoins and semijoin reductions.
- No schema information is known. This case requires some new techniques.

---

5. In theory, the data guide of a data graph with n nodes may have as many as 2^n nodes.

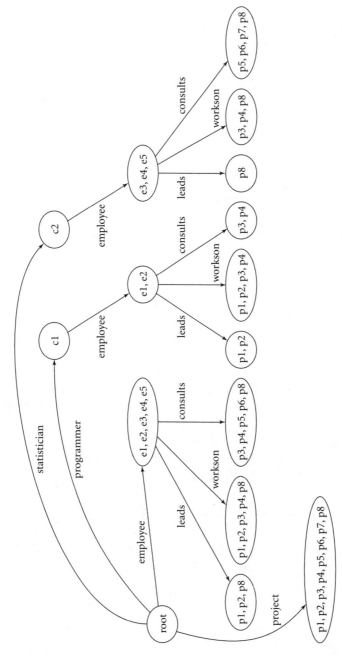

Figure 8.13 A data guide.

Distributed evaluation with schema knowledge

stands for
↳ which

We refer to the car dealership example at the beginning of this chapter (Figure 8.3). That example illustrated the integration of several sources, one being NHTSA, which contains crash test data. This may be described in XML as follows:

```
<car id="o3525">
  <name> <make> Ford </make>
         <model> Contour </model>
         <year> 1998 </year>
  </name>
  <rating>
    <front> <driver> 5 </driver>
            <passenger> 4 </passenger>
    </front>
    <side>  <front-seat> 3 </front-seat>
            <rear-seat> 4 </rear-seat>
    </side>
  </rating>
</car>
```

Each entry contains up to four ratings for a given car. Each rating is a number from 1 to 5, with 1 being worse and 5 being best.

Initially we assumed that the application decided to copy locally the entire NHTSA data (i.e., "warehouse" the data). However, there are a number of reasons why we may choose not to warehouse some NHTSA entries. For example, data for very old models may be accessed infrequently. Or new models may not have all the ratings yet; as the NHTSA data gets updated, we would like to offer users up-to-date information. In these cases we store an XML link to the actual data at the NHTSA site, instead of copying that data. A typical entry in our warehouse will look like this:

```
<dealer>
  <name> Autoland </name>
  <address> <street> Highway 22 </street>
            <city> Springfield </city>
            <state> NJ </state>
  </address>
  <phone> 555-4242 </phone>
  <car> <make> Ford </make>
        <model> Contour </model>
        <year> 1998 </year>
```

```
            <rating> <front> <driver> 5 </driver>
                     </front> <passenger> 4 </passenger>
                     <side> <front-seat> 3 </front-seat>
                            <rear-seat> 4  </rear-seat>
                     </side>
            </rating>
            <price> 16000 </price>
      </car>
      <car> <make> Honda </make>
            <model> Accord </model>
            <year> 2000 </year>
            <rating href="www.nhtsa.dot.gov#id(o4254)"/>
            <price> 22000 </price>
      </car>
      <car> <make> Toyota </make>
            <model> Corolla </model>
            <year> 1985 </year>
            <miles> 243000 </miles>
            <condition> excellent </condition>
            <price> 1000 </price>
            <rating href="www.nhtsa.dot.gov#id(o2453)"/>
      </car>
</dealer>
```

Note that `<rating>` either contains the data locally or contains a link (`href`) to the actual data at the NHTSA site.

Consider now the query retrieving all models after 1996 whose driver and passenger front ratings are ≥ 4 and that are available from dealers in Springfield. The query also returns all dealers' names and addresses:

```
Q = select X.name, X.address, Y.make, Y.model
    where   dealer X,
            X.address.city = "Springfield",
            X.car Y,
            Y.year >= 1996,
            Y._*.rating R,
            R._*.driver >= 4, R._*.passenger >=4
```

Although it is invisible to the user, query processing has to be done on distributed data.

At this point we assume the processor to have some minimal schema information describing how the data is distributed. All the processor needs to know is the following:

- Every external link is labeled with href.
- Every external link is from the local site to www.nhtsa.dot.gov.
- After traversing a rating edge, there will be no href link.

The schema formalisms described in Chapter 7 can be easily adapted to express such knowledge.

Using this information, the processor can rephrase Q as the union of two queries: one looking for local ratings, the other looking for ratings at the remote site. The local query is

```
Q1 = select X.name, X.addr, Y.make, Y.model
     where  dealer X,
            X.address.city = "Springfield",
            X.car Y,
            Y.year >= 1996,
            Y.[^href]*.rating.R,
            R._*.driver >= 4, R._*.passenger >= 4
```

Here [^href]* is a regular expression meaning any sequence of links that does not contain the label href.

The interesting part is how to evaluate the query searching for an external rating. This is related to a semijoin reduction for a distributed database. We illustrate here one such reduction. Start by evaluating the following query locally:

```
Q2 = select entry: {dealer:X, car:Y, ref:Y.href}
     where  dealer X,
            X.address.city = "Springfield",
            X.car Y,
            Y.year >= 1996,
            inDomain(Y.href, "www.nhtsa.dot.gov")
```

Note that Q2 needs to check that the href link is remote, since hrefs can also be local. Let R be Q2's result; it contains both local objects (X, Y) and external references (Y.href). Next we send R over to the NHTSA site[6] together with the query:

---

6. We assume that the remote site is capable of processing queries.

```
Q3 = select nhtsa: {dealer:X, car:Y}
     from   R.entry E, E.dealer X, E.car Y, E.href H
     where  H.rating Z, Z._*.driver >= 4, Z._*.passenger >= 4
```

The result, call it H, is a subset of pairs X, Y corresponding to (dealer, car) pairs. Finally we evaluate Q4 on the local data:

```
Q4 = select X.name, X.addr, Y.make, Y.model
     from   H.nhtsa N, N.dealer X, N.car Y
```

The resulting sequence of queries and messages between sites corresponds to a semijoin reduction in distributed relational databases. In deriving the reduction we used the schema information in an essential way.

Distributed evaluation without schema knowledge

We now address the question of what to do when the schema information is unknown or insufficient. We illustrate here the case when the query consists of a single regular path expression; joins would only further complicate matters. For example, consider the data in Fig. 8.14(a) where the root is x1 and the following query:

```
select X
from a.b*.c X
```

The query's result is {x3, y3, z2}.

Let us start with a naive distributed evaluation strategy: later we will improve it. First we construct the automaton[7] corresponding to the regular expression. In our example the automaton for a.b*.c is shown in Fig. 8.14(b). Next we traverse recursively the nodes in the data graph simultaneously with the states in the automaton. We remember all pairs (node, state) we have seen so far. We start with the root and the initial automaton state at the first site. So far this is standard query evaluation of a regular expression. But now the process may migrate to different sites. Continuing our example, we will visit (not necessarily in this order) the pairs

```
(x1,s1), (x2, s2), (y1, s2), (x3, s2), (y3, s2), ...
```

We assume nothing about the order in which nodes are visited, but observe that at some point the computation has to migrate from site 1 to site 2 (nodes y1,

---

7. It can be nondeterministic.

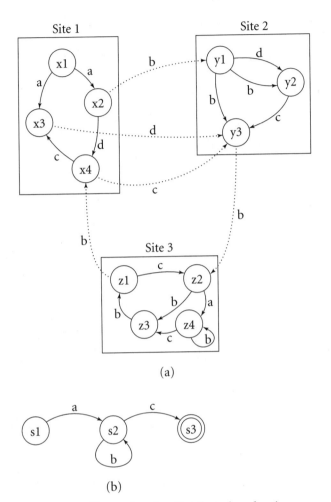

(a)

(b)

Figure 8.14 Illustration for distributed evaluation:
(a) a database and (b) an automaton.

y3 are on site 2); from there it continues to site 3, then back to site 1 with (x4, s2). Eventually, it visits nodes in the final state, which will cause it to include the corresponding node in the result. In our example, the computation will eventually visit (x3, s3), (y3, s3), (z2, s3); hence, the query's result is x3, y3, z2.

Obviously this evaluation method is hopelessly inefficient, since it leads to a large number of communication steps.

This evaluation method can be improved by reducing the number of communication steps. To accomplish that, we have to perform more work locally. First, in a preprocessing phase, each site identifies all its external references (i.e., nodes residing at other sites to which it has links); copies of these nodes are added to the local graph and called *output nodes* for that site. By exchanging the output node, sites can further identify all their local nodes that are targets of external references; we call these *input nodes*. The graph's root is added to the inputs of site 1. For the example in Figure 8.14(a), the inputs and outputs are

```
Site 1     Inputs:   x1(root), x4
           Outputs:  y1, y3

Site 2     Inputs:   y1, y3
           Outputs:  z2

Site 3     Inputs:   z2
           Outputs:  x4
```

Given a query, we compute its automaton and send it to each site. Then we start an identical process at each site. The process "runs" the query automaton starting at each input node at that site and for each state in the query automaton. More precisely, let n be an input node at site i and s be a query state. Construct $Closure_i(n, s)$, a set of node/state pairs, as follows: $Closure_i(n, s)$ is initially $\{(n, s)\}$. If there is a node/state pair in (n', s') in $Closure_i(n, s)$ and we can find another node/state pair (n'', s'') such that (1) n'' is a node at site i, (2) there is an edge from n' to n'' at site i, and (3) there is a transition with the same label from s' to s'' in the query automaton, then we add (n'', s'') to $Closure_i(n, s)$. We repeat this process until $Closure_i(n, s)$ does not change. For example:

$$Closure_3(z2, s1) = \{(z2, s1), (z4, s2), (z3, s3)\}$$
$$Closure_3(z2, s2) = \{(z2, s2), (z3, s2), (z1, s2), (x4, s2), (z2, s3)\}$$

Note that these computations are performed independently at each site.

From $Closure_i(n, s)$ we extract two sets: $Stop_i(n, s)$, the set of all pairs (n', s') in $Closure_i(n, s)$ for which n' is an output node, and $Result_i(n, s)$, the set of nodes in $Closure_i(n, s)$ that are paired with the final state. For example, $Stop_3(z2, s1) = \{\}$, $Stop_3(z2, s2) = \{(x4, s2)\}$, and $Result_3(z2, s2) = \{z2\}$. At each site i, we can construct two binary relations to describe $Stop_i$ and $Result_i$. The first relation contains the pairs $((n, s), (n', s'))$ for which $(n', s') \in Stop_i(n, s)$. The second relation contains the pairs $((n, s), n')$ for which $n' \in Result_i(n, s)$. For example, at site 2 these relations are as shown in Figure 8.15.

Start	Stop
(y1,s2)	(z2,s2)
(y3,s2)	(z2,s2)

Start	Result
(y1,s2)	y3
(y1,s3)	y1
(y3,s3)	y3

Figure 8.15 Binary relations describing *Stop* and *Result* at site 2.

Start	Stop
(x1,s1)	(y1,s2)
(x4,s2)	(y3,s5)
(y1,s2)	(z2,s2)
(y3,s2)	(z2,s2)
(z2,s2)	(x4,s2)

Start	Result
(x1,s3)	x1
(x4,s2)	x3
(x4,s3)	x4
(y1,s2)	y3
(y1,s3)	y1
(y3,s3)	y3
(z2,s1)	z3
(z2,s2)	z2
(z2,s3)	z2

Figure 8.16 Union of the relations at the three sites.

Each site now transmits its relations to a central location where their union is taken. In our example, we get the union of the relations at the three sites, as shown in Figure 8.16.

The central site now takes the transitive closure of the Start/Stop relation and finds all the Stop pairs accessible from the root pair (x1, s1). From these pairs it uses the Start/Result relation to find the nodes accessible from the root. In our example, this is the set {y3, z2, x3}. This is the result of the query.

At the cost of extra local processing (there are several ways to improve what we have suggested here), we can dramatically reduce the number of communication steps. It is interesting to observe that, no matter how complex the data and how large the number of sites, the number of communication steps is only two per site: one to receive the query, and the other to send its tables.

8.3 MEDIATORS FOR SEMISTRUCTURED DATA

Semistructured data is often encountered in data exchange and integration. At the sources the data may be structured (for instance, it may come from relational databases), but we choose to model the data as semistructured to facilitate exchange and integration. In such applications the entire data is never fully materialized in its semistructured form. Instead, users see an integrated semistructured view that they can query, but their queries are eventually reformulated into queries over the structured sources (for example, as SQL queries), and only results need to be materialized.

The architecture that makes this kind of application possible is based on mediators. The concept of a mediator was described by Gio Wiederhold [Wie92] as an architectural component in future information systems. In the original definition a *mediator* is a complex software component that "simplifies, abstracts, reduces, merges, and explains data" [Wie92]. Subsequent database research has mostly focused on a narrower interpretation of the term, in which a mediator integrates and transforms data from one or several sources using a declarative specification. This section illustrates mediators for semistructured data in two contexts:

- *Data conversion.* The mediator converts data between two different models, for example, by translating data from a relational database into XML format.
- *Data integration.* The mediator integrates data from different sources into a common view.

The key technology in mediators consists in *query rewriting;* we will illustrate query rewriting both for data conversion and for data integration.

8.3.1 A Simple Mediator: Converting Relational Data to XML

We start by illustrating with a simple but quite useful mediator, which exports a relational database into XML. Consider a relational database with the following schema:

```
Store(sid, name, phone)
Book(bid, title, authors)
StoreBook(sid, price, stock, bid)
```

Store holds information about bookstores and Book about books. The relation StoreBook tells us which store sells what book, together with the selling price and current stock.

We want to export this data in XML and decide to group books by stores. That is, the exported XML view will have elements of the form

```
<store> <name>  ... </name>
        <phone> ... </phone>
        <book> ... </book>
```

```
        <book> ... </book>
        <book> ... </book>
        ...
  </store>
```

Each book element will have the form

```
<book> <title> ... </title>  <authors> ... </authors>
       <price> ... </price>
</book>
```

In each store we decide to include only books with stock > 0.
The mediator is specified declaratively as follows:

```
M = from Store $S
    construct
      <store>
        <name>  $S.name  </name>
        <phone> $S.phone </phone>
        (from   Book $B, StoreBook $SB
         where  $S.sid = $SB.sid and
                $SB.bid = $B.bid and
                $SB.stock > 0
         construct <book>
                     <title>   $B.title </title>
                     <authors> $B.authors </authors>
                     <price>   $SB.price </price>
                   </book>
        )
      </store>
```

We used here a mixed relational/semistructured query language for the translation. The from and where clauses have a syntax resembling SQL, while the
construct clause contains XML templates, like XML-QL.

We emphasize that for real applications it is necessary to be able to construct
arbitrarily complex XML structures from a given relational database. Usually the
structure of the XML data has to conform to a DTD agreed upon by a group of
organizations and is not under the database administrator's control. Hence, it
is necessary to have an expressive mediator query language, possibly combining
nested queries (as above) with Skolem functions, to allow us to express arbitrarily
complex XML structures.

We could execute this query and obtain the XML representation of the entire database. But this is probably a bad idea. Instead we will allow users to pose queries on the XML view and rewrite them to queries over the relational schema. To see such a rewriting, consider the following XML-QL query asking for all bookstores that sell *The Java Programming Language* for under $25:

```
Q = where <store>
          <name> $N </name>
          <book>
            <title> The Java Programming Language </title>
            <price> $P <price>
          </book>
        </store> in M,
      $P < 25
construct <result> $N </result>
```

When presented with this query, the mediator will *rewrite*; in this case it simply means composing it with M. After some algebraic manipulations and simplifications, the resulting query is

```
Q' = from Store $S, Book $B, StoreBook $SB
       where $S.sid = $SB.sid and $SB.bid = $B.bid
         and $B.title = "The Java Programming Language"
         and $SB.stock > 0 and $SB.price < 25
       construct <result> $S.name </result>
```

This query can be executed by an SQL engine (except for the `construct` part, which requires some XML formatting). Moreover, only a few bookstore names need to be actually transmitted from the server to the client.

8.3.2 Mediators for Data Integration

We illustrate next the use of mediators in data integration. We illustrate with a few examples, focusing on the case when all sources export the semistructured data model.

Suppose we have three kinds of sources:

- `S-Catalog` provides information about books: title, code, book type, and description.
- `S-YellowPage` provides information about stores: name, address, and phone number.
- For each store, a source describes the books stored at that source: `S-Amazon`, `S-Hachette`, and so on.

The S- stands for source.

First, let us see how to specify the mediator. We will not define here a precise syntax. We could use something as follows:

```
define Catalog          := import S-Catalog
define YellowPage       := import S-YellowPage
define AllStores        := {site: {name : "Hachette",
                                   content : import S-Hachette},
                            site: {name : "Amazon",
                                   content : import S-Amazon},
                            site: {name : "Offilib",
                                   content : import S-Offilib}}
```

This states that the name Catalog views the same data as the external source S-Catalog, and similarly for YellowPage. It also states that there are three edges labeled site from AllStores to three objects; the latter each have a name and a content, with the content viewing the same data as S-Hachette, S-Amazon, and S-Offilib, respectively. The integrated (virtual) data is shown in Figure 8.17. Entry points to external sources are shown in gray.

This is a rather simplistic view because in general we may have to restructure the sites of the vendors that probably export a different structure than that expected. For instance, we may want to introduce a new vendor:

```
define AllStores.site +:= {name : " Gibert",
                           content: Q(import S-Gibert)}
```

where Q is a restructuring query for this site. Dealing with such restructurings is similar to the translation considered in the previous section. Another simplification lies in the fact that the imported sources are considered totally disjoint. In practice we may want to "fuse" objects from several sources; we will discuss this issue later.

Consider the following query:

> Where in Paris may I buy bibles for less than $10? I want the names of the stores and their phone numbers, and the titles, prices, and descriptions of the bibles.

We can use the following query on the integrated data:

```
select Y.storename, Y.phone, C.title, B.price, C.description
from   YellowPage.store Y, Catalog.book C,
       AllStores.site S, S.content.book B
where  Y.storename = S.name and Y.address.city = "Paris"
   and C.code = B.code and C.type = "Bible" and B.price < 10.0
```

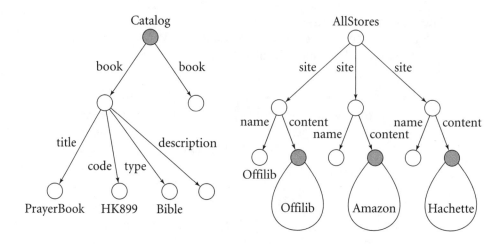

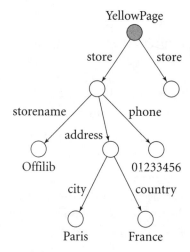

Figure 8.17 Integrated data.

The mediator's task is to decompose this query into a number of queries to be sent to the individual sources. The queries transmitted and their order are called a *query plan*. A possible query plan is the sequence Q1, Q2, Q3, described next. First Q1 is issued to S-YellowPage:

```
Q1 at S-YellowPage:
  select answer: {name: N, phone: P}
  where store: {storename: N, phone: P, address.city: "Paris"}
```

Next we query the S-Catalog site for bibles:

```
Q2 at S-Catalog:
  select answer: {title: T, code: C, description: D}
  from book: {title: T, code: C, type: "Bible", description: D}
```

Finally, for each `answer:{name:N, phone:P}` returned by `Q1`, we ask the following query at source `S-N`:

```
Q3 at S-N:
    select answer:{storename:N, phone:P, title: A.title,
                   price: B.price, description: A.description}
    from book B, Q2.answer A
    where A.code = B.code and B.price < 10.0
```

This plan is, of course, not unique, and it is not necessarily the best. The whole process of rewriting the original query into a sequence of queries to the sources may be quite complicated when restructuring is involved and, as is often the case, when the sources have limited capabilities. (For example, some sources may only allow some fixed predefined set of selection queries.) Another difficulty is optimization since cost models for the sources are in general not available.

To conclude this section we consider (1) data fusion and the use of Skolem functions to specify the combination of data from many sources, and (2) an original viewpoint on mediation proposed in the Information Manifold.

Data fusion

A very common situation in mediator systems is to glue information coming from many sites in a certain domain of interest. Recall that in the previous example we had a source `S-Catalog` with entries of the form

```
book: { title: ..., code: ..., type: ..., description: ...}
```

Suppose now that, in addition, we also have a source `S-Reviews`, providing book reviews. A typical entry in `S-Reviews` is

```
review: { booktitle: ..., bookcode: ..., text: ...
(some long text)... }
```

We wish to integrate books with their reviews. The integrated view will have entries of the form

```
book: { title: ..., code: ..., type: ..., description: ...,
        review: ...,   review: ...,   review: ...,
        ...}
```

Some books, of course, may have no reviews; in this case we only keep the data
from S-Catalog. Conversely, we may find reviews that don't match any book in
the catalog; for these we want to gather the information from S-Reviews and
have entries like

```
book: { title: ..., code: ..., review: ..., review: ..., ... }
```

This leads us to the introduction of objects with "logical identifiers," or Skolem
functions. Assuming code to be unique, we assign a logical id BK(code) to the
newly created book entries:

```
BigCatalog  =
  /*  Q1  */
  select book BK(C): { title: T, code: C,
                       type: T, description: D}
    from  S-Catalog.book: {title: T, code: C,
                           type: T, description: D}


BigCatalog +=
  /*  Q2  */
  select book BK(C): { title: T, code: C, review: R}
    from  S-Reviews.review: {booktitle: T, bookcode: C, text: R}
```

Here BK is a Skolem function that creates a unique new oid for every value of its
argument.

When the system attempts to create a book with the same logical identifier
BK(C) as an existing one, the edges of the new object are instead added to the old
object. To illustrate this, assume that S-Catalog contains the book

```
book: { title: "The Java Programming Language",
        code: "ISBN0201634554",
        type: "...", description: "..."}
```

While executing Q1 the system will create the following object in BigCatalog:

```
book BK("ISBN0201634554") :
    { title: "The Java Programming Language",
      code: "ISBN0201634554",
      type: "...", description: "..."}
```

Next, assume S-Review contains the entry

```
review: { booktitle: "The Java Programming Language",
          bookcode: "ISBN0201634554",
          text: "...some long review..."}
```

When executing Q2 the system attempts to construct the object

```
book BK("ISBN0201634554") :
    { title: "The Java Programming Language",
      code: "ISBN0201634554",
      review: "...some long review..."}
```

But since this has the same object identifier as an existing object, the "two objects" are merged into a single one:

```
book BK("ISBN0201634554") :
    { title: "The Java Programming Language",
      code: "ISBN0201634554",
      type: "...", description: "..."
      review: "...some long review..."}
```

This is called *object fusion*. If other reviews are found for the same book, they are later added to the same object. Note that title and code do not occur twice because they have the same value.

Logical identifiers offer us substantial power in dealing with redundant or inconsistent data. For example, assume that there may be conflicts between the title in S-Catalog and that in S-Reviews. If we have more confidence in S-Catalog, then we can express this by changing Q2 to

```
BigCatalog +=
    /*  Q2'  */
    select book BK(C):
            { code: C, review: R,
             (select {title: T}
              where not(exists S-Catalog.book B: B.code = C))
            }
    from  S-Reviews.review: {booktitle: T, bookcode: C, text: R}
```

That is, the title field is created only if S-Catalog has no book with the same code. Of course, in that case we may end up with multiple titles if S-Reviews lists the book under different titles. We can further refine the query to select a canonical title among several ones.[8]

---

8. An ad hoc solution would be to select the first title in alphabetical order. A more realistic solution is to assume that S-Reviews also contains a date field. Then we could pick the title of the earliest review for the given book.

The power of controlling how to fuse objects comes with two costs. First, as mediator queries become more complex, it is harder for the mediator to rewrite user queries into queries over the sources. Second, as the number of sources increases, we may have to specify all possible interactions between the sources.

Information Manifold

The Information Manifold is a mediator system that scales to tens or even hundreds of sources from the Web. To do so it uses an original approach, which handles quite nicely the simple cases and provides data integration at a limited processing cost.

So far we have defined the integrated logical view as a query over the sources (*global as view*). This is a natural way to think about the construction of a view based on original data. But when there are n sources, the view may need to express n^2 interactions between the sources. In Information Manifold the sources are considered as views over the integrated data (*local as view*). Given n sources, we only have to specify n views.

To illustrate, consider the example above in which we integrate S-Catalog with S-Reviews. Recall how we expect the integrated data to look. It should have entries like

```
book: { title: ..., code: ..., type: ..., description: ...,
        review: ...,   review: ...,   review: ...,
        ...}
```

Then S-Catalog and S-Reviews can be obtained as projections:

```
declare S-Catalog  included_in
   /*  Q3 */
   select book: {title: T, code: C, type: Y, description: D}
   from BigCatalog.book: {title: T, code: C, type: Y,
                          description D}

declare S-Reviews  included_in
   /*  Q4 */
   select review: {booktitle: T, bookcode: C, text: R}
   from BigCatalog.book: {title: T, code: C, review: R}
```

Thus, the main idea in Information Manifold is that we define the existing sources as views of the integrated data, hence *local-as-view*. Note that sources do not need to be complete. S-Catalog is not expected to contain all results returned by Q3. The mediator only specifies that S-Catalog is a subset of Q3, and similarly for S-Reviews.

It is easy to add new sources. Assume for instance that we want to add a third source, S-CatalogCourse, offering the title and code of some textbooks:

```
declare S-CatalogCourse  included_in
    /* Q5 */
   select textbook : {title: T, code: C}
   from BigCatalog.book: {title: T, code: C, type: "textbook"}
```

We expect that the new source injects more data into BigCatalog. This does not affect the definition of the old sources S-Catalog and S-Reviews, since we only claimed that their values are included in Q3, Q4. It also leaves open the possibility that some information from the new source overlaps with that from old sources. But it also leaves us puzzling over what really is added to the integrated view. The answer in the Information Manifold is that the integrated view is the minimal instance that is consistent with all definitions. In concrete terms, this implies that objects are fused whenever possible.

It is interesting to observe that this approach somewhat reverses the specification process. In the original approach, the mediator is defined as a view of the source databases. With the Information Manifold, a query is used to define a source in terms of the mediator databases. In fact, if we analyze this carefully, the Information Manifold scenario specifies, based on a state of a source (that is known), certain information about the mediator database. This specification is incomplete. By combining such incomplete information from all the sources, we obtain an incomplete state for the mediator database.

The use of Information Manifold presents the advantage of yielding more independence between the specification of what each source provides to a global mediator. On the other hand, it imposes limitations on the kind of views that can be considered by the system.

8.4   INCREMENTAL MAINTENANCE

When the data is imported to a data warehouse or replicated in a server, its contents must be maintained when sources change in order to preserve its consistency with respect to the base data. Maintenance can be performed either by recomputing the view entirely from the sources or by computing the incremental updates to the view based on the updates to the sources. In this section, we mention some issues related to this maintenance problem.

Again, the lack of schema makes incremental maintenance more complicated than in the relational case. A data warehouse may filter data from several sources and restructure (or provide structure to) it. Filtering is crucial since semistructured data is often encountered in applications interested in a very small portion of the available data (e.g., some specific data from the Web). Furthermore, restructuring may be the only solution when sources are outside of our control. So, the mapping between the source data and the warehouse may be trivial (replication) or rather intense, involving projections, selections, joins, and unions.

The maintenance of such data can be seen as a *view maintenance problem.* Mechanisms and algorithms for materialized view maintenance have been studied extensively in the context of the relational model. Incremental maintenance has been shown to improve performance dramatically for relational views. Views are much richer in the object world and, subsequently, languages for specifying and querying materialized views are significantly more intricate. But the maintenance problem is not significantly more complex in this richer setting. For both models, incremental maintenance is based on an extensive use of type information that is lacking for semistructured data. In particular, subobject sharing along with the absence of a schema makes it difficult to detect if a particular update affects a view. We illustrate this aspect in an example.

Suppose we have defined a view as follows (using the view specification syntax of Lorel):

```
define view FavoriteRestaurants as
    select r
    from Guide.Restaurant r
    where r.City = "Paris"  and r.Entree.Price < 100
    with r.Name, r.Address, r.Phone
```

Intuitively, this states that we are interested only in Parisian restaurants that have some entree under 100F, and that for such restaurants, we want the name, address, and phone number when available.

Changes to semistructured data come in several flavors. We can change the content of some atomic object. We can create new objects, or add or delete labeled edges between vertices. Consider changing the name of an ingredient from *strawberry* to *cherry*. Clearly such an update will have no impact on the view. Unfortunately, in many cases, we cannot detect whether an update will have an effect on a view. Suppose that we are adding a *Price* edge to some object and that the price is 95; for example, we add a *Price* edge between object &234 and object &555 of value 95. The addition of such an edge may potentially change the view. Observe that the system does not distinguish between prices for entrees and prices of, say, toys or cars. So, the view has potentially changed, and we have to recompute it or propagate the update. Observe what we pay here for the absence of typing.

To see the potential for optimization, a simple analysis shows that in this case, the restaurants that may have been added can be computed with the query

```
define view FavoriteRestaurants as
    select R from Guide.Restaurant R
    where R.City = "Paris"  and R.Entree.Price = &555
      and R.Entree = &234
```

With a careful use of "backpointers," we could avoid having to consider all the restaurants. Once we obtain these restaurants (if any), it is easy to obtain their name, address, and phone and update the view.

To conclude this section, we consider the use of typing information (when available) to optimize the maintenance process. First, suppose that we distinguish between classes of objects. If &234 is a toy and we know that *Guide.Restaurant* only returns restaurants, we can derive that there is no propagation. A variation of the argument is as follows. Suppose this update is the result of the update statement:

```
update T.Price := 95
from select T
    from Guide.Store S, S.Toy T
    where S.name = "ToysRUs"
      and T.name = "Barbie-Sissi"
```

If we know that the path *Guide.Store.Toy* and *Guide.Restaurant.Entree* do not overlap, information that may be provided by some kind of data guide, then again we know this particular update has no effect on the view.

8.5   BIBLIOGRAPHIC REMARKS

The section on storage follows mostly [FK99] (for the relational back end) and [CACS94] (for the object-oriented back end). A self-organizing storage method is described in [DFS99]. Semijoin reduction and query evaluation on distributed databases are covered in textbooks (e.g., [OV91]).

A complete optimizer for semistructured data in the context of the Lore project is described in [MW99]. Lorel's indexes are described in [Raj96]. Query decomposition for distributed semistructured data is discussed in [Suc96].

Salminen and Tompa [ST94] describe the region algebra in the context of PAT, a text searching system developed at the University of Waterloo's Centre for the

New Oxford English Dictionary and Text Research. More complex operators and implementation details are given in [NBY97, Nav95]. Indexes for graph semistructured data based on bisimulation are described in [MS99]. An index for XML documents is described in [ZJ99] in the context of the XSet project.

Mediators were first introduced by Gio Wiederhold [Wie92]. Since then they have been deployed in several systems: for example, in Tsimmis [PGMW95], a data integration system using the semistructured data model. Object fusion in mediators using Skolem functions is described by Papakonstantinou et al. [PAGM96] in the context of MSL (Mediator Specification Language). The Information Manifold is described by Levy et al. [LRO96].

Query rewriting has received much attention in the theoretical database community and usually refers to *query rewriting using views*. The problem was first described and analyzed in [LMSS95]. A more practical approach is described in [GD97], and query rewriting in the specific context of semistructured data is addressed in [PV99]. In this chapter we followed a more liberal meaning of the term *rewriting*, meaning a source-to-source query transformation performed by the mediator. This is also the interpretation given by the Tsimmis mediator system, for which rewriting is described in [QRS$^+$95, PAGM96].

Relational vendors are fast adapting to XML (e.g., Oracle or IBM). Object database vendors such as O_2, Poet, or Object Design are providing XML repositories. You can find discussions on views and incremental maintenance in textbooks on relational databases (e.g., [Ull88]). For an entry point for views in object databases, see, for instance, [dSAD94].

Finally, we mention that the car shopping example is adapted from a paper by David Maier [QL98], who attributes the example to Jeff Naughton.

9

The Lore System

THE LORE SYSTEM, developed at Stanford University, was designed specifically for managing semistructured data. Indeed, Lore manages data in the Object Exchange Model (OEM) used throughout this book and supports the Lorel language, which strongly influenced the query language developed in Chapter 4. Lore was originally meant as a Lightweight Object Repository where "lightweight" referred both to the simple object model and to the fact that Lore was supporting single-user, read-only access. Since then, the system has evolved to include also updates and concurrency control, but its data model remains the same.

There are several alternatives in developing a database management system for semistructured data. We could build it as an application on top of existing relational or object database systems. This offers the advantage of facilitating the development. We discussed this solution in Chapter 8 and noted that it may lead to poor performance, notably because of inappropriate clustering. An implementation on top of an object database system has been tested at Stanford, and we will mention the resulting system, called Ozone, toward the end of this chapter. Yet another approach consists of using a low-level object server such as Exodus. Finally, a last approach consists of building the system from scratch. This is the approach taken in Lore and is discussed here. This approach requires rethinking many aspects of database management. We describe the architecture of Lore, then query processing and indexes in that system, and finally a number of issues related to semistructured data management that have been studied in the context of Lore.

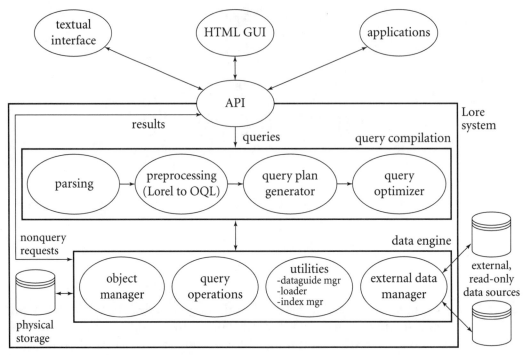

Figure 9.1 Lore architecture.

9.1   ARCHITECTURE

The basic architecture of the Lore system is shown in Figure 9.1. Although query processing for semistructured data introduces a number of new challenges, this architecture is rather standard. The challenges lie in the design of some of the components

Access to the Lore system is via an application program interface (API) and some predefined applications that use the API. There is a simple textual interface (primarily used by the system developers) and a graphical interface for end users (GUI). The GUI provides tools for browsing query results, a data guide for seeing the structure of the data and formulating simple queries "by example," a way of saving frequently asked queries, and mechanisms for viewing the multimedia atomic types such as video, audio, and java.

Data can be put into a Lore database using update statements or using load files in some standard format. (XML files can also be loaded in Lore.) Lore arranges objects in physical disk pages. Because of the diversity of data and the importance of text and multimedia in this context, the system imposes no constraints on

Query plan?

the size or structure of atomic or complex objects. This seriously complicates the layout of objects on disks. In particular, large atomic objects or complex objects representing very large collections may span several disk pages. At load time, the system clusters objects on pages in a depth-first manner. Specifying and maintaining the clustering are interesting research issues.

Lore's query language is Lorel, which is extensively covered in Chapter 4. The query compilation layer of Lore consists of a parser, a preprocessor, a query plan generator, and a query optimizer. The preprocessor primarily handles some syntactic sugaring that is part of Lore and transforms Lorel queries into OQL-like queries that are easier to process. A query plan is generated from the transformed query and then passed to the query optimizer. The optimizer has to decide whether and how to use indexes. It turns out to be rather difficult to estimate alternative query plans in the context of semistructured data because of the absence of a schema. The optimized query plan is finally sent to the data engine layer that executes the query.

The data engine layer contains the OEM object manager, the query operators, and various utilities (some, such as the external object manager, will be discussed later). The object manager provides the translation layer between OEM data and the low-level file data. It supports basic primitives such as fetching an object, comparing two objects, performing simple coercion, and iterations over the subobjects of a complex object. In addition, it includes, for performance reasons, features such as a cache of frequently accessed objects. The query operators are in charge of executing the generated query plans. They provide standard data functionalities such as scanning a collection or join operations. Many of these exploit indexing, which we discuss next.

9.2   QUERY PROCESSING AND INDEXES

One obvious difficulty comes from the absence of schema to guide query processing. Furthermore, Lore includes powerful forms of navigation based on path expressions, which induce the use of automata and graph traversal techniques inside the database engine. In spite of these peculiarities, query plans in Lore bear some resemblance to plans in relational systems and even closer resemblance to plans in object database systems. (See, for instance, Figure 9.2 but ignore the details of the plan.) Lore, however, makes unconventional use of indexes.

In traditional systems, indexes are created to obtain members of collections efficiently. This is the case in relational systems, with indexes on attributes to locate tuples with certain values for that attribute. In object database systems,

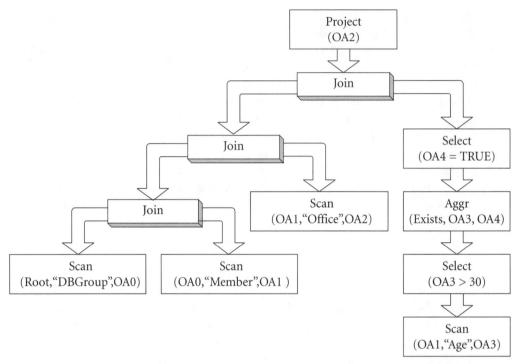

Figure 9.2 Example Lore query plan.

indexes on more complex paths may be provided, but the idea remains essentially the same. The regularity of data is used to provide fast access.

In a semistructured data context, we do not have such a regularity, so accessing data by value given some precise structural path is not sufficient. We need to be able to determine fast what are the possible paths; that is, we need to have a fast access to the structure as well.

Lore query processing therefore relies on two essential kinds of indexes: a value index (the Vindex) and a link index (the Lindex). A Vindex takes a label, a comparator, and a value. It returns all atomic objects having an incoming edge with the specified label and a value satisfying the specified operator and value (e.g., ⟨*ticket*, <, 7.50⟩). A Lindex takes an oid *o* and a label *l*, and returns all (parent) objects having an *l*-edge going to *o*. If the label is omitted, all parents are returned. Note that we now have two ways to traverse the OEM graph:

1. *(forward)* Using the stored description of an object, we can get to its sub-objects.

2. *(backward)* Using the Lindex, we can get from an object to its parent objects (i.e., to objects referring to it).

Because Vindexes are useful for *range* (inequality) as well as *point* (equality) queries, they are implemented in Lore as B+-trees. (See also the following remark.) Lindexes, on the other hand, are used for single-object lookups and thus are implemented using linear hashing.

Remark 9.2.1 To conclude this brief description of indexes in Lore, the flexibility of the Vindex should be stressed. The same data, say, the current year, may be recorded as an integer in parts of the data and as a string in others. A semistructured database user should not have to worry about such type distinctions. So the Lore Vindex is able to retrieve all objects that match integer 1998 including those that have "1998" or "01998" for value. This is achieved by having a "normal form" for data values across a variety of types.   □

These two forms of traversal of the graph will be illustrated best by a short example. Consider the query

```
select X
from db.a.b X
where X.c = 5
```

Suppose the data rooted at *db* is a tree, that there are 10,000 *a*-elements in *db* and each has 500 *b*-components, and that only one, say, *o*, has a *c*-component that is equal to 5. To obtain *o* in the absence of indexes, we have to visit the 10,000 *a*-elements and, for each one, visit its 500 *b*-components. Now, with Vindexes and Lindexes, we get the good *b*-component using the Vindex (with label *c*, comparator "=" and value 5) and, with two calls to the Lindex, we verify that there is a path *a.b* from *db* to this object. So, the most efficient evaluation in this case is backward. Of course, there are databases where the best evaluation for the same query is forward (see Figure 9.3). Lore also provides three other kinds of indexes:

- A Bindex that gives all pairs of objects connected by a particular label. For instance, a Bindex for label *b* can be used for the previous query and the database given in Figure 9.3(c). Bindexes allow a hybrid mode of evaluation that starts by retrieving edges with a given label and then uses both backward and forward traversing of the graph.
- A full-text index that provides standard retrieval of all text objects containing a certain pattern.

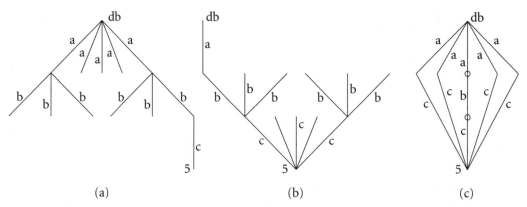

Figure 9.3 Data for various query plans: (a) use forward traversal; (b) use backward traversal; (c) use a hybrid method.

■ A Pindex (i.e., path index), for a given object *o* (e.g., a root of persistence) and a path expression *p*, allows us to obtain all the objects reachable from *o* by following path *p*. Only simple paths (sequences of labels) are supported for the moment in Lore. In this limited setting, Pindexes are similar to path indexes provided by some object systems.

9.3   OTHER ASPECTS OF LORE

As previously mentioned, many standard components of a database system need to be revisited. We have seen the query language Lorel and some of the new features in query processing, in particular indexes. Considerable effort has been devoted at Stanford to the development of Lore. We briefly mention interesting aspects studied in the context of this project: the data guide, the management of external data, proximity searches, views, temporal OEM, and the introduction of structured data as well.

9.3.1 The Data Guide

Perhaps one of the most novel aspects of Lore is the use of data guides, which were already discussed in Section 7.4.1. Lore data guides are maintained dynamically and are used in a number of situations that would require the use of a schema in standard database systems. First, data guides are essential for users to explore the structure of the database and formulate queries. They are also used in Lore to store data statistics that serve to estimate the costs of query plans.

9.3.2 Managing External Data

Since a motivation for semistructured databases is to facilitate the integration of data from heterogeneous information sources (including the Web), Lore includes an external data manager that enables dynamical loading of data from external sources when needed. The distinction between Lore-resident and external data is invisible to the user.

9.3.3 Proximity Search

While query languages such as Lorel (or even SQL in the relational world) can be used to exploit precise data relationships, users are often interested in finding data based on *fuzzy* relationships. Search engines on the Web are one good example: someone interested in finding a movie starring Nicolas Cage and John Travolta may simply type "movie Cage Travolta." Engines return pages containing those words. Ranking strategies are needed for organizing the results that are obtained, since correctness also becomes a fuzzy issue. Despite the limitations on expressiveness of such queries, they are useful for homing in on relevant data.

Neither SQL nor Lorel include the machinery to handle a query of the form "movie Cage Travolta." We first have to search the OEM graph for objects (or labels) containing some of these keywords. But then we have to rank the resulting objects/edges based on their *proximity* to other objects/edges containing these terms, where proximity is measured based on distances in the OEM graph. Technology was developed around Lorel that allows such a form of querying.

9.3.4 Views

The Lore system is equipped with a view specification language. Observe that a Lorel query returns some structure including selected objects. Typically, you may want to include subobjects of these objects in a view as well. The view mechanism allows to do that using a *with* clause. So, for instance, to retrieve each movie directed by Hitchcock with its title, list of actors, and the script of the movie (that may be a rather deep subtree), we could use

```
select X
from db.movies X
where X.director = "Hitchcock"
with title, actor, actor.name, actor.picture, script #
```

(Recall that, in Lorel, # matches any path.) The current Lore system includes the view facility. The incremental maintenance of materialized Lore views has been studied at Stanford, but at the time this book was written was not yet incorporated into the system.

9.3.5 Dynamic OEM and Chorel

In many applications involving semistructured data, users are interested in changes of the data as much as in the data itself. Consider for instance the following "subscription query" to a movie data source: send me every week the list of *new* movies with South American directors. Here we are at the crossroads between semistructured data and temporal data. The OEM model has been extended to the DOEM model that handles temporal data by introducing annotations for

- all vertices: (created *date*), (deleted *date*)
- atomic vertices: (changed-value *date* old-value)
- edges between two fixed vertices: (added *date*), (removed *date*)

The language Lorel has been extended to form Chorel (Change-Lorel). As an example of a Chorel query, to obtain the movies with South American directors added to the database since 1990/06/12, we can use

```
select X
from db. < added T > movies X
where X.director.country in db.South-America.country
    and T > "1990/06/12"
```

where *South-America* contains the list of South American countries. The path expression db.movies indicates that we are looking for outgoing edges from db labeled movies. Now we are also interested in *annotations* on these edges. The path expression

```
db.<added T>movies
```

indicates that we are look for outgoing edges from db that are labeled movies and also have an annotation <added T> for some time T, that is, by edges added at some time T. Note that this is binding variable T as well as X.

9.3.6 Mixing Structured and Semistructured in Ozone

In parallel with the main development of Lore, the Stanford group has implemented a system for OEM management, called Ozone, on top of an object database system, namely, the O_2 system. Ozone supports the Lorel language but attempts little optimization beyond that offered by the standard OQL optimizer of O_2. OEM data is stored in O_2 in a simple manner, and Lorel queries are translated into OQL queries.

An interesting aspect of Ozone is that semistructured data may coexist in the same database with standard (structured) ODMG data. In fact, it is possible (1) to have ODMG data refer to OEM objects (e.g., an n-relation where some fields are of type OEM), and (2) conversely, to have OEM objects refer to some ODMG objects. In this context, the language used by Ozone can be viewed as an extension of both Lorel and standard OQL that coincides with Lorel on pure OEM and with OQL for pure ODMG data. In the case of hybrid data, a query may traverse OEM and ODMG objects. The preprocessing determines which variables are ODMG and which are OEM. Implicit and explicit coercions are provided to simplify queries that cross from one world to the other.

9.4   BIBLIOGRAPHIC REMARKS

Overviews of the Lore system and the Lorel language can be found in [MAG$^+$97] and [AQM$^+$97], respectively.

Proximity search in Lore is discussed in [GSVGM98] and data guides in [GW97]. The external data manager is described in [MW97]. Views for the Lore system and in particular the problem of view maintenance are studied in [AMR$^+$98]. The management of temporal and semistructured data is considered in [CAW98]. Lorel's optimizer is presented in [MW99] and its indexes in [Raj96]. A description of Ozone can be found in [LAW98b].

10

Strudel

A TYPICAL WEB SITE CONSTRUCTION involves three tasks for the site creator: managing the information presented at the site, managing the structure of the Web site, and creating the graphical presentation of the HTML pages. When site creators write HTML files or CGI-BIN scripts directly, they must deal with all three tasks at once. The information management (i.e., how to extract/interpret data from databases or other sources) is hardwired in CGI-BIN scripts, and the structure and graphical presentation are hardwired in the HTML file(s). Here "structure" refers both to the intrapage structure (paragraphs, tables, items) and to the interpage structure (hyperlink graph).

Strudel, a system developed in AT&T Labs, separates these three Web site creation tasks. The data managed in Strudel is semistructured data.

Strudel's architecture is shown in Figure 10.1. The first part deals with *data management*. Here the Web site creator integrates data from multiple, heterogeneous sources into a single semistructured data repository called the *data graph*. The data graph is stored in a text file in a syntax that is a minor variation of that used in this book. The data integration part of Strudel is standard: there is a wrapper for each source and a global mediator. Each wrapper translates the data from the source's logical model to Strudel's logical model. Adding a new source is easy: the Web site manager has only to make the one-time effort of writing a wrapper for that source. The *mediator*[1] integrates logically the data from several sources and is defined by a query.

---

1. The term *mediator* is used here in a broader sense than in Chapter 8. There we used the term to mean an integration module defining a virtual integrated view, that is, with no materialized data. Strudel, instead, materializes the integrated view.

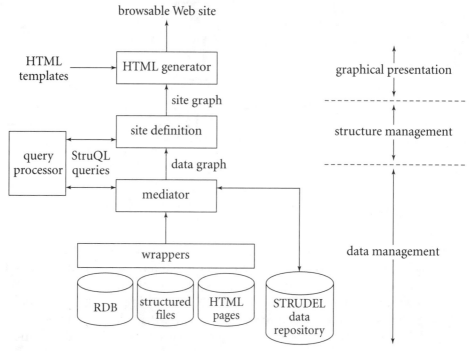

Figure 10.1 Strudel's architecture.

The second part manages the *structure*. Here the site creator constructs a *site graph* that encodes the Web site's structure; nodes correspond to HTML pages, or components thereof, and edges to hyperlinks or to component inclusion. The site graph is constructed declaratively by a StruQL query from the data graph; complex sites may require a sequence of StruQL queries rather than a single one.

The third part deals with the *graphical presentation*. The Web site creator describes the graphical layout in *HTML templates*, which are input together with the site graph into the HTML generator to create HTML files.

10.1 AN EXAMPLE

We illustrate the creation of a simple Web site in StruQL. This is a researcher's home Web site. Most of the information displayed is about the researcher's papers, which are organized in various ways. The Web site is illustrated in Figure 10.2. The root page contains three kinds of information: links to all publications, to publications sorted by year, and to publications grouped by topic. The

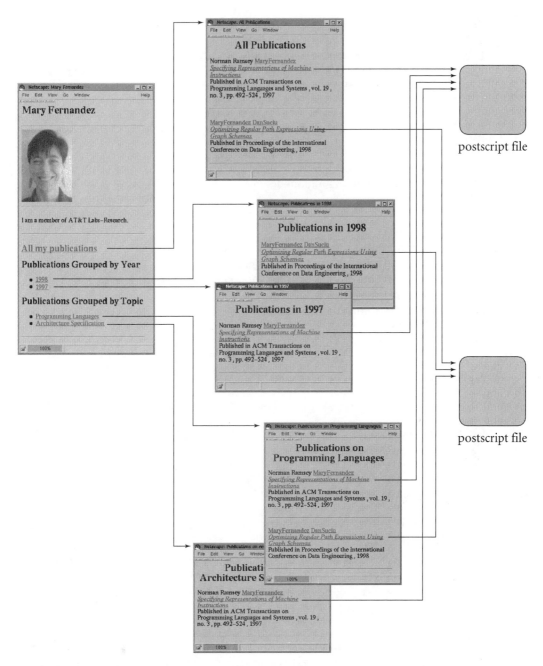

Figure 10.2 Web site generated with Strudel.

```
@article{rf97b,
author = "N.~Ramsey and M.~Fernandez",
title = "Specifying Representations of Machine Instructions",
journal = "ACM Transactions on Programming Languages and Systems",
year = 1997,
volume = 19,
number = 3,
pages = "492-524",
postscript = "papers/toplas97.ps.gz",
topic = "Architecture Specification",
topic = "Programming Languages"
}

@inproceedings{fs98,
author = "Fernandez, Mary and Suciu, Dan",
title = "Optimizing Regular Path Expressions Using Graph Schemas",
booktitle = "Proceedings of the International Conference on Data
        Engineering",
postscript = "papers/dataeng98.ps.gz",
year = 1998,
topic = "Programming Languages"
}
```

Figure 10.3 File bibtex.bib; created by the user.

latter two have links to a page for each year and a page for each topic, respectively. The "leaf" pages are papers in PostScript files.

10.1.1 Data Management

In our example we use two information sources: a bibtex file and a file of coauthors. The bibtex file (bibtex.bib) is illustrated in Figure 10.3.

The data described by the bibtex syntax can be easily viewed as semistructured data. There are two objects, whose identifiers are rf97b and fs98, with incoming edges labeled article and inproceedings, respectively. The objects have outgoing edges labeled author, title, journal, and so on, with corresponding values.

The second source contains information about coauthors. This source is used to normalize the coauthor's first name (since bibtex allows us to use both the syntax N.~Ramsey and Norman~Ramsey). In addition this data source contains

```
graph people
collection Person { }
object norman in Person  {
        lastname "Ramsey"
        firstname "Norman"
}
object suciu in Person {
        lastname "Suciu"
        firstname "Dan"
        homepage is url "http://www.research.att.com/~suciu"
}
object mary in Person  {
        lastname "Fernandez"
        firstname "Mary"
        homepage is url "http://www.research.att.com/~mff"
}
```

Figure 10.4 File people.ddl; created by the user.

the coauthor's home page URL, if available. The data about coauthors is stored in the file people.ddl, shown in Figure 10.4.

This is Strudel's syntax for the text representation of semistructured data and is very close to the syntax used throughout the book. Person is the name of a collection (recall from Section 6.5 that Strudel's data model also includes a number of collections). All three top-level objects are included in this collection. Note that the syntax also specifies the type of the atomic values; for instance, the value of homepage is url. When missing, the type is string by default (e.g., like in lastname).

Of the two sources, bibtex.bib requires a wrapper. The wrapper generates the file bibtex.ddl, shown in Figure 10.5.

Besides a simple syntactic rewriting, the wrapper also splits the author fields into multiple authors, each with a first and last name, following the conventions used by Bibtex to separate the first from the last name. Since the data model is unordered, an ordernumber field is used to store the relative order of authors; this number is later used to display the authors in the original order. The wrapper creates a collection Bibentry with all publication objects.

The last data management step is data integration. In our example we simply have to join bibtex.ddl with people.ddl. This is done by evaluating the StruQL query integrate.st, shown in Figure 10.6, which produces the file datagraph.ddl (not shown).

```
graph   bibtex
collection Bibentry { }
    collection Bibentry { }
object bib1 in Bibentry {
    publicationtype "article"
    bibtexkey "rf97b"
    author object {
        lastname "Ramsey"
        firstname "N."
        ordernumber 1
        }
    author object {
        lastname "Fernandez"
        firstname "M."
        ordernumber 2
        }
    title "Specifying Representations of Machine Instructions"
    journal "ACM Transactions on Programming Languages and Systems"
    year "1997"
    volume "19"
    number "3"
    pages "492-524"
    postscript is ps "papers/toplas97.ps.gz"
    topic "Architecture Specification"
    topic "Programming Languages"
    }
object bib2 in Bibentry {
    publicationtype "inproceedings"
    bibtexkey "fs98"
    author object {
        lastname "Fernandez"
        firstname "Mary"
        ordernumber 3
        }
    author object {
        lastname "Suciu"
        firstname "Dan"
        ordernumber 4
        }
    title "Optimizing Regular Path Expressions Using Graph Schemas"
    booktitle "Proceedings of the International Conference on Data
Engineering"
    postscript is ps "papers/dataeng98.ps.gz"
    year "1998"
    topic "Programming Languages"
    }
```

Figure 10.5 File `bibtex.ddl`; created by Strudel.

```
{ where Bibentry{X}, X->"author"->A,
      A->"lastname"->LN, A->"ordernumber"->I,
      X->L->V, L != "author"
  create Pub(X), Author(A), Pers(LN)
  collect Pub{Pub(X)}
  link Pub(X) -> "author" -> Author(A),
      Author(A) -> "isPerson" -> Pers(LN),
      Author(A) -> "ordernumber" -> I,
      Author(A) -> "HTMLtemplate" -> "person.html",
      Pub(X) -> L -> V,
      Pub(X) -> "HTMLtemplate" -> "article.html"
}
{ where Person{X}, X->"lastname"->LN, X->L->V
  create Pers(LN)
  link Pers(LN) -> L -> V
}
```

Figure 10.6 Query integrate.st.

10.1.2 Structure Management

Next we create the site graph. In general, it has more nodes than HTML pages, since some nodes represent page fragments. The site graph for our example is shown in Figure 10.7; you may wish to compare it to the Web site in Figure 10.2. The StruQL query defining the site graph in our example is sitegraph.st, shown in Figure 10.8. It takes as input the file datagraph.ddl and produces the file sitegraph.ddl. The query is straightforward. It has four parts dealing with the root node, with all publications, with publications grouped by year, and finally grouped by topic.

10.1.3 Management of the Graphical Presentation

In Strudel the graphical presentation is described separately in HTML templates. These are HTML files extended with a few Strudel tags. Certain nodes in the site graph have an attribute HTMLtemplate, which associates them with a template file. This is shown with dotted edges in Figure 10.7. For example, the root node's template file is root.html, shown in Figure 10.9.

The purpose of the template is to instruct Strudel how to generate a HTML file for that node. The HTML generator copies from the template into the output HTML file, paying attention to certain Strudel tags. There are three Strudel tags: <SFMT>, <SFOR7>, and <SIF>.

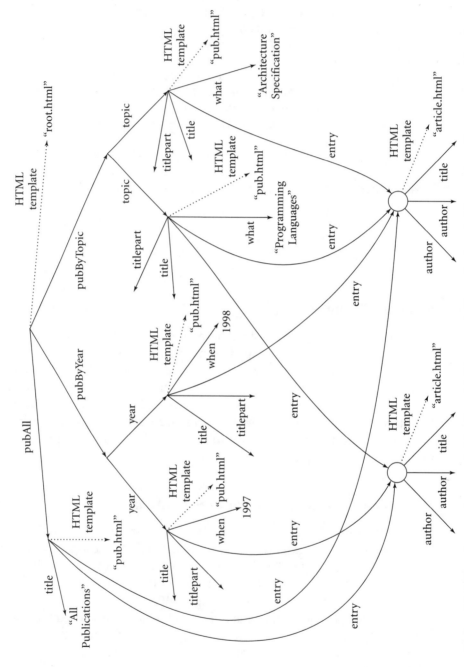

Figure 10.7 The site graph generated by Strudel (fragment). Dotted edges hold template file names used by the HTML generator.

```
{ // Create RootPage node, with its three entries
  create RootPage(), PubAllEntry(), PubByYearEntry(), PubByTopicEntry()
  link RootPage() -> "pubAll" -> PubAllEntry(),
       RootPage() -> "pubByYear" -> PubByYearEntry(),
       RootPage() -> "pubByTopic" -> PubByTopicEntry(),
       RootPage() -> "HTMLtemplate" -> "root.html"
  collect HTMLPage{RootPage()}, HTMLPage{PubAllEntry()}
}
{ // Create the All Publication page
  where Pub{X}, X -> L -> V
  create PubEntry(X)
  link   PubAllEntry() -> "title" -> "All Publications",
         PubAllEntry() -> "entry" -> PubEntry(X), PubEntry(X) -> L ->
V,
         PubAllEntry() -> "HTMLtemplate" -> "pub.html"
}
{ // Create the Publications-by-year page
  where Pub{X}, X -> L -> V, X -> "year" -> Y
  create YearEntry(Y)
  link   PubByYearEntry() -> "year" -> YearEntry(Y),
         YearEntry(Y) -> "title" -> "Publications in",
         YearEntry(Y) -> "titlepart" -> Y,
         YearEntry(Y) -> "entry" -> PubEntry(X),
         YearEntry(Y) -> "when" -> Y,
         YearEntry(Y) -> "HTMLtemplate" -> "pub.html"
  collect HTMLPage{YearEntry(Y)}
}
{ // Create the Publications-by-topic page
  where Pub{X}, X -> L -> V, X -> "topic" -> T
  create TopicEntry(T)
  link   PubByTopicEntry() -> "topic" -> TopicEntry(T),
         TopicEntry(T) -> "title" -> "Publications on",
         TopicEntry(T) -> "titlepart" -> T,
         TopicEntry(T) -> "entry" -> PubEntry(X),
         TopicEntry(T) -> "what" -> T,
         TopicEntry(T) -> "HTMLtemplate" -> "pub.html"
  collect HTMLPage{TopicEntry(T)}
}
```

Figure 10.8 Query sitegraph.st.

```
<title> Mary Fernandez </title>
<h1>Mary Fernandez</h1>
<hr>
<IMG SRC="http://www.research.att.com/~mff/files/picture.jpg">
<hr>
<p>I am a member of AT&T Labs-Research.</p>
<hr>
<p><h2><SFMT pubAll LINK="All my publications"></h2></p>
<p>
<h2>Publications Grouped by Year</h2>
<ul>
    <SFOR ye IN pubByYear.year>
        <li> <SFMT @ye LINK=@ye.when>
    </SFOR>
</ul>
</p>
<p><h2>Publications Grouped by Topic</h2><ul>
    <SFOR te IN pubByTopic.topic>
        <li> <SFMT @te LINK=@te.what>
    </SFOR>
</ul>
</p>
<hr>
```

Figure 10.9 HTML template root.html; created by the user.

The basic tag is SFMT (Strudel format), which takes as argument a label or, more generally, a path expression. When Strudel encounters SFMT, it traverses the corresponding label (or path) from the current object. This leads to a subobject. Strudel starts processing recursively that subobject's HTML template, construct- ing another HTML output. This new piece of HTML text can be either *embedded* in the current HTML page (the default), or it can be made a stand-alone file to which the current page has a link; in the latter case, SFMT must have a LINK ar- gument. For example,

```
<SFMT pubAll LINK="All my publications">
```

instructs Strudel to traverse the pubAll link of the current object, recursively construct the HTML file for the subobject, and insert a link to that file with anchor value "All my publications".

The second Strudel tag is SFOR. This is an iterator that successively binds a variable to each subobject reachable by a certain path, then repeatedly processes

```
<title> <SFMT title> <SIF titlepart> <SFMT titlepart> </SIF> </title>
<H1 align="center"> <SFMT title> <SIF titlepart> <SFMT titlepart> </SIF>
</H1>
<SFOR e IN entry>
  <p> <SFMT @e EMBED> </p>
  <hr>
</SFOR>
```

Figure 10.10 HTML template pub.html; created by the user.

the template fragment between `<SFOR>` and `</SFOR>`, once for each binding. For example,

```
<SFOR ye IN pubByYear.year>
    <li> <SFMT @ye LINK=@ye.when>
</SFOR>
```

instructs Strudel to bind ye to each subobject reachable by the path pub-ByYear.year, and for each binding to process

```
<li> <SFMT @ye LINK=@ye.when>
```

Here, @ye evaluates to the current value of the variable ye (i.e., some object). In our example this produces two links with the text anchors "1997" and "1998". Note also that we skipped the intermediate object pubByYear; hence, it does not need to have an associated template.

The third Strudel tag is SIF, denoting a conditional statement. We illustrate this on the second template (the file pub.html, shown in Figure 10.10), which is used for all publication pages (the page of all publications, for a given year, and for a given topic). Here we want to change the title in different publication pages; for example, the title will be "All Publications", or "Publications in 1997", and so on. We obtain the title as the value of the title attribute. But there is a variable part to it: "1997" or "1998", or "Programming Languages". The variable part is stored in titlepart. The SIF construct tests whether the titlepart is present and only evaluates the body if it is.

The template illustrates how to control the order of similar attributes. The author objects are sorted based on their ordernumber attribute.

Note how we make use of `<SIF>` to ensure that we do not attempt to display a nonexisting link. More complex conditions are also allowed in `<SIF>`. Notice also an example where `<SFOR>` is ordered: we order on ordernumber, thus ensuring that the original author order is preserved.

```
<a name="<SFMT bibtexkey EMBED>">
<SFOR a IN author ORDER=ascend KEY=ordernumber>
  <SFMT @a EMBED>
</SFOR>
<BR>
<i> <SFMT postscript LINK= title> </i>
<BR>
<SIF journal> Published in <SFMT journal EMBED> </SIF>
<SIF booktitle> Published in <SFMT booktitle EMBED> </SIF>
<SIF volume>, vol. <SFMT volume> </SIF>
<SIF number>, no. <SFMT number> </SIF>
<SIF pages>, pp. <SFMT pages> </SIF>
<SIF month>, <SFMT month EMBED> </SIF>
<SIF year>, <SFMT year EMBED> </SIF>
<BR>
```

Figure 10.11 HTML template `article.html`: created by the user.

10.2 ADVANTAGES OF DECLARATIVE WEB SITE DESIGN

We conclude this chapter with a discussion of the advantages of specifying Web sites declaratively. A clear advantage is that we can define multiple views of the Web site with minimal effort, either by writing a new query or by changing the HTML templates. Our example actually offers three views of the researcher's publications: a full list, grouped by year of publication, and grouped by topic. In a purchase order catalog, for example, we may wish to display a complete list of products grouped by departments, and separately a shorter list with special offers. In addition we may wish to display the products grouped by geographical region, manufacturer, and so on. Often Web site designers want to structure their sites differently to target different classes of users. An extreme example of this approach is to offer *personalized Web sites*, which each individual user can control both in terms of what information is shown and how the view is structured.

Another advantage is the clear separation of the three Web creation tasks: data, structure, and graphical management. This is especially important for Web site service companies, in which the three tasks are performed by distinct employees with different skills.

Another advantage is maintenance. It is easier to understand and modify a declarative program like StruQL than a CGI-BIN script.

Finally, once a Web site has an underlying data model, it is possible to query and transform it in a declarative fashion. One often-cited limitation of search engines is their inability to search simultaneously in groups of linked pages.

For example, a search for "database warehouses" will only retrieve pages where "database" and "warehouse" occur together. But some sites may mention these words on separate pages, which are one or two links apart. Using a declarative query language allows us to express more complex queries, like the following StruQL query:

```
where x -> (_ | _._) -> y
      x CONTAINS "database", y CONTAINS "warehouse"
collect result{x}
```

10.3   BIBLIOGRAPHIC REMARKS

The Strudel system is described in [FFK+98], and its query language, StruQL, is presented in [FFLS97]. The system can be downloaded for noncommercial use from www.research.att.com/sw/tools/strudel/.

Several other Web site management systems have been proposed. Araneus [AMM97] translates Web sites into a more structured data model, where they can be managed using traditional database technology. Specialized transformation languages are provided for mapping between Web sites and the structured data model. YAT [CDSS98] is a semistructured data management system that has been used to manage Web sites [SC98].

11

Database Products Supporting XML

As stressed in this book, the management of data on the Web, including acquisition, integration, dissemination, and so on, is a key technology to enable access to data on the Web. Considering this and the fact that most important Web sites already use some database technology, the XML-related activity among database vendors is not surprising. Indeed, most (all) database vendors have an offer now for exporting data in XML, or at the least in HTML/DHTML. It should be expected that most will soon provide storage support of XML data as well. The offer is at minimum an XML loader and extractor and an API preferably compliant with the Document Object Model API from the W3C.

In this chapter, we briefly discuss four such products. Three are from object database vendors: Axielle by Ardent Software,[1] eXcelon by ODI, and XML Repository by Poet. One is from a relational DBMS vendor, Oracle8i. We also mention the Bluestone product that is positioned as an XML server. Bluestone XML server, although not based on an actual database storage, offers features that are important for XML repositories. A partnership between Bluestone and ODI was announced in 1999.

We did not have the time to experiment with these products and apologize if our presentation contains mistakes. By way of an excuse, the domain is rapidly evolving and new releases happen almost every day. This also explains why we

---

1. Axielle is developed on the O_2 object database system. Ardent Software also has an offer for nonobject database systems.

will ignore many other products that have been advertised, for example, Tamino and the X-Machine by Software AG.

Our presentation is biased toward object database systems even though the database market is clearly still dominated by relational solutions. There are many reasons for this:

1. XML data is a better fit with the richer structure of ODMG than with tables.
2. The standard API for XML, the Document Object Model, is object-based and is easy to adapt to the ODMG world.
3. Object database vendors have moved faster into the XML market.

11.1 ARCHITECTURE

The first issue is the architecture. Most vendors (with perhaps the exception of Poet) provide an architecture in which the XML server is middleware capable of obtaining data from many sources and storing it in an XML format. This is in keeping with the vision of XML as some standard (universal) data exchange format. The main tasks of the server are therefore

1. the loading of data in many formats
2. data integration
3. data storage
4. data production in XML form

The main role of these servers is to facilitate the development of data-intensive Web applications. As XML is the standard for the Web, storing data directly in a Web format is therefore a plus in terms of performance. Most products insist on the need to be able to integrate data from a variety of sources. It is rather easy to view data from most sources as XML data, possibly equipped with DTDs (and DCDs). The advantage is that data is not lost when mapped to XML, and some semantics is preserved using DTDs. Data is exported via interfaces that conform to the standards of the World Wide Web Consortium (W3C).

A typical (simplified) architecture is shown in Figure 11.1.

11.2 STORAGE

An issue on which database systems for XML clearly diverge is storage. The object database paradigm is naturally suited to store XML documents. An XML element is easily seen as an object, and the object gains persistence using the object database. This vision is even more straightforward when considering DOM. The

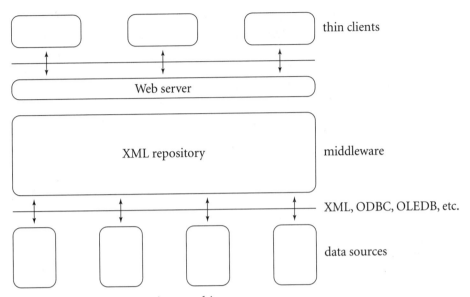

Figure 11.1 An XML repository architecture.

DOM trees of some XML data consist of objects. Thus, DOM trees can be directly stored in the object database.

Object database vendors seem to have adopted a generic internal representation for XML elements; that is, all XML elements are objects of some fixed set of predefined classes. In other words, the object schema does not depend on the DTD. The same schema is capable of storing any XML-compliant document. Although this is clearly needed for supporting XML documents without DTDs/DCDs, a more sophisticated organization may be more appropriate when a specific (and regular) DTD is used in a data-intensive application. This is particularly true for application domains where a standard DTD already exists, such as in finance or chemistry. For example, it may be convenient to consider a class Invoice capable of storing invoice objects for XML. Axielle is considering such specific storage for future releases.

Another issue is the possibility of varying the storage granularity in order to avoid having to create and manage too many small objects. For example, in XML a carriage return is an element. It is not clear whether the repository needs to maintain objects for every text-formatting command. Products such as Axielle allow defining some tags of the document as *stop tags*. The loader will store data defined by such tags as blobs.

Clearly, storage is a harder issue for relational systems. In Oracle8i, we may specify (using some file descriptions) how a structured XML document should be stored or conversely reconstructed from some stored data. We may store the document as a text blob. To retain some structure existing in the data, the storage may also involve a series of related database tables and columns. This is the approach that should be used when the data contains large (set) collections. A hybrid approach is possible for documents mixing structured data and structured text.

The relational storage of XML data presents a number of drawbacks. Lists and references are poorly handled because of the limitations of the relational model. The storage of a complex element in multiple tables may result in obscuring the semantics of the element. The management of a large number of tables and the need to perform many joins to answer queries are certainly also handicaps for performance. Indeed, the simple reconstruction of the original document may become quite expensive.

11.3 APPLICATION PROGRAMMING INTERFACE

There is a standard for API in the XML world, namely, DOM. Using DOM, it is easy to interface with Web tools and editors. For a repository, ease of interfacing is an essential requirement. Therefore, all vendors claim some support for the DOM API (and sometimes for SAX as well).

Using DOM, a programmer may extend the XML server with some application-specific code written, for instance, in Java. The advantage is to be able to manipulate directly via the API data inside the store. Such features are to be found in eXcelon and Axielle. For relational vendors, this works via object views defined for the relational data. So, for instance, it is not clear whether we can access via DOM internal nodes of a document. In all cases, performance—a key issue in databases—seems to have taken second place to ease of deployment. Consequently, much effort is devoted to graphical editors and to proposing all kinds of binding libraries.

Most of these products include a parser. Oracle8i developed its own. Some vendors include editors. For instance, Poet integrates with Arbortext Adept. The Studio of eXcelon allows a visual specification of DCDs. From DCD schemas generated with the Studio, the system automatically generates HTML pages and Java classes adapted to the schemas. Both Axielle and eXcelon explorers provide the means to organize the XML data into a folders/subfolders hierarchy and import data to the repository.

11.4 QUERY LANGUAGE

The query language is also a point of divergence since there is no accepted standard yet.

As previously mentioned, Oracle8i has two ways of storing XML data: in tables or text blobs. It provides two corresponding search styles: standard SQL search on the portions stored in tables and structured text search for the portions stored as text blobs. The second is a rather powerful search for marked-up text, ConText. Furthermore, both kinds of searches can be combined in a single query. However, to write the query, we need to understand the specific storage of the document that is used. In particular, only blobs seem to be full-text indexable.

The lack of standardization (not surprising given the youth of the field) is very visible among the object database providers. Axielle and Poet support OQL and some full-text search, whereas eXcelon supports XQL.

11.5 SCALABILITY

The scalability of these systems to large quantities of XML data is unclear at the moment. Based on the strengths of the underlying stores, Oracle8i should lead for relational systems and Axielle for object database systems. Benchmarks for XML and performance measurements for these systems are clearly needed.

It is interesting to consider also systems targeting low volumes of data but large numbers of users. Bluestone proposes such a product. Its XML server focuses on integration of data from databases and XML. One advantage of this server is its openness to many standards such as COM, CORBA, and EJB, among others. Furthermore, Bluestone offers a family of products around XML and a virtual toolkit for defining dynamic XML documents. This server is probably typical of an emerging generation of products around XML that will facilitate the tasks of import, integration, and diffusion of data on the Web.

11.6 BIBLIOGRAPHIC REMARKS

As we noted at the start of this chapter, any discussion of commercial systems will be out of date a day after it is written. The basis for this chapter is our understanding of the product descriptions and advertising for Ardent Software [Axi99], ODI [eXc99] Poet [Poe99], Oracle [Ora99], and Bluestone [Blu99], as available at the time of the writing of the book.

Bibliography

[Abi97]   S. Abiteboul. Querying semistructured data. In *Proc. of Intl. Conf. on Database Theory*, 1997.

[ACC⁺97]   S. Abiteboul, S. Cluet, V. Christophides, T. Milo, G. Moerkotte, and Jerome Simeon. Querying documents in object databases. *Intl. J. on Digital Libraries*, 1, 1997.

[Ade98]   B. Adelberg. NoDoSE—A tool for semi-automatically extracting semi-structured data from text. In *Proc. of the SIGMOD Conference*, Seattle, June 1998.

[AHV94]   S. Abiteboul, R. Hull, and V. Vianu. *Foundations of Databases*. Addison-Wesley, Reading, MA, 1994.

[AK89]   S. Abiteboul and P. C. Kanellakis. Object identity as a query language primitive. In *Proc. of the ACM SIGMOD Conf. on Management of Data*, pages 159–173, 1989.

[AK98]   S. Abiteboul and P. Kanellakis. Object identity as a query language primitive. *Journal of the Association for Computing Machinery*, 45(5):798–842, 1998.

[AMM97]   P. Atzeni, G. Mecca, and P. Merialdo. To weave the Web. In *VLDB*, pages 206–215, 1997.

[AMR⁺98]   S. Abiteboul, J. McHugh, M. Rys, V. Vassalos, and J. Wiener. Incremental maintenance for materialized views over semistructured data. In *Proc. of Intl. Conf. on Very Large Data Bases*, 1998.

[AQM⁺97]   S. Abiteboul, D. Quass, J. McHugh, J. Widom, and J. Wiener. The Lorel query language for semistructured data. *Intl. J. on Digital Libraries*, 1(1):68–88, April 1997.

[AV97a]   S. Abiteboul and V. Vianu. Regular path queries with constraints. In *Proc. of the ACM Conf. on Principles of Database Systems*, Denver, 1997. To appear.

[AV97b]   S. Abiteboul and V. Vianu. Querying the web. In *Proc. of the ICDT*, 1997.

[Axi99]   Axielle. Ardent software. 1999. www.ardentsoftware.com/.

[BCD89]   F. Bancilhon, S. Cluet, and C. Delobel. Query languages for object-oriented database systems: the O_2 proposal. In *Proc. of the Second Intl. Work. on Data Base Programming Languages*, 1989.

[BDFS97]   P. Buneman, S. Davidson, M. Fernandez, and D. Suciu. Adding structure to unstructured data. In *Proc. of the ICDT*, 1997.

[BDHS96]   P. Buneman, S. Davidson, G. Hillebrand, and D. Suciu. A query language and optimization techniques for unstructured data. In *SIGMOD*, pages 505–516, Montreal, 1996.

[BDS95]   P. Buneman, S. Davidson, and D. Suciu. Programming constructs for unstructured data. In *Proc. of the DBPL*, 1995.

[BFW98]   P. Buneman, W. Fan, S. Weinstein. Path Constraints on Semistructured and Structured Data. In *Proc. of the ACM Symp. on Principles of Database Systems*, June 1998.

[BFW99]   P. Buneman, W. Fan, and S. Weinstein. Interaction between path and type constraints. In *Proc. of the ACM Symp. on Principles of Database Systems (PODS)*, June 1999.

[BGL+99]   C. Baru, A. Gupta, B. Ludäscher, R. Marciano, Y. Papakonstantinou, and P. Velikhov. XML-based information mediation with MIX. In *SIGMOD Systems Demonstration*, 1999. To appear.

[BK90]   C. Beeri and Y. Kornatski. A logical query language for hypertext systems. In *VLDB*, 1990.

[BLS+94]   P. Buneman, L. Libkin, D. Suciu, V. Tannen, and L. Wong. Comprehension syntax. *SIGMOD Record*, 23(1):87–96, March 1994.

[Blu99]   XML server. Bluestone software, 1999. www.bluestone.com/.

[BM99]   C. Beeri and T. Milo. Schemas for integration and translation of structured and semi-structured data. In *Proc. of the Intl. Conf. on Database Theory*, 1999. To appear.

[BNTW95]   P. Buneman, S. Naqvi, V. Tannen, and L. Wong. Principles of programming with collection types. *Theoretical Computer Science*, 149:3–48, 1995.

[Bos97]   J. Bosak. XML, Java, and the future of the web, 1997. Available from http://sunsite.unc.edu/pub/sun-info/standards/xml/why/xmlapps.htm.

[BTS91]   V. Breazu-Tannen and R. Subrahmanyam. Logical and computational aspects of programming with sets/bags/lists. In *LNCS 510: Proc. of the 18th Intl. Colloquium on Automata, Languages, and Programming*, Madrid, Spain, pages 60–75. Springer Verlag, New York, 1991.

[Bun97]   P. Buneman. Semistructured data. In *Proc. of the ACM Symp. on Principles of Database Systems*, 1997.

[CACS94]   V. Christophides, S. Abiteboul, S. Cluet, and M. Scholl. From structured documents to novel query facilities. In *SIGMOD '94*. ACM, 1994.

[Car86]   L. Cardelli. Amber. In *LNCS 242: Combinators and Functional Programming*, pages 21–47. Springer-Verlag, New York, 1986.

[Cat94]   R. G. G. Cattell, editor. *The Object Database Standard: ODMG-93*. Morgan Kaufmann Publishers, San Francisco, 1994.

[CAW98]   S. Chawathe, S. Abiteboul, and J. Widom. Representing and querying changes in semistructured data. In *Proc. of the IEEE Intl. Conf. on Data Engineering*, pages 4–13, 1998.

[CDSS98]   S. Cluet, C. Delobel, J. Siméon, and K. Smaga. Your mediators need data conversion! In *Proc. of the ACM SIGMOD Conf. on Management of Data*, pages 177–188, 1998.

[CEH+94]   M. Consens, F. Eigler, M. Hasan, A. Mendelzon, E. Noik, A. Ryman, and D. Vista. Architecture and applications of the Hy+ visualization system. *IBM Systems Journal*, 33(3):458–476, 1994.

[CGL98]   D. Calvanese, G. Giacomo, and M. Lenzerini. What can knowledge representation do for semi-structured data? In *Proc. of the 15th National Conf. on Artificial Intelligence (AAAI-98)*, 1998.

[CGMH+94]   S. Chawathe, H. Garcia-Molina, J. Hammer, K. Ireland, Y. Papakonstantinou, J. Ullman, and J. Widom. The TSIMMIS project: Integration of heterogenous information sources. In *Proc. of the Information Processing Society of Japan Conf.*, Tokyo, Japan, October 1994.

[CM90a]   M. Consens and A. Mendelzon. Graphlog: a visual formalism for real life recursion. In *Proc. of the ACM Symp. on Principles of Database Systems*, pages 404–416, 1990.

[CM90b]   M. Consens and A. Mendelzon. The G+/graphlog visual query system. In *SIGMOD Conf.*, 1990.

[CM95]   M. Consens and T. Milo. Algebras for querying text regions. In *Proc. on Principles of Database Systems*, 1995.

[CW89]   W. Chen and D. S. Warren. C-logic of complex objects. In *Proc. of the ACM Symp. on Principles of Database Systems*, pages 369–378, 1989.

[DCD99]   Document content description (DCD), by the W3C, 1999. http://www.w3.org/TR/NOTE-dcd.

[Deu90]   O. Deux. The story of O_2. *IEEE Trans. on Data and Knowledge Eng.*, 2(1):91–108, March 1990.

[DFF+98]   A. Deutsch, M. Fernandez, D. Florescu, A. Levy, and D. Suciu. XML-QL: A query language for XML, 1998. http://www.w3.org/TR/NOTE-xml-ql/.

[DFF+99]   A. Deutsch, M. Fernandez, D. Florescu, A. Levy, and D. Suciu. A query language for XML. In *Intl. World Wide Web Conf.*, 1999. To appear.

[DFS99]   A. Deutsch, M. Fernandez, and D. Suciu. Storing semistructured data with stored. In *Proc. of the ACM SIGMOD Intl. Conf. on Management of Data*, 1999.

[DOM99]   The World Wide Web Consortium (W3C)'s DOM (document object model) web page, 1999. http://www.w3.org/DOM/.

[DOTW97]   S. Davidson, C. Overton, V. Tannen, and L. Wong. Biokleisli: A digital library for biomedical researchers. *Intl. J. on Digital Libraries*, 1(1):36–53, 1997.

[dSAD94]   C. S. dos Santos, S. Abiteboul, and C. Delobel. Virtual schemas and bases. In *Intl. Conf. on Extending Database Technology*, Cambridge, 1994.

[EA93]   T. Etzold and P. Argos. SRS: an indexing and retrieval tool for flat file data libraries. *Applied Bioscience*, 9:49–57, 1993.

[eXc99]   eXcelon, 1999. www.odi.com.

[FFK+97]   M. Fernandez, D. Florescu, J. Kang, A. Levy, and D. Suciu. Strudel: a web site management system. In *Proc. of the ACM SIGMOD Conf. on Management of Data*, 1997. Systems demonstration.

[FFK⁺98]   M. Fernandez, D. Florescu, J. Kang, A. Levy, and D. Suciu. Catching the boat with Strudel: experience with a web-site management system. In *Proc. of ACM-SIGMOD Intl. Conf. on Management of Data*, 1998.

[FFLS97]   M. Fernandez, D. Florescu, A. Levy, and D. Suciu. A query language for a web-site management system. *SIGMOD Record*, 26(3):4–11, September 1997.

[FHPJW92]   J. Fasel, P. Hudak, S. Peyton-Jones, and P. Wadler. The functional programming language Haskell. *SIGPLAN Notices*, 27(5), May 1992.

[FK99]   D. Florescu and D. Kossmann. A performance evaluation of alternative mapping schemes for storing XML data in a relational database, 1999. Manuscript.

[FMM98]   M. Fuchs, M. Maloney, and A. Milowski. Schema for object-oriented XML. W3C Note NOTE-SOX-19980930, 1998. http://www.w3.org/TR/NOTE-SOX.

[FO97]   J. Friedl and A. Oram. *Mastering Regular Expressions: Powerful Techniques for Perl and Other Tools*. O'Reilly & Associates, 1997.

[FS98]   M. Fernandez and D. Suciu. Optimizing regular path expressions using graph schemas. In *Proc. of the Intl. Conf. on Data Engineering*, pages 14–23, 1998.

[GD97]   M. Genesereth and O. Duschka. Answering recursive queries using views. In *Proc. of the ACM Symp. on Principles of Database Systems*, pages 109–116, 1997.

[GP98]   C. F. Goldfarb and P. Prescod. *The XML Handbook*. Prentice Hall, Englewood Cliffs, NJ, 1998.

[GSVGM98]   R. Goldman, N. Shivakumar, S. Venkatasubramanian, and H. Garcia-Molina. Proximity search in databases. In *Proc. of Intl. Conf. on Very Large Data Bases*, 1998.

[GW97]   R. Goldman and J. Widom. Dataguides: Enabling query formulation and optimization in semistructured databases. In *Proc. of Intl. Conf. on Very Large Data Bases*, pages 436–445, 1997.

[H⁺95]   J. Hammer et al. Information translation, mediation, and Mosaic-based browsing in the Tsimmis system. In *Proc. of the ACM SIGMOD Conf.*, page 483, May 1995.

[HGMC⁺97]   J. Hammer, H. Garcia-Molina, J. Cho, R. Aranha, and A. Crespo. Extracting semistructured information from the Web. In *Proc. of the Workshop on Management of Semistructured Data*, Tucson, Arizona, May 1997.

[HHK95]   M. Henzinger, T. Henzinger, and P. Kopke. Computing simulations on finite and infinite graphs. In *Proc. of the 20th Symposium on Foundations of Computer Science*, pages 453–462, 1995.

[Hom99]   A. Homer. *XML XSL IE5 Programmer's Reference*. Wrox Press, Birmingham, England, 1999. To appear.

[HU79]   J. E. Hopcroft and J. D. Ullman. *Introduction to Automata Theory, Languages, and Computation*. Addison-Wesley, Reading, MA 1979.

[HY90]   R. Hull and M. Yoshikawa. ILOG: Declarative creation and manipulation of object identifiers (extended abstract). In *Proc. of Intl. Conf. on Very Large Data Bases*, pages 455–468, 1990.

[ISO86]   ISO 8879. Information processing—text and office systems—Standard Generalized Markup Language (SGML), 1986.

[ISO87]   ISO 8824. Specification of abstraction syntax notation one (ASN.1), 1987. Information Processing System.

[KL89]   M. Kifer and G. Lausen. F-logic: A higher-order language for reasoning about objects. In *Proc. of the ACM SIGMOD Conf. on Management of Data*, 1989.

[KLW93]   M. Kifer, G. Lausen, and J. Wu. Logical foundations of object-oriented and frame-based languages. Technical Report 93/06, Dept. Computer Science SUNY–Stony Brook, 1993.

[KM98]   T. Kistlera and H. Marais. WebL: a programming language for the Web. In *WWW7*, Brisbane, Australia, 1998. http://www.research.digital.com/SRC/WebL/index.html.

[KS95]   D. Konopnicki and O. Shmueli. W3QS: A query system for the World Wide Web. In *VLDB*, pages 54–65, 1995.

[KW89]   M. Kifer and J. Wu. A logic for object-oriented logic programming (Maier's O-logic revisited). In *Proc. of the ACM Symp. on Principles of Database Systems*, pages 379–393, 1989.

[LAW98a]   T. Lahiri, S. Abiteboul, and J. Widom. Ozone: Integrating structured and semistructured data, 1998. www-db.stanford.edu/tlahiri/ozone.pdf.

[LAW98b]   T. Lahiri, S. Abiteboul, and J. Widom. The Ozone system and language. Stanford report, in preparation, 1998.

[LJM$^+$]   A. Layman, E. Jung, E. Maler, H. S. Thompson, J. Paoli, J. Tigue, N. H. Mikula, and S. De Rose. XML-Data. W3C Note NOTE-XML-data-980105. http://www.w3.org/TR/1998/NOTE-XML-data.

[LLF98]   M. Leventhal, D. Lewis, and M. Fuchs. *Designing XML Internet Applications*. Prentice Hall, Englewood Cliffs, NJ, 1998.

[LMSS95]   A. Levy, A. O. Mendelzon, D. Srivastava, and Y. Sagiv. Answering queries using views. In *Proc.of the ACM Symp. on Principles of Database Systems*, 1995.

[LP81]   H. R. Lewis and C. H. Papadimitriou. *Elements of the Theory of Computation*. Prentice Hall, Englewood Cliffs, NJ, 1981.

[LRO96]   A. Y. Levy, A. Rajaraman, and J. J. Ordille. Querying heterogeneous information sources using source descriptions. In *Proc. VLDB*, 1996.

[LSS96]   L. Lakshmanan, F. Sadri, and I. Subramanian. A declarative language for querying and restructuring the Web. In *Proc. of the Sixth Intl. Workshop on Research Issues in Data Engineering, RIDE '96*, New Orleans, February 1996. In press.

[MAG$^+$97] J. McHugh, S. Abiteboul, R. Goldman, D. Quass, and J. Widom. Lore: A database management system for semistructured data. *ACM SIGMOD Record*, 26(3):54–66, 1997.

[Mai86]   D. Maier. A logic for objects. In *Workshop on Foundations of Deductive Databases and Logic Programming*, pages 6–26, 1986.

[McG98]   S. McGrath. *XML by Example: Building E-Commerce Applications*. Prentice Hall, Englewood Cliffs, NJ, 1998.

[Mic98]   A. Michard. *XML, Langage et applications*. Eyrolles, Paris, 1998.

[Mil89]   R. Milner. *Communication and Concurrency*. Prentice Hall, Englewood Cliffs, NJ, 1989.

[Mit96]   J. C. Mitchell. *Foundations for Programming Languages*. MIT Press, Cambridge, MA, 1996.

[MM97]   A. Mendelzon and T. Milo. Formal models of web queries. In *Proc. of the ACM Symp. on Principles of Database Systems*, pages 134–143, 1997.

[MMM96]   A. Mendelzohn, G. A. Mihaila, and T. Milo. Querying the World Wide Web. In *Proc. PDIS*, 1996.

[MS99]   T. Milo and D. Suciu. Index structures for path expressions. In *Proc. of the Intl. Conf. on Database Theory*, pages 277–295, 1999.

[MW93]   T. Minohara and R. Watanabe. Queries on structure in hypertext. In *Foundations of Data Organization and Algorithms, FODO '93*, pages 394–411. Springer-Verlag, New York, 1993.

[MW95]   A. Mendelzon and P. Wood. Finding regular simple paths in graph databases. *SIAM J. Comp.*, 24(6), 1995.

[MW97]   J. McHugh and J. Widom. Integrating dynamically fetched external information into a DBMS for semistructured data. *ACM SIGMOD Record*, 26(4):24–31, 1997.

[MW99]   J. McHugh and J. Widom. Query optimization for XML. In *Proc. of the Intl. Conf. on Very Large Data Bases*, Edinburgh, 1999.

[NAM97]   S. Nestorov, S. Abiteboul, and R. Motwani. Inferring structure in semistructured data. In *Proc. of the Workshop on Management of Semi-structured Data*, 1997. Available from http://www.research.att.com/~suciu/workshop-papers.html.

[Nav95]   G. Navarro. A language for queries on structure and contents of textual databases. Master's thesis, University of Chile, Santiago, Chile, April 1995.

[NBY97]   G. Navarro and R. Baeza-Yates. Proximal nodes: a model to query document databases by content and structure. *ACM Transactions on Information Systems*, 15(4):400–435, October 1997.

[NCS99]   An introduction to HDF5. The National Center for Supercomputing Applications, University of Illinois at Urbana-Champaign. http://hdf.ncsa.uiuc.edu/HDF5/doc/H5.intro.html.

[NOA73]   NMC Format for Observational Data, 1973. http://dao.gsfc.nasa.gov/data_stuff/formatPages/on29.html.

[NUWC96]   S. Nestorov, J. Ullman, J. Wiener, and S. Chawathe. Representative objects: concise representations of semi-structured hierarchical data. Technical report, Stanford University, 1996. Available by anonymous ftp from db.stanford.edu.

[OBB89]   A. Ohori, P. Buneman, and V. Breazu-Tannen. Database programming in Machiavelli, a polymorphic language with static type inference. In J. Clifford, B. Lindsay, and D. Maier, editors, *Proc. of the ACM-SIGMOD Intl. Conf. on Management of Data*, pages 46–57, Portland, Oregon, June 1989.

[OHMS92]   J. Orenstein, S. Haradhvala, B. Margulies, and D. Sakahara. Query processing in the ObjectStore database system. In *Proc. of the ACM SIGMOD*, 1992.

[OMG92]   OMG ORBTF. *Common Object Request Broker Architecture*. Object Management Group, Framingham, MA, 1992.

[Ora99]   XML storage. Oracle8i, 1999. `www.oracle.com/`.

[OV91]   T. Ozsu and P. Valduriez. *Principles of Distributed Database Systems*, 2nd edition. Prentice Hall, Englewood Cliffs, NJ, 1991.

[PAGM96]   Y. Papakonstantinou, S. Abiteboul, and H. Garcia-Molina. Object fusion in mediator systems. In *VLDB*, Bombay, 1996.

[PGMU95]   Y. Papakonstantinou, H. Garcia-Molina, and J. Ullman. MSL: A mediation system based on declarative specifications. Available by anonymous ftp from `db.stanford.edu` as the file `pub/papakonstantinou/1995/medmaker.ps`, 1995.

[PGMW95]   Y. Papakonstantinou, H. Garcia-Molina, and J. Widom. Object exchange across heterogeneous information sources. In *Intl. Conf. on Data Engineering*, pages 251–260, Taipei, Taiwan, 1995.

[Poe99]   XML repository. Poet software, 1999. `www.poet.com/`.

[PT87]   R. Paige and R. Tarjan. Three partition refinement algorithms. *SIAM Journal of Computing*, 16:973–988, 1987.

[PV99]   Y. Papakonstantinou and V. Vassalos. Query rewriting using semistructured views. In *SIGMOD*, 1999.

[QL98]   Query for XML: position papers, 1998. `http://www.w3.org/TandS/QL/QL98/pp.html`.

[QRS⁺95]   D. Quass, A. Rajaraman, Y. Sagiv, J. Ullman, and J. Widom. Querying semistructured heterogeneous information. In T. Ling, A. Mendelzon, and L. Vieille, editors, *Proc. of the Fourth Intl. Conf. on Deductive and Object-Oriented Databases (DOOD)*, Singapore, pages 436–445, Springer-Verlag, New York, 1995.

[Raj96]   A. Rajaraman. Indexing semistructured data for flexible comparisons. Working document of the Stanford DB Group, March 1996.

[RD90]   R. Rew and G. Davis. The unidata netCDF: Software for scientific data access. In *Sixth Intl. Conf. on Interactive Information and Processing Systems for Meteorology*, Anaheim, CA, pages 33–40. American Meteorology Society, February 1990.

[RDF99]   Resource description framework (RDF) model and syntax specification, 1999. `http://www.w3.org/TR/REC-rdf-syntax/`.

[RTSCF96]   P. Rodriguez-Tomé, P. Stoehr, G. Cameron, and T. Flores. The European Bioinformatics Institute (EBI) Databases. *Nucleic Acids Research*, 24:6–13, 1996. `http://www.ebi.ac.uk`.

[SA98]   A. Sahuguet and F. Azavant. W4F: the wysiwyg web wrapper factory. Technical report, University of Pennsylvania, Department of Computer and Information Science, 1998. To appear. `http://db.cis.upenn.edu/W4F`.

[SC98]   G. Simeon and S. Cluet. Using YAT to build a web server. In *Proc. of the Intl. Workshop on the Web and Databases (WebDB)*, Valencia, Spain, March 1998.

[ST94]   A. Salminen and F. W. Tompa. Pᴀᴛ expressions: An algebra for text search. *Acta Linguistica Hungarica*, 41(1–4):277–306, 1994.

[Str99]   The Strudel system, 1999. `www.research.att.com/sw/tools/strudel`.

[Sty99]   Web style sheets, by the W3C, 1999. `http://www.w3.org/Style/`.

[Suc96]   D. Suciu. Query decomposition and view maintenance for query languages for unstructured data. In *Proc. of Intl. Conf. on Very Large Data Bases*, pages 227–238, 1996.

[Suc98]   D. Suciu. An overview of semistructured data. *SIGACT News*, 29(4):28–38, December 1998.

[TMD92]   J. Thierry-Mieg and R. Durbin. Syntactic definitions for the ACeDB data base manager. Technical Report MRC-LMB xx.92, MRC Laboratory for Molecular Biology, Cambridge, UK, 1992.

[Tur85]   D. Turner. Miranda: a non-strict functional language with polymorphic types. In J. P. Jouannaud, editor, *LNCS 201: Proc. of the Conf. on Functional Programming Languages and Computer Architecture*, Nancy, pages 1–16. Springer-Verlag, 1985.

[Ull88]   J. D. Ullman. *Principles of Database and Knowledge-Base Systems*, Vol. I: *Classical Database Systems*. Computer Science Press, New York, 1988.

[Ull89]   J. D. Ullman. *Principles of Database and Knowledge Base Systems*, Vol. II: *The New Technologies*. Computer Science Press, New York, 1989.

[W3C]   The World Wide Web Consortium (W3C). `http://www.w3c.org/`.

[Wad92]   P. Wadler. Comprehending monads. *Mathematical Structures in Computer Science*, 2:461–493, 1992.

[Wie92]   G. Wiederhold. Mediators in the architecture of future information systems. *IEEE Computer*, 25(3):38–49, March 1992.

[Won94]   L. Wong. *Querying Nested Collections*. PhD thesis, Department of Computer and Information Science, University of Pennsylvania, Philadelphia, PA, August 1994. Available as University of Pennsylvania IRCS Report 94-09.

[XLI98]   XML linking language (XLink), by the W3C, 1998. `http://www.w3c.org/TR/1998/WD-xlink-19980303`.

[XML98]   The World Wide Web Consortium (W3C)'s XML web page, 1998. `http://www.w3c.org/XML/`.

[XPO98]   XML pointers, by the W3C, 1998. `http://www.w3c.org/TR/1998/WD-xptr-19980303`.

[XSL98]   Extensible Stylesheet Language (XSL). `http://www.w3c.org/TR/WD-xsl`, 1998.

[ZJ99]   B. Zhao and A. Joseph. XSet: a high performance XML search engine, 1999. Available from `http://www.cs.berkeley.edu/~ravenben/xset/`.

[Zlo77]   M. Zloof. Query-by-example: a data base language. *IBM Systems Journal*, 16:324–343, 1977.

Index

About the Authors

Serge Abiteboul received his Ph.D. in computer science from the University of Southern California in 1982, and his French *Thèse d'Etat* from the University of Paris XI in 1986. He is Senior Researcher at I.N.R.I.A. where he manages the Database Group. He also has a joint professor position at the École Polytechnique. He has worked recently at I.N.R.I.A and Stanford University (two-year sabbatical) on object databases, digital libraries, semistructured data, data integration, and electronic commerce. He has been program chair of ACM PODS '95, ICALP-1994, ICDT '90. He is the program chair of ECDL-99 (European Conference on Digital Libraries). He received the 1998 ACM SIGMOD Innovation Award.

Peter Buneman is a professor in the Computer and Information Science Department at the University of Pennsylvania. He received his undergraduate degree from Cambridge and his Ph.D. from the University of Warwick; he also worked at the University of Edinburgh and has held numerous visiting positions. His interests include databases, programming languages, cognitive science and classification theory. He has served as program chair for ACM SIGMOD '93 and ICDT '99.

Dan Suciu is a researcher in AT&T labs. He received his Ph.D. from the University of Pennsylvania in 1995, and his BS from the Polytechnic of Bucharest (Romania). He has worked on various aspects of semistructured data for the last few years and has published widely on the topic. He has organized workshops on the topic and has served on the committees of ICDT, PODS, and EDBT.